PALACES
OF
POWER

PALACES
OF
POWER

THE BIRTH AND EVOLUTION
OF LONDON'S CLUBLAND

STEPHEN HOARE

To Pauline,
with love

First published 2019
This paperback edition published 2021

The History Press
97 St George's Place, Cheltenham,
Gloucestershire, GL50 3QB
www.thehistorypress.co.uk

British Library Cataloguing in Publication Data.
A catalogue record for this book is available from the British Library.

ISBN 978 0 7509 9727 0

Typesetting and origination by The History Press
Printed and bound in Great Britain by TJ Books Limited, Padstow, Cornwall.

FSC
www.fsc.org

MIX
Paper from
responsible sources
FSC® C013056

Trees for Life

CONTENTS

Contents

FOREWORD

The London members' club is an extraordinary success story. It is a product of the very beginnings of modern London in the eighteenth century. It transformed itself, both in numbers and in the luxuriousness of its clubhouses, in the nineteenth century – for many, the club's golden age. In the twentieth century it is possible to discern signs of decline and decay, especially in the club's historic centre in the aristocratic parish of St James's, Westminster. Even then, though, the idea of the club never lost its attractiveness. And now, in the last twenty or thirty years in particular, the club has burst far beyond its historic confines in one or two central London parishes and found a new lease of life in districts that once had lurid reputations for vice and crime but have now been resurrected as ultra-smart. Rather than being rendered irrelevant to the modern age, the club has readily accommodated London's restless desire for all things new; rather than discarded as unfashionable, the London club has recovered its reputation as a symbol of good taste. Why is this?

One reason, it seems to me, lies in the very nature of London. Even in the eighteenth century, London was an urban wonder. The largest city in Europe, it dwarfed the towns and cities of Britain. So, in many ways, it still does. After a period of decay for thirty years or so following the Second World War, when London lost over 2 million people and scores of thousands of jobs, it has recovered to reach and even surpass its previous high–point of some 8¾ million people; the next largest city (Birmingham) is just about one-eighth of its size.

In all this time, London's growth has depended on immigration. Even in the eighteenth century only a minority of Londoners were London-born. In the nineteenth century, ten decades of astonishing growth when the metropolis multiplied its population six-fold, immigration was so much the life-blood of the city that observers worried that the pure-bred cockney was a mere specimen of physical and mental degradation. Even in the years of London's decline in the second half of the twentieth century, largescale immigration from home and abroad fuelled those positive signs of energy and rebirth that coalesced in 'Swinging London'. In the twenty-first century, when the British-born population now makes up just 62 per cent and when more than a third of Londoners are born abroad, the economic driving-force of immigration is plain for all to see. London, then, is a city of strangers. And so it has been for the past 300 years.

It is in this migrant-fuelled growth of London 300 years ago that we find the birth of the club as an idea and when we see that idea taking root in metropolitan soil. It should come as no surprise that freemasonry assumed its modern world-wide form in London in 1717, for it was in this city of strangers that men – and it was men at that time – had to create their own connections, make their own 'friends' on whom they could rely in frequent times of trouble. The lodge and the club formed part of this solution to a pressing need for those newly arrived in London: the need for an identity in a whirling city where perhaps you might know just one or two people, sometimes none at all; the need for neighbourliness in a city notorious for a shifting preoccupied population that never seemed to root itself in one place; and for visibility in a place where swarming crowds rendered every individual invisible.

The club survived and, indeed, now flourishes because it continues to fulfil these needs. All this is not to deny the club's ups and downs in its 300-year history. It has not had an easy ride. Just as London has suffered its own blows of outrageous fortune, the club has had to adapt to changing circumstances, uncomfortable and incomplete though that adaptation has sometimes proved – the antediluvian reluctance of a few clubs to admit women members is a case in point. If the London club has shown an indestructible longevity then in the process it has become a great deal altered. Not the least of these changes has been that move away from its historic centre. As London has grown on the ground, so has its 'Clubland' become far-flung and dispersed. And yet the historic connection with clubs and St James's is still so strong that when people speak of London's Clubland, as they still do, it is the streets between and around Piccadilly and Pall Mall that they have in mind.

Stephen Hoare's genial history of this Clubland-at-home reveals to us just how that connection between the club and St James's arose and how it changed over time. It is a fascinating story and it is told with wit and verve. Those of us who think we know our London history tolerably well will find much that is new here. And Hoare convinces us that the London club, and its connection with London's most exclusive parish, is a story that goes to the heart of just what London has meant to its people over the past 300 years.

Jerry White
Reform Club
June 2019

ACKNOWLEDGEMENTS

This book grew out of my MA dissertation at Birkbeck, University of London, the title of which was *A comparison of the coffee-houses of St James's and Cornhill in the long eighteenth century*. For this I would like to thank my supervisor Professor Jerry White for the advice he gave when I decided to extend the scope of my studies to focus on members' clubs. Also, to Professor Penelope Corfield of Royal Holloway College University of London, Dr Gillian Williamson and members of the Long Eighteenth Century Seminar Group at the Institute for Historical Research, Senate House for their support and encouragement. Thanks also to my fellow journalist and historian Peter Guy Brown for his constructive comments on my draft and especially to Michael Jeremy Hodges of Brooks's for his forensic eye for detail when reading the final manuscript.

I am indebted to the many London clubs whose response to my inquiries has given my book depth and focus. I offer especial thanks to Charles Sebag-Montefiore, secretary of the Society of Dilettanti, Mark Rivett, secretary of the Oriental Club, Julie Owens of the 'In and Out' Naval and Military Club, Sheila Markham, librarian of the Travellers Club and Brooks's, Simon Blundell, librarian of the Reform Club, Mohammed Anzouai, Chief Steward at the Reform Club, Sheron Easter, membership secretary of the Reform Club, Dr Peter Urbach, archivist at the Reform Club, Jennie de Protani of the Athenaeum, Seth Alexander Thevoz, librarian of the National

Liberal Club, and, not least, to Helen O'Neill and Yvette Dickerson of the London Library, St James's Square, and Lizzie Morcom of Senate House Library.

For the chapter on the jazz age I am grateful to the highly knowledgeable Ray Pallett. Ray's website Memory Lane www.memorylane.org.uk should be essential reading to anyone interested in the big bands of the 1930s.

Essential in giving this book the authentic flavour of Clubland were the members who generously entertained me at their clubs. Thank you one and all for the gin and tonics, whisky and sodas, and for a memorable lunch at White's. Your anecdotes were invaluable. In particular, I would like to thank Michael Jeremy Hodges of Brooks's, John Martin Robinson of the Travellers Club, Pratt's and the Beefsteak, Krishan Chudasama of the Oriental Club, and Robbie Lyle of White's for their hospitality and for sharing their knowledge of their clubs. For these introductions, I am indebted to my journalistic colleague Hilaire Gomer, whose family connections provided an 'open sesame' to Brooks's and White's.

Finally, I thank my wife and co-conspirator Pauline for her dedicated support over the years this project took shape. I value her patience, encouragement, and encyclopaedic knowledge of the novels of Jane Austen, Georgette Heyer and of course our shared enthusiasm for that supreme chronicler of Victorian Clubland, Anthony Trollope.

The owners of copyright material have been contacted and have given permission, for which the author expresses his gratitude. While every effort has been made to trace secondary sources, some have proved hard to trace and for this the author offers his sincere apologies.

INTRODUCTION

Take a stroll from Trafalgar Square along Cockspur Street and Pall Mall and then turn sharp right at St James's Palace into St James's Street. You will pass a series of grand buildings flanked by cast-iron gas lamps, with stone steps and porters guarding the doors. On your left is the Institute of Directors, formerly the United Service Club, while directly opposite fronting onto Waterloo Place there is the Athenaeum with its classical Greek frieze and statue of Pallas Athene. Moving onwards, along Pall Mall, are the Travellers Club, the Reform Club, the Royal Automobile Club and the Oxford and Cambridge Club. On the west side of St James's Street is the Carlton Club, while further up is Brooks's and the former Crockford's clubhouse, while on the opposite side are Boodle's and White's. And if you should take a detour to St James's Square you will see the 'In and Out' Naval and Military Club, and the East India Club. This is the historic heart of London's Clubland.

Clubland is, of course, much bigger, and is constantly evolving, but it is a world normally hidden from public view. Over 300 years, Clubland has extended its reach to encompass Piccadilly, Mayfair, Bond Street, Covent Garden and Westminster. The clubs are a valuable part of London's built environment with most historic clubhouses listed grade one architecturally. Despite being highly visible, Londoners take these classical clubhouses for granted as part of the streetscape. Ever discreet, the clubs do not draw attention to themselves. Nevertheless, their members are often highly influential individuals who are leaders in politics, finance, business, the law, the established church, the arts and the media and much more.

In telling the story of Clubland I have presented a slice of political and social history. It cannot be told through events alone – although many clubs were established at times of great political upheaval and national crisis. Events like the Napoleonic wars and the Great Reform Act were a catalyst to club formation.

In the end, this book is a biography of Clubland. Focused on St James's and Piccadilly, the clubs have spawned a colourful cast of characters and the story of St James's features – among others – lords and ladies, bawds and madams, dandies, speculators, generals, prime ministers, shopkeepers, suffragettes, nightclub owners, boxers, gamblers and jazz singers. You will meet such characters as Beau Brummel, society hostess Sarah, Lady Jersey, the Prince Regent, the Duke of Wellington and the courtesan Harriette Wilson, the alpine pioneer Lizzie Le Blond, the jazz singer 'Hutch', and former Prime Minister Harold Macmillan.

Clubland has been shaped by its close connection to the sources of power, royalty, the aristocracy, the army, Parliament, the diplomatic and civil service and the law. Unsurprisingly, clubs reflect traditions built over centuries. Highly individualistic, and yet able to adapt to changing times, the members' club has been a model that has been exported across the world. Global centres of power, influence and resources like London, Tokyo, New York, Paris and Berlin have a common thread of attracting and building enclaves of luxury and fashion.

For over 300 years, St James's, Piccadilly and the West End has remained the location for London's most exclusive clubs. Throughout economic depression, and even war, there has always been – and always will be – a demand for the personalised services only a club can provide.

CHAPTER 1

A ROYAL VILLAGE

The Pail Mail, a fine long Street, which from the Hay Market runs in a streight Line Westwards into St. James's-street. The Houses on the South Side have a pleasant Prospect into the King's Garden; and besides, they have small Gardens behind them, which reach to the Wall, and to many of them there are raised Mounts, which give them the Prospect of the said Garden, and of the Park.

From John Strype, *A Survey of the Cities of London*
and Westminster 1720

It all began at the Palace. The focal point of St James's has been for many hundreds of years St James's Palace. Established early in the twelfth century as a hospital run by Augustinians for 'fourteen leprous women', St James's Palace was originally situated in the middle of open countryside known as St James's Fields. There was a spring close by, capped by a brick conduit which provided fresh drinking water for the hospital dedicated to St James the Less. The building was acquired along with 185 acres of surrounding land by Henry VIII in 1528 from the Provost of Eton College. Following a complete refurbishment, the hospital's monastic halls and corridors took on a new life as a royal residence. The red-brick gate tower at the bottom of St James's Street proclaims the palace's Tudor origins. It is ironic that what began life as a charitable institution was later to become synonymous with the power, wealth and decadence of Restoration London. By 1698 and the Palace being occupied by William and Mary, St James's was about to enter a new chapter of what had been a chequered history.

Early Days

John Strype's *Survey of the Cities of London and Westminster* was published in 1720. Quoted above, it provides the most comprehensive picture of London as it looked following the rebuilding that took place after the Great Fire of 1666. By the time Strype described St James's and Westminster, the sprawling Palace of Whitehall had been severely damaged by fire on 4 January 1698. Only Inigo Jones's Banqueting Hall, the Great Hall at Westminster and the Jewel Tower survived the conflagration. An open space near St James's Palace was the site of St James's Fair, a riotous annual celebration 'held on St James's Day near his Majesty's house at St James's'.[*] St James's Day was 25 July. The fair continued until 1698 when William and Mary adopted St James's Palace as their royal residence. The fair subsequently moved to Mayfair.

John Strype's St James's was an urban village lying to the north of what had been a walled royal deer park. The 'raised Mounts' in the back gardens of the houses on the south side of Pall Mall were populated with summer houses and gazebos. The 'Pail Mail' mentioned in the *Survey* had in the first half of the seventeenth century been a long straight pitch for the eponymous game of bowls enjoyed by royalty and aristocracy up to the mid-seventeenth century.

But St James's Palace was no quiet backwater. Pall Mall, the wide thoroughfare leading up to it, was populated with taverns and four- and five-storey mansions of the rich including the magnificent Schomberg House, built on the south side of Pall Mall in 1698 for the Duke of Schomberg. The first duke was part of a family of French

---

[*] E. Beresford Chancellor, *Memorials of St James's Street*, Grant Richards, London, 1922, p. 25

generals and was born in the Palatinate. He was second in command to William of Orange on his 1688 expedition to England. Part of his house still stands next door to the Oxford and Cambridge Club. A short way to the north of Pall Mall, one of London's vital mail coach routes, the road to Reading, Bath and Bristol terminated at the coaching inns of Piccadilly. This major highway known as Piccadilly was linked to St James's Palace by St James's Street, a short avenue of substantial brick-built homes occupied mainly by aristocratic courtiers and wealthy merchants.

A Royal Palace Takes Shape

After fire had rendered the Palace of Whitehall uninhabitable, the reigning monarchs William and Mary established their London court here in 1698. St James's was all set for its next phase as a principal royal residence. Their successor, Queen Anne, ordered an extensive building programme to be carried out with a new suite of royal apartments designed by Sir Christopher Wren. The reign of Queen Anne (1702–1714) was the catalyst for St James's rapid development, as nobility, courtiers, ambassadors to the Court of St James, soldiers, tradesmen and servants gravitated to the new dwellings and lodgings that were springing up around the royal palace.

Development was well under way long before the royal court took up residence in St James's Palace. John Strype describes St James's Street as a 'spacious street well inhabited by Gentry'. Around fifteen substantial brick-built houses fronted onto the rough, un-metalled street which ran from the palace gates to the 'important way to Readinge', as Strype refers to Piccadilly. St James's was a safe haven from the Great Plague of 1664 which had spread like wildfire in the City of London's densely packed tenements. The fresh drinking water provided by the nearby well would have been a valuable asset for the street's early inhabitants.

The rate books prove conclusively not only the growing popularity of St James's Street but also the fashionable character it was assuming. 'Sir Ralph Clare, in 1635, is joined in the following year by Sir John Bingley … In 1641 we find besides Lord Berkshire, (Sir William) Pulteney and (Sir Henry) Henn, Sir David Cunningham, the Earl of Danby and Lord Gorringe.'*

Prior to the accession of Charles II, St James's Palace played a minor role as annexe to the main seat of power at Whitehall Palace. The history of Clubland has its roots in 1660 with the Restoration of the monarchy following the Commonwealth of Oliver Cromwell that had been established after a bloody civil war and the execution of Charles I. The power vacuum following the death of Cromwell led to a re-invigorated, re-invented monarchy which needed to establish a new order based on aristocratic patronage. King Charles II set about enlarging and refurbishing St James's Palace to create a royal residence for his brother the Duke of York, later James II.

The first official mention of St James's Street dates from 1659 in the final year of Oliver Cromwell's short-lived Commonwealth. The Restoration of the Monarchy in 1660 saw King Charles II reward his loyal followers with large parcels of Crown land on generous leases. As the Court orbited around St James's Place, the development of the urban village known as St James's began.

The newly ennobled supporters of King Charles II were granted long leases to build stately mansions for themselves and invest in high status speculative developments such as St James's Square. Charles also gifted a splendid house on Pall Mall close by the royal palace to his mistress Nell Gwynn. The gift, more generous than to any of his other numerous lovers, was made doubly so when Miss Gwynn demanded and was given the freehold of the property. Her former house is still the only one in Pall Mall to be freehold.

Another recipient of royal largesse was not quite so lucky. Queen Anne granted her one-time favourite and confidante Sarah Churchill, Duchess of Marlborough, £44,000 and a leasehold to build a grand mansion next to St James's Park in recognition of her husband's

---

* E. Beresford Chancellor, *Memorials of St James's Street*, Grant Richards, London, 1922, p. 16

successful campaigns in the War of Spanish Succession. Designed by Sir Christopher Wren and completed in 1711, Marlborough House was the duke and duchess's London home. With the house came the right to drive a carriage on the Mall in St James's Park, a privilege reserved for the king and his closest friends. With the accession of King George I, the Marlboroughs' prodigious spending came under public scrutiny. Scandalous reports reached the government that Sir John Vanbrugh the architect of Blenheim Palace was owed a vast sum by the duchess for building work carried out but deliberately withheld.

Vanbrugh was ruined and the Prime Minister, Sir Robert Walpole, was determined to exact revenge. He removed the duchess's privilege of driving in St James's Park and closed off the principal carriageway into her house. The duchess then petitioned the king for permission to buy and demolish two neighbouring houses to create a grand carriage entrance onto Pall Mall. Walpole nipped this scheme in the bud by extending the Crown leases on the houses by thirty years, thus preventing their sale and demolition. Piqued, the duchess had no choice but to abandon her grand plans. After the end of Walpole's long reign as prime minister, the duchess was finally able to buy and demolish a small house to the west next door to the German Chapel to the side of St James's Palace to create a modest carriageway to her house. The narrow entrance created a dog-leg which proved an obstacle for carriages. To cap it all, Walpole, when in power, had bought one of the houses overlooking Marlborough House that had escaped demolition for his son, Edward. When the lease on Marlborough House expired in 1828, it was brought back into government ownership.

A Noble Development

As St James's became fashionable, the nobility built grand mansions along Piccadilly. Lord Arlington, Richard, Earl of Burlington and the Duke of Albemarle developed land that lay to the north of

Piccadilly. Burlington's grand mansion, Burlington House, is now the Royal Academy while Arlington Street takes its name from its aristocratic landlord.

In 1661 the Bailiwick of St James's was leased by Queen Henrietta Maria's trustees to the trustees of Henry Jermyn, the Earl of St Albans 'who over the course of the next eight years granted some twenty leases along the whole of the east side of St James's Street and also on the west side south of Park Place'.* The Court of St James's attracted aristocrats and courtiers, military officers and their wives, many of whom were involved in ceremonial duties at the court. Neighbouring streets including Jermyn Street, Duke Street, Bury Street and King Street attracted not only Stuart courtiers but members of Parliament, scientists and an odd assortment of wealthy individuals. Sir Isaac Newton, the Duke of Marlborough, in the days when he was plain Colonel Churchill, and the apothecary and part-time highwayman William Plunkett lived on Jermyn Street.

In 1662 Jermyn applied to Charles II for a lease of 45 acres upon which to build 'great and good houses ... fit for the dwellings of noblemen and persons of quality'.** By gifting these leaseholds, a large swathe of St James's Fields gave way to imposing houses built in what was later called Queen Anne style with projecting eaves and dormer windows. The Jermyn family continued to own the leasehold land until 1740 when it reverted to the Crown as did similar estates.

St James's Square was built in stages between 1665 and 1720. Built in partnership with the builder Nicholas Barbon, this was London's first speculative development and a blueprint for the fashionable London squares that were developed over the subsequent centuries. Early residents of St James's Square included Thomas Thynne, Viscount Weymouth; William Hervey, Earl of Bristol; Edward Howard, Duke of Norfolk; The Duke of Kent; Sir John Heathcote, MP for Bodmin; and Sir Everard Fawkener, Postmaster General. Thynne did not live

---

* British History Online
** Calendar of State Papers, Vol. 340, pp. 3, 5, 6

long to enjoy the fashionable London life. He was assassinated by Colonel Graz and Lieutenant Stern who ambushed his coach in Pall Mall and shot him dead on 12 February 1681. The murderers were hanged but not Count Konigsmark, the man who had ordered the killing in revenge for Thynne's winning the hand of Lady Ogle to whom he believed himself engaged.

St James's was slowly but surely adopting something of the reputation of 'the wild West End'. Alongside the urban village's grand houses, there grew up a haphazard collection of shops, livery stables, theatres, concert halls and places of entertainment as well as numerous taverns like the Eagle and Child, the Chequer, the Coach and Horses, the Star and Goat, and the Thistle and Crown, all to be found on Pall Mall. The fine houses of St James's Street soon found themselves jostling cheek by jowl with the encroaching shops and coffee-houses. In the eighteenth century, the nobility began to move out as their former homes changed hands and were bought by up-and-coming tradesmen. Typical of incomers was the local 'fruit woman' Betty Neale who ran a fruit and vegetable business from number 62 St James's Street. Born in St James's Street in 1730, Neale claimed she had only ever been out of the street on two occasions. In business from around 1750 till her retirement in 1783, Betty's fruit shop was patronised by men and women of the *ton* who came to hear the latest gossip about court life or scandalous stories of sexual intrigue. When Horace Walpole and his friends visited Vauxhall Pleasure Gardens in 1750, they invited Betty who 'accompanied the party with hampers of strawberries and cherries'.***

One family business survives from this era at number 3 St James's Street. Wine merchant Berry Bros & Rudd started life in 1698 when the Widow Bourne established a grocer's opposite St James's Palace. Her daughter Elizabeth married William Pickering and the young couple began supplying the newly fashionable chocolate and cof-

---

*** E. Beresford Chancellor, *Memorials of St James's Street*, Grant Richards, London, 1922, p. 185

fee-houses with ground coffee beans. The firm grew and took on a partner, John Clarke, whose grandson George Berry took over running the family firm in 1810. Renamed Berry, the grocer's shop survives intact although by the early nineteenth century, wine had overtaken coffee as the main stock in trade. Visitors to the original Berry Bros shop can still see the massive set of scales used to weigh coffee beans. And when sacks of coffee were no longer weighed, the scales were put to good use weighing gentlemen who wished to check the progress of their diet. Berry Bros still keeps the original ledger on which is recorded the weight of Beau Brummel, the Prince Regent and many others. Berry Bros & Rudd is now a luxury brand.

St James's Street was an expensive address and households struggled to make ends meet. As a result, many residents of St James's Street took in lodgers. Paying for board and lodging was a cheap and convenient way of acquiring a fashionable address at a fraction of the cost of buying or renting a property. Some famous people lodged here. Alexander Pope, the historian and MP Edward Gibbon and the essayist Joseph Addison were among the many people of note who rented lodgings on St James's Street. Close by, Bury Street could be described as the epicentre of eighteenth-century 'bed-sit land'. Jonathan Swift arrived from Dublin in 1710, describing his situation thus:

> I lodge in Berry Street, where I removed a week ago. I have the first floor, a dining room and a bed-chamber at eight shillings a week; playing deep, but I spend nothing for eating, never go to a tavern, and very seldom in a coach; yet, after all, it will be expensive. *

Addison's friend and literary collaborator Richard Steele and his wife also lodged in Bury Street. The impecunious Steele had a fraught relationship with their landlady, a Mrs Vanderput who had the writer arrested for unpaid rent in November 1708. In a letter, Steele referred to his landlady as 'that insufferable brute'.

---

* Jonathan Swift, *Journal to Stella*, 29 September 1710

St James's Street must clearly have attained a degree of notoriety for a pillory was set up in Park Place, St James's Street in around 1690. Miscreants – more often than not seditious Jacobites – could be forced to stand with their hands locked in the crossbar of the pillory while the public hurled abuse or rotten fruit at them. The pillory was sited near a stand for sedan chairs which stood parked in rows while their chairmen rested while waiting for their next fare. It was a busy public thoroughfare.

Central to the story of Clubland was the burgeoning number of taverns, coffee and chocolate-houses. White's was established in St James's Street in 1693 and in Pall Mall, Ozinda's opened in 1694. In St James's Street, coffee and chocolate-houses followed in quick succession. The Cocoa Tree opened in 1698, the Star and Garter Tavern in 1700, the Smyrna in 1702, the Thatched House Tavern in 1704, and the St James's Coffee-House in 1705. Highly fashionable beverages imported from Italy and Portugal revolutionised social habits, segregating men from women and providing a public sphere where politics could be debated and card games played for high stakes. These coffee and chocolate-houses were the unlikely precursors of some of London's most famous clubs.

By the early eighteenth century, St James's Street was a prosperous enclave. William Hogarth's *A Rake's Progress,* painted in 1734, depicts a streetscape composed of plain, three-storey, brick-built, flat-fronted Queen Anne houses. There appears to have been a steep gradient at the north end of St James's Street, and houses there fronted onto a terraced walkway ascended by steps. This arrangement caused a lot of accidents with sedan chairs and people falling down the steps. The result was that in 1765, the Westminster Paving Commissioners carried out works to level the street. But this also led to some strange anomalies. In some houses, cellars were raised above ground level and in others, doorways were sunken. A correspondent for the *London Chronicle* wrote:

Some gentlemen are forced to dive into their own parlours ... some persons, not thinking of the late alterations, attempting to knock at their own door, have frequently tumbled up their new-erected steps, while others, who have been used to ascend to their threshold, have as often, for the same reason, tumbled down.*

Following the invasion of coffee-houses, most of the nobility had moved onwards and upwards to grand houses in St James's Square and Piccadilly. St James's Street was the home of successful tradesmen. By the end of the century the tradesmen had moved on and most of their houses had been sold and demolished to make way for the imposing classical buildings and clubhouses we see today.

The Parish

The growing area needed a church and in 1684 Sir Christopher Wren completed St James's Church, Piccadilly, setting the seal on Henry Jermyn's success. The parish covered an area bounded by St James's Palace, Pall Mall, Piccadilly and the Haymarket, and included St James's Square, Jermyn Street, Pall Mall, Haymarket, and St James's Street. The parish originally included parts of Mayfair, Soho and extended as far as Coventry Street, leading to Leicester Fields better known today as Leicester Square. In later centuries this small and tightly defined area was to become the nucleus of London's Clubland.

At the time, the neighbouring parishes were St Margaret's Westminster, St Anne's Soho and St Martin-in-the-Fields. St George's Hanover Square was established in 1724 as the parish church of Mayfair after parish boundaries were redrawn following the *New Churches in London and Westminster Act of 1710*, which led to the creation of a commission to oversee the building of fifty new churches to serve London's fast expanding population. St James's Church, Piccadilly stood on what was then called Portugal Street later renamed Piccadilly, a thoroughfare which took its name from a *Pickadill*, meaning the outer hem of a skirt or collar. At the time the

---

* *The London Chronicle,* 15–17 August 1765

area could truly be said to represent the outskirts of London, and this is the likely origin.

St James's included London's biggest concentration of royal households: St James's Palace, Cumberland House, York House and Clarence House. The impact of having a royal household on the doorstep led to rapid gentrification.

A Bustling Hub

Passengers and goods for the regular stage coaches departing London-bound for Windsor, Reading, Bath, Bristol and all points west were served by huge coaching inns which stood near the site of the present day Piccadilly Circus. Coaches either started from Piccadilly or were making their first port of call on a journey which had begun in a City coaching inn such as the Bell Savage on Ludgate Hill. The principal coaching inns were the White Bear on the site of what is now the Trocadero, the White Horse located on the south side of Piccadilly facing up Bond Street, both built around 1670–80, and the Three Kings built in 1683. The Gloucester Coffee-House, Piccadilly, held the exclusive Royal Mail contract to run mail coaches serving Windsor, Bath, Bristol, Worcester and the West Country.

The mail coach, with driver and guard, and with luggage and passengers piled up on the roof, as well as four people inside the coach itself, would travel at about 7–8 miles an hour, meaning that a journey might take several days with overnight stops at inns or stages along the route. A system of well-maintained turnpike roads (where a toll was paid) speeded up the mail but even so, a fresh team of horses would be needed every 15 to 20 miles. Turnpikes reduced the time of the journey from London to Bristol from thirty-eight hours to sixteen hours.[**]

The basic design of the coaching inn can be seen from London's sole surviving coaching inn, the George on Borough High Street,

---

[**] The Postal Museum www.postalmuseum.org

which was the terminus for the Rochester mail route. It has a large gateway for horse-drawn stagecoaches and a yard where the coaches set down passengers and where the horses could be untethered, fed, watered and rested at stables to the rear. Around all four sides of the inn yard would be a staircase leading to balustraded galleries which provided access to bedrooms for guests needing overnight accommodation and private dining rooms. On the ground floor were the ticket office, goods porters, a mail office and public waiting rooms where passengers would wait for their coach. It was a ceaseless hive of activity. These inns fulfilled exactly the same function as a modern railway terminus.

The proximity of these coaching inns was vital to the economy of St James's and fed into the area's growing reputation as a premium shopping district. Wealthy individuals patronising the St James's shops and warehouses might order goods such as medicines, tea, coffee, haberdashery, fashionable clothes, boots, hats, sporting guns, clocks, and even optical instruments which were then parcelled and dispatched to their country estates by coach.

Royal St James's

As a residence, St James's Palace was not always a firm favourite with royalty. It was far too public and indeed anyone strolling in St James's Park would have had a clear view of palace life. George III preferred the seclusion of Windsor Castle and Kew Palace, leaving the Court of St James's as a place where foreign dignitaries and ambassadors were received. In 1783 George III's son, the Prince of Wales, was given Carlton House which he expanded and developed as a royal palace. Here, the Prince of Wales attracted a disreputable crowd of courtiers all seeking influence as his father withdrew from public life. Carlton House effectively became a parallel court.

St James's set the gold standard for London streets, which at the time were overwhelmingly muddy, rutted and hazardous. Duke Street, St James's was the first thoroughfare in London to have pavements for pedestrians. Pall Mall was the first to be lit by gas. An experimental technology, coal gas was pioneered by a German, Frederick Winsor, who staged a demonstration of his new lighting at his home in 93–94 Pall Mall in 1807. The innovation attracted the attention of the Prince of Wales.

In 1824, the Prince of Wales, now George IV, decided to demolish Carlton House in anticipation of a move to Buckingham House. The large vacant plot created enabled the construction of Waterloo Place and the Duke of York Steps which provided a vista to St James's Park. Carlton House Terrace was built on the site of what was known as 'the King's Garden', also known as 'the Wilderness', situated between the backs of mansions on Pall Mall and St James's Park. This land had once been owned by the scientist Robert Boyle who was granted it by Queen Anne on a thirty-one-year lease from 1709. The queen also gave Boyle a noble title, Lord Carlton. Reverting to the Crown estate, Lord Carlton's garden gave its name to Carlton House and subsequently to the terrace. It is a delightful irony that the Royal Society of which Boyle – Lord Carlton – was a founder member should now be located in Carlton House Terrace.

St James's Park

King Charles II opened up the previously private royal deer park to create a public pleasure garden in 1660. His first decision was to order the Mall to be re-metalled to provide a suitable surface for carriages and horses. St James's Park was wooded with rows of trees and occasional clumps. Parallel to the Mall was a long, wide canal originally fed by water from the River Tyburn. To the right of this canal was a shallow, oblong lake, Rosamund's Pond, located on what is now Birdcage Walk. The land between the Mall and the canal bank was laid out as a series of tree-lined walks. Tame deer roamed the park, and ducks lived in a 'duck decoy' constructed to one side of the canal. Then, as now, seventeenth-century children would be taken to 'feed the ducks'. The park was also home to a small herd of dairy cattle, and milkmaids were on hand to milk the cows and sell this natural drink to the public at a penny a cup. St James's Park quickly became a place for public promenading where the aristocracy and middle classes could engage in gentle conversation and even mingle with royalty. Officers of the Life Guards were often to be seen off duty but in military uniform.

Baron Bielfeld, a visitor to London, wrote in 1741:

I enter a long and spacious walk they call the Mall. It is now mid-day and I find it thronged with the *beau monde* of both sexes, who pass hastily along. The ladies here wear a kind of *negligee*, in which they appear still more charming than in a most laboured dress. Every part of their apparel is extremely neat; instead of a large hoop, they have short petticoats, and their gowns are elegant but not gaudy, they have short cloaks trimmed with lace.*

The old formal park of 1660 was given a total revamp around 1770 as part of works carried out by the landscape architect Lancelot 'Capability' Brown. George III had purchased Buckingham House for his queen and he wanted to improve the vista. Brown's garden design scheme envisaged converting the canal and Rosamund's Pond into a long, narrow lake that widened at the east end to encircle an island covered with trees. Rosamund's Pond and the canal were drained and filled in, but it was left to the architect John Nash who finally completed the digging of the lake in the 1820s, by which time its water was supplied by the Chelsea Water Works. Some years later, visitors to the park would have encountered its most famous residents, a flock of pelicans, descendants of a pair of which were presented to King Charles II in 1664 by the Russian ambassador. Although these birds are now resident in St James's Park, they were originally housed at the Tower of London menagerie where all exotic animals presented

---

* *Letters of Baron Bielfeld*, 1740-1741

to the monarch were kept. When the menageries closed in 1835, the pelicans were re-homed in St James's Park.

The Court of St James's attracted the aristocracy and the beau monde to this urban village. The social divide between the upper classes and people of the 'middling sort' created a fertile ground for the development of a 'public realm' where gentlemen and ladies could mix freely with people of their own rank and status in the area's many coffee-houses, inns and taverns. This burgeoning 'public realm' created the necessary precondition for the birth of London's Clubland.

CHAPTER 2

COFFEE-HOUSE
SOCIABILITY

This is to give notice to all ingenious gentlemen
In and about the cities of London and Westminster
Who have a mind to be instructed in the noble sciences
Of music, poetry, and politics, that they repair
To the Smyrna Coffee House in Pall Mall.

Advertisement from the *Tatler*, 8 Oct 1709

In 1730 a slim guidebook *A Brief and Merrie History of England* was published explaining the strange nature of English customs to a foreign audience. Purporting to be the work of 'Mohamad Hadgi, Physician to his Excellency Cossem Hojah, late envoy for the Government of Tripoli in South-Barbary', the book was, in fact, the work of satirist Anthony Hilliar:

They (Londoners) represent these Coffee-houses as the most agreeable Things in *London* ... but in other respects they are loathsome, full of Smoak, like a Guard-Room. I believe 'tis these Places that furnish the Inhabitants with Slander, for there one hears exact Accounts of everything done in Town as if it were but a Village.

At those Coffee-Houses near the Court, called *White's*, *St James'*, *Williams's*, the conversation turns chiefly upon Equipages, Essence, Horse-Matches, Tupees, Modes, Mortgages and Maidenheads; the

Cocoa Tree upon Bribery and Corruption, Evil-Ministers, Errors and Mistakes in Government ... *

Rather than being quiet retreats where the individual could order a coffee and drink it in peace, anyone who entered a coffee-house would have to be prepared to engage in rowdy debate, often with complete strangers. A crowded room furnished with plain bench seating and sawdust covering the floor, coffee-houses and their slightly more exclusive counterpart chocolate-houses were essentially masculine spaces where gentlemen would sit cheek by jowl.

A large pot of thick, dark coffee would be simmering in front of a fire from which a servant would pour the viscous liquid into small china mugs called cans. Bitter and full of grounds, coffee was a reviving if somewhat bitter drink whereas chocolate was a thick sweet brew flavoured with vanilla. In the packed room a rabble-rousing orator might be complaining loudly against the government or, huddled in a corner, a group might be discussing in hushed tones the latest scandal in court. In the hubbub of conversation, social distinctions were often blurred.

A Public Realm

For all its humour, Hilliar's *Brief and Merrie History* is an accurate description of an early eighteenth-century St James's Coffee-House. The egalitarian atmosphere promoted by coffee drinking coincided with the birth of a new social class popularly referred to as the 'middling sort'.

Seventeenth-century society was based upon a land-owning aristocracy and the mass of the population lived in varying degrees of poverty. By the eighteenth century, social mobility was beginning

---

* A. Hilliar, *A Brief and Merry History of Great Britain*, London, J. Roberts, J. Shuckburgh, J. Penn and J. Jackson, 1730, pp. 22–23

to accelerate. St James's attracted professionals, such as lawyers, doctors, stock-jobbers, speculators, bankers, and successful merchants, retailers and shop-keepers who formed what became known as 'the middling sort'. These individuals had aspirational values and styled themselves gentlemen. Coffee-houses created a public realm where men of the 'middling sort' could mix with the established nobility and gentry.

In St James's Street alone, there were twenty-five coffee- and chocolate-houses doing business throughout the eighteenth century.* Business failure was high with the majority lasting in business no more than five years. But popular establishments like the Cocoa Tree, Gaunt's, White's, Ozinda's, St James's, the Smyrna and Williams' survived and thrived, often moving to bigger premises on the same street.

The definition of a coffee-house was fluid. Taverns, coffee-houses and the more upmarket chocolate-houses co-existed in close proximity and many served a similar clientele.** Proprietors of both types of establishment needed a victualler's licence if they were to sell spirits, as most did.*** Many gentlemen frequented both types of establishment. Customer loyalty would be based on the quality of the roasted coffee served, and on whether the establishment served additional beverages like tea, chocolate, or liquor.

Licensed victuallers moved with ease between these different types of establishment. The St James's Coffee-House at 87 St James's Street was, for example, run by John Elliott who in 1705 succeeded Arthur Goffe, the vintner who founded the Thatched House Tavern,**** a palatial clubhouse and assembly rooms rather than some kind of

---

* Bryant Lillywhite, *London Coffee Houses*, George Allen and Unwin, 1963, p. 806 (see also appendix X)
** Peter Clark, *The English Alehouse: a social history 1200–1830*, London, Longman, 1983, p. 199
*** Peter Clark, *The English Alehouse: a social history 1200–1830*, London, Longman, 1983, p. 52
**** The Survey of London

rustic retreat as its name implies. Williams' Coffee-House was run by James Rowles from 1749–1768 who is described as a coffee-man and vintner, while Richard Saunders who ran Gaunt's Coffee-House from 1758–1764 held a victualler's licence.

By night, the coffee-house scene was transformed as the few establishments that remained open would undoubtedly have encouraged card playing and possibly gambling. Linkmen would light the way at night, while ticket porters carried urgent messages between coffee-houses. Chairmen congregated at the foot of St James's Street with their sedan chairs ready to carry individuals to the club or gaming house. Where the wealthy congregated, so too did bailiffs and bullies with writs to execute.

To cap it all, coffee-house proprietors had to contend with occasional rowdyism. An article appearing in the *Gentleman's Magazine* under the by-line 'The Universal Spectator' complained about 'Coffee-House Savages', a group of upper-class rakes intent on mayhem:

> A society of Sober Citizens, who frequent a Coffee-House to read the News and smoke their Pipes peaceably, complain to Mr Stonecastle that they are pestered with a company of young Rakes with Toupee wigs, swinging oaken clubs and shallow understandings, who make such an intolerable Noise with their filthy Ribaldry and Horse-laughs, swearing and cursing and damning themselves and cursing the Waiters, and blaspheming all that's sacred, that they disturb Every Body about 'em ...Coffee-house 'masters' are advised to call for a constable 'to shew them out of Doors.'[*****]

In St James's Street, politics and pleasure were the chief pursuits of the mainly male coffee-house clientele. The atmosphere was rowdy and sometimes brutal. The more discerning began to consider how to civilise their pastimes by introducing some forms of social order.

[*****] *The Gentleman's Magazine*, January 1, 1732 p. 552. IHR Library

Secret Societies

Clubs and coffee-houses share a common history. In the late seventeenth century, some divergence becomes noticeable in social behaviour. Coffee-houses frequently had spare rooms which the proprietor might rent out for club meetings. Right from the earliest days, coffee-men were on the lookout for new sources of income and ways of boosting sales of the invigorating beverage. Making a back room available for private meetings encouraged trade.

The Turk's Head Coffee-House in New Palace Yard, St James's, hosted one of London's earliest known debating societies, the Rota Club. A short-lived republican group founded in 1659 by James Harrington in the dying days of the Commonwealth, the Rota Club was based upon the Italian model of learned societies or virtuosi.

The Rota's proposition, that a proportion of MPs should be elected on a rota basis, was designed to encourage and empower citizen politicians. Members of the Rota Club included John Aubrey, Andrew Marvell, John Milton, scientists Robert Boyle and Robert Hooke, the Astronomer Royal John Flamsteed, and the diarist Samuel Pepys. This hotbed of republicanism did not long survive the Restoration of the Monarchy in 1660. But while the Rota Club and quasi-religious organisations like the Levellers aimed at wielding influence in Cromwell's Commonwealth, another group – the Sealed Knot – was dedicated to its overthrow.

The Sealed Knot met in secret to further its agenda of restoring the Stuart monarchy.

If word had got out about what was discussed at meetings of the Sealed Knot or who its members were, then charges of treason might have been brought and certain prominent aristocrats would have faced the executioner's block.

The Rota Club was immediately disbanded. Harrington fled to Plymouth where he was captured and imprisoned. Algernon Sydney and William Russell, two other founder members of the Rota, were less lucky. Marked men, they were tried and executed for involvement in the Rye House plot in 1683. Other members like Samuel

Pepys and Sir William Petty survived and thrived in the Restoration. These marked differences in fortune depended on whom you knew, what you knew, how valuable your services might be in future and how lucky you were.

Learned Societies

The Restoration of the Monarchy ushered in an era of scientific discovery and a thirst for knowledge. Formed in 1660 and given a royal charter two years later, the Royal Society's original founders included Robert Boyle, Sir William Petty and the architect Christopher Wren. To give it its full name, 'The Royal Society of London for Improving Natural Knowledge', functioned as an elite club. Members, known as 'fellows', were each accorded equal status. All were freemasons.

Coffee-houses of the period were keen to participate in intellectual and scientific debate. Publicised well in advance, talks would attract a more educated clientele and encourage repeat custom. The following advertisement appeared in the *Tatler* dated 8 October 1709:

> This is to give notice to all ingenious gentlemen in and about the cities of London and Westminster who have a mind to be instructed in the noble sciences of music, poetry and politics that they repair to the Smyrna coffee-house in Pall Mall between the hours of eight and ten at night, where they may be instructed with elaborate Essays 'by word of mouth' on all or any of the above mentioned arts. To purge their bodies with three dishes of Bohea and purge their brains with two pinches of snuff.

Popular places of public resort, coffee-houses and taverns were obvious meeting places for early clubs. But following the Restoration of the Monarchy in 1660 virtually any club was regarded with the utmost suspicion, and the government employed spies to mix with the patrons of coffee-houses in and around St James's to report on any political discussions taking place. This febrile atmosphere of suspicion came to a head in 1675 when King Charles II on the advice of his Privy Council issued 'A Proclamation For the Suppression of Coffeehouses.'

The royal command was directed:

> to all manner of persons, That they or any of them do not pre-
> sume ... to keep any Publick Coffee-house, or to Utter or sell by
> retail, in his or her own house or houses (to be spent or consumed
> within the same) any Coffee, Chocolate, Sherbett or Tea as they
> will answer the contrary at their utmost perils.

It was also declared illegal to brew or drink coffee at home. The 'Proclamation' led to a public outcry and was never widely enforced. However, in 1715, at the height of the Jacobite Rebellion, the king's messengers burst into a packed Ozinda's and dragged away its pro-prietor along with some of his customers and incarcerated them in Newgate Prison.

Attempts to control coffee consumption and the political discus-sion that often accompanied it were doomed to failure. Coffee-houses were by now part of the fabric of urban life. By 1720 it is estimated that there were some 2,000 coffee-houses in London and other major cities. One important side effect was that clubs which continued to meet in coffee-houses became more secretive about their activities and their individual members less outspoken and more circumspect.

The clubs did however meet a real need for conversation and debate, particularly concerning the advancement of science or poli-tics. Typical of these learned societies was Jonathan Swift's Brother's Club founded in 1711. The club which comprised 'nine lords and ten commoners' met every Thursday at the Thatched House Tavern in St James's Street 'at the cost of seven good guineas'.[*] Members included the Duke of Beaufort and the Earls of Danby, Bathurst and Harcourt. Swift framed a set of rules. 'The end of our club is to

---

[*] John Timbs, *Clubs and Club Life in London*, John Camden Hotten, London, 1872, p. 17

advance conversation and friendship, and to reward learning without interest or recommendation.'**

Over at the Turk's Head Tavern in Gerrard Street, Soho, a coterie of influential writers gathered around Doctor Samuel Johnson. Known as 'The Club' or Literary Society, this band of clubmen held weekly court from 1746, switching the venue of their meetings a few years later to St James's Street. The nine founding members were Samuel Johnson, Joshua Reynolds, Edmund Burke, Christopher Nugent, Topham Beauclerk, Bennet Langton, Oliver Goldsmith, Anthony Chamier and John Hawkins. The proceedings would begin quietly enough with a supper, after which conversation would grow increasingly animated as drinking and rowdy conduct would carry on into the small hours. The club was popular with authors, actors and MPs. The club was so successful it outlived Johnson's death in 1783 and survived into the twentieth century. By 1775 Johnson's club had grown to twenty-one members, many more than its founder's original vision of an intimate dining club. New members included the doctor's amanuensis and diarist James Boswell, the Whig politician Charles James Fox, Sir Thomas Bunbury, and the author Edward Gibbon. As time went on, membership of 'The Club' became more aristocratic and elite.

Private Spaces

Occasionally, public taverns and coffee-houses abandoned the public realm altogether to become private clubs from which the public were excluded. This phenomenon represents the first shoots of the governing principles of what we recognise today as a members' club. A prime example of this nascent social segregation was the Cocoa Tree Club in St James's Street, which closed its doors as a public coffee-house in around 1746 to become the de facto headquarters of the Tory party.

** Ibid., p. 17

The Cat and Fiddle tavern in King's Street Westminster followed the same route, being reborn as the Kit Kat Club. The most famous literary club of the reign of Queen Anne, the Kit Kat was named after its proprietor, Christopher Katt. Pub landlord and pastry chef, Katt's celebrated mutton pies were known colloquially as 'Kit Kats'. Club members included the printer and publisher Jacob Tonson, writers Addison, Steele, Pope, and Congreve, and the architect Vanbrugh.

The association between coffee-houses and intellectual curiosity, however, was being replaced by crass sensationalism. This is evident by 1735 when the following advertisement appeared in a London newspaper beneath a crude woodcut illustration of an unlikely looking serpent: 'To be SEEN at the Virginia Coffee-House behind the Royal Exchange A very Large and Beautiful RATTLE-SNAKE, the only one now in England and the finest ever seen … ' And in the Haymarket, a street noted for curious exhibitions, huckster and showman George Baily advertised a monster 'brought from Mount Tibet' which was considered ' … to approach the human species nearer than any other hitherto exhibited, and is supposed to be the long-lost link between the human and brute creation.'

So, whether it was through 'the noble sciences of music, poetry and politics' or a rattlesnake in a cage, coffee-men needed to attract paying customers. The shrewd coffee-man or woman needed to forge a common bond with the customers and give them what they wanted. By hiring out rooms for private gatherings like clubs and debating societies, the coffee-houses of St James's had built the foundation for the rise of London's Clubland.

The Craze for Clubs

By the 1720s the Scottish diarist John Macky described London as having 'an infinity of clubs and societies for the improvement of learning and keeping up good humour and mirth'. St James's was home to a bewildering array of debating societies, gambling and sporting clubs, musical and literary societies, masonic and pseudo-masonic orders, as well as clubs dedicated to politics, phi-lanthropy, professional networking, self-improvement or indeed, any common basis for co-fraternity.

Precise numbers are hard to pin down but male sociability revolved around a common social and intellectual bond. This is still the hall-mark of the modern members' club.

To that keen observer of London life, Ned Ward, many such clubs must have appeared utterly ridiculous. In his book, *A Compleat and Humorous Account of all the Remarkable Clubs and Societies in the City of London and Westminster,* Ward lampoons such notable organs as the No Nose Club, the Farting Club, the Beggars Club, the Mollies Club and Sam Scot's Smoking Club. Apparently, the Farting Club was based at:

> ... a public house in Cripplegate Parish where they used to meet once a week to poison the neighbouring Air with their unsavoury *Crepitations*, and were so vain in their ambition to out Fart one another, that they used to diet themselves against their Club-Nights with Cabbage, Onions, and Pease-Porridge, that everyone's Bumfiddle might be better qualified to sound forth its Emulation.[*]

It is an intriguing possibility that similar clubs might have inspired Ward's satire of bawdy tavern life. In his book's table of contents, Ward includes the equally implausibly named Kit Kat Club and the Beefsteak Club, both of which were genuine. In the case of the last, although the original was disbanded, the name was later revived and is now attached to an aristocratic dining club which still enjoys great popularity. Originally known as 'The Sublime Society of Beef Steaks', this dining club was founded in 1735 by the actor Henry Rich and the landscape painter George Lambert. Now located in Irving Street just off the Charing Cross Road, the Beefsteak Club can justly claim to be a spiritual descendent of Ward's original.

---

[*] Ned Ward, *A Compleat and Humorous Account of all the Remarkable Clubs and Societies in the City of London and Westminster,* printed for J. Wren, London, 1756, p. 31

A good example of the more informal public house camaraderie found in some of the clubs during this period of transition is Charles Dickens's fictitious 'Pickwick Club' which met at the George and Vulture, off Lombard Street in the City. *The Pickwick Papers* recounts a series of hilarious but embarrassing set pieces that readers could readily identify with, such as electioneering at a rotten borough, a pheasant shoot, hiring a manservant, fending off amorous widows and so forth.

This proliferation of sociability was not confined to London, or even to England, as the craze for forming clubs followed colonial expansion and newly established trade routes to the Americas. The historian Peter Clark has estimated that during the eighteenth century there 'may have been up to 25,000 different clubs and societies meeting in the English-speaking world'.[*]

Coffee-houses and taverns were ideal meeting places, particularly important in this period of social change when one might need to talk in confidence about one's horses, one's investments or one's political plans. This aspect is particularly evident throughout Trollope's political novels. Coffee-house clubs were generally informal, membership was fluid and there were few, if any, rules. Some clubs were peripatetic, assembling in various public taverns and coffee-houses to suit the needs or whims of members. However, it was quickly realised that rules were needed to enforce polite conduct and maintain social distance.

The Robin Hood Club, which met at the Robin Hood Tavern in Butcher's Row, gathered around Edward Cave, a self-styled and highly talented journalist who went on to publish the highly popular *Gentleman's Magazine*. What had started as an informal debating society was almost ruined after some new members made the mistake of monopolising the conversation. Rules were needed to enforce conduct and impose penalties. The writers' magazine the *Grub Street Journal* reported:

---

[*] Peter Clark, *British Clubs and Societies 1580–1800*, Clarendon Press, Oxford, 2000, p. 2

For six months this occasional club 'subsisted with great regularity though without any restraint', but then one night three newcomers came and spoke so incessantly and tediously that there was a universal demand for a set of rules.[**]

By the early eighteenth century some popular coffee and chocolate-houses had begun restricting entry to only those willing to pay the admission charge. This could range from a penny to six-pence for a smart establishment like White's. Writing in the *Tatler* shortly after its launch in May 1709, Richard Steele reporting 'from White's Chocolate-House', observes: 'I cannot keep an ingenious man to go daily to Will's under 2d each day merely for charges, to White's under 6d ... ' Price was a crude instrument of social segregation but it was also the first move on the path towards the privatisation of the public realm and the subsequent development of Clubland.

Although it was to rise steadily throughout the century, the admission charge was a small price to pay for congenial conversation among social equals, a comfortable seat in front of a blazing fire, and a selection of the latest newspapers kept on the bar counter. By the eighteenth century, coffee-houses began to reflect the identity of special interest groups. They started to appeal to niche markets, catering for a single tightly defined demographic. A love of the arts, science, or a political leaning was enough to encourage like-minded men to form a club.

The Dilettanti

An early example of intellectual stratification of this type is the Society of Dilettanti. The moving spirit behind the Society's foundation in 1732 was Sir Francis Dashwood, Lord le Despencer. Initially

[**] *The Grub Street Journal*, 20 February 1734, Collection: Institute of Historical Research

it was a dining club for a group of young men who had travelled to Italy, Greece and the Levant as part of the Grand Tour, then a near universal rite of passage for young English aristocrats. Dashwood's 'grand tourists' shared a keen interest in Greek and Roman art, and a certain *joie de vivre*. Meetings of this small but highly influential Society were held at various taverns, the Society never having possessed premises of its own in which to hang its paintings and hold its dinners. The first recorded dinner took place in the Bedford Head Tavern in Covent Garden, moving in about 1757 to the Star and Garter Tavern in Pall Mall.

With a boundless enthusiasm for fine wines and fine dining, the Society's dinners were presided over by one member, appointed for that evening only. Whenever a newly elected member was introduced, the president wore a scarlet toga and sat on a special throne covered in crimson velvet. The club secretary was dressed as Machiavelli while the master of ceremonies, known as the Arch Master, was kitted out in a crimson taffeta pleated gown and a Hungarian cap. The club's regalia included a casket for keeping the Society's dinner money, known as the 'Tomb of Bacchus', a carved and ornamented box mounted with an ivory figure of a reclining Bacchus. These rituals have survived intact to the present day.

A series of portraits commissioned by the Dilettanti and now on permanent display at Brooks's give us a flavour of a carnival atmosphere of an eighteenth-century club dinner. Painted by the Society's Painter Member and official artist George Knapton, the portraits reveal a startling array of images of young men dressed in turbans, togas, cardinal's robes, and in one instance in the costume of a Venetian gondolier. These are all references to the attributes, skills, travels or diplomatic posts held by the member depicted in each portrait. Perhaps all this exuberance was to be expected, for the Dilettante-in-chief Francis Dashwood was the man who had created the Medmenham Friars, better known as the 'Hell-fire Club', a secret society reputed to indulge in drunkenness, satanism and lechery whose candlelit meetings were held in the caves beneath West Wycombe Mausoleum. Despite rumours of strange goings-on, the

Society of Dilettanti was certainly no hell-fire club. A respected, if eccentric, Whig politician, Dashwood held the post of Chancellor of the Exchequer from 1762–1763. By the time he died in 1788, the Society had consolidated its position as a leading advocate for the arts in Britain.

In its early days, the Society of Dilettanti promoted Italian opera at the Theatre Royal Haymarket, and by the 1750s it was campaigning vigorously for a royal sponsorship of the arts. Later in the eighteenth century the Society financed expeditions by artists and engineers to excavate temples and other classical sites in Greece and Asia Minor, draw them and publish the results in magnificent folio volumes. The Society also funded the purchase of antiquities, which it presented to the British Museum.

Among the most influential of the new generation of Dilettanti, Sir Joshua Reynolds laid the foundations for what was to become the Royal Academy. In 1759 Reynolds and a group of artists including Francis Hayman, Richard Wilson and Sir William Chambers formed the Society of Artists of Great Britain, Britain's first formal artistic organisation.

Meanwhile the Royal Academy went from strength to strength. Support for the institution, which with its rules and written constitution resembled a gentlemen's club, was led by the rising generation of talented British artists, Reynolds, Gainsborough and Zoffany. The instrument founding the Royal Academy was signed by King George III on 10 December 1768. Its first home was established in Pall Mall next to the Royal Opera Arcade. The Royal Academy now occupies Burlington House, Piccadilly.

From the outbreak of the Napoleonic wars in 1792 until Napoleon's defeat at Waterloo in 1815, Britain was cut off from continental Europe. During those dark, uncultured years, for Britain at least, the Dilettanti preserved the vision of classical culture. Between 1810 and 1861 the Society of Dilettanti held its meetings at the Thatched House Tavern, 74 St James's Street. This club has played an unparalleled role in promoting the arts in Britain.

The Thatched House

The famous Thatched House Tavern on St James's Street was an institution in its own right. It is intimately associated with the formation of clubs and the development of London's Clubland. It exemplifies the transition from public house to coffee-house to members' club. Conjuring images of a rural idyll, the 'thatched house' comprised a grand set of assembly and club rooms. Illustrations show a banqueting hall with an enormous high ceiling complete with chandeliers and marble chimneypieces. The Thatched House Tavern's Scottish proprietor William Cullen hosted many clubs and societies, all of which made their mark on society. Among the clubs Cullen encouraged were the Catch Club, the Linnaean Club, the Literary Society, which had been founded by Dr Samuel Johnson, and the Royal Society.

The Thatched House was associated with freemasonry. Far more than a members' club, a masonic lodge depended upon privacy, discretion and the exclusion of the public. The Thatched House had many private rooms where lodge meetings could be held, and its management was receptive to the needs for discretion and privacy. A notice appearing in a London newspaper lists the '117 Lodge of Regularity at the Thatched House Tavern in St James' Street.'* No fewer than nine masonic lodges held their meetings at the Thatched House Tavern, suggesting that freemasonry was an influence on the rising middle classes. The Prince of Wales was the master of a royal lodge based on Carlton House and with a branch for the Brighton Pavilion. Many of his closest associates including the dandified cronies of Watier's Club would have been freemasons.

Despite superficial similarities including privacy, exclusivity, and shared purpose, there is no direct link between gentlemen's clubs and freemasonry. Their memberships undoubtedly overlapped but the clubs were, if anything, even more scrupulous than

---

* *Oracle and Daily Advertiser,* Wednesday 23 April 1800, issue 22, The Burney Collection Online

Masonic lodges when it came to excluding outsiders or people who did not fit in.

Coffee-Women

The coffee-houses of London were not always the masculine havens they are purported to be. Women often ran coffee-houses. While they rarely set up the business themselves, they often took over after their husband's death or else demonstrated to their spouse that they had better business nous. To a certain extent, this also reflected the surrounding milieu. In St James's, for example, shops, theatres, concert halls and assemblies attracted both sexes. Many of the coffee- and chocolate-houses of St James's doubled as box offices for plays, masquerade balls and assemblies. Advertisements were aimed at women and men. Typical of this offer was this advertisement which appeared in *The London Daily Post and General Advertiser*:

> At the King's Theatre Haymarket, Thursday next will be AN ASSEMBLY (being the last of this year). Tickets will be delivered to subscribers at White's Chocolate-House in St James's Street on Wednesday next. NB Every ticket will admit either one Gentleman or TWO Ladies.**

Ladies would send their servants to coffee-houses to post mail using the penny post service available within London. Ladies were not the only members of society using coffee-houses as post offices. The following advertisement is typical of much coffee-house correspondence soliciting get-rich-quick schemes:

> A CONSIDERABLE pecuniary GRATUITY. A Gentleman who is at present wholly disengaged from any occupation, will be happy

---

** *London Daily Post and General Advertiser*, The Burney Collection of Seventeenth and Eighteenth Century Newspapers (Online)

to meet with any Lady or Gentleman, who has a sufficient degree of Influence with Government or any Public Body, to recommend him to a Comfortable Establishment for which he will make an adequate return. Application to MDG, St James's Coffee-House, St James's Street, will be duly attended to. *

The serving of chocolate and tea, widely considered to be more refined beverages, indicates that efforts were being made to attract women's custom. Strong and bitter, coffee roasted over a fire was not to female tastes as a pamphlet published in 1689 suggests. *The Women's Petition Against Coffee* claimed coffee ' ... that dry enfeebling liquor ... '** was responsible for a loss of libido in men. On the other hand, chocolate 'boiled for several hours, with white sugar, cinnamon ... cloves, almonds, orange flower water and vanilla straws and then enriched with milk and beaten eggs'*** was a more expensive and a high-status drink. Reports about its impact on male libido are unsubstantiated.

It was not uncommon to find women serving and even owning coffee-houses despite their predominantly masculine clientele. Known as 'coffee-women', most were doughty widows who had inherited the trade from their husbands like the notorious Moll King who ran Tom King's Coffee-House in Covent Garden after being widowed in 1737. Moll turned a blind eye to the prostitution and pick-pocketing that went with the territory and may have played an active part.

Coffee-women included Mary Stringar of Stringar's Coffee-House in Little Trinity Lane, Sarah's in Cornhill, Madame Rochford's Coffee-House at Charing Cross and Mary Long of the Rose in Covent Garden. When Francis White died in 1711, the lease of

---

* *World*, 3 March, 1788, The Burney Collection of Seventeenth and Eighteenth Century Newspapers (Online)
** The Women's Petition Against Coffee, London, 1674
*** Mary Cathcart Borer, *The Story of Covent Garden*, Robert Hale, London, 1984, p. 52

the house was re-assigned to his widow Elizabeth who ran White's Chocolate-House until 1729. She subsequently re-married a Major George Skene of Chelsea about whom almost nothing is known. Skene played no part in the running of White's and it is quite possible that the independent and resourceful Elizabeth still known as 'Widow White' kept her married life and her business interests completely separate. For a time, Elizabeth ran a business on the side as a ticket agent for the King's Theatre Haymarket. On 11 April 1724, the *Daily Post* advertised:

> Tickets for balls at the King's Theatre in Haymarket to be obtained at the chocolate-house in St James's Street and Masquerade Habits hired or bought at Widow White's House in Little Wild Street, and at the Opera Coffee-house next door but one to the Opera House.[****]

It is believed that Elizabeth left the business to her sons Bartholomew and Francis who kept White's in the family until at least 1732.

The Birth of Journalism

Hilliar's description of coffee drinkers eagerly swapping news and gossip and debating matters of common interest strikes a chord, for the eighteenth-century coffee-house was a place to find the latest news and meet friends. In many ways coffee-houses today operate in much the same way, with the addition of the internet and social media.

Established in 1705 and located at 87 St James's Street, St James's Coffee-House is closely associated with two of London's finest journalists, Joseph Addison and Richard Steele. Between them this pair launched two of the century's most influential and enduring

---

[****] Bryant Lillywhite, *London Coffee Houses*, George Allen and Unwin, London, 1963, p. 641

publications: the *Tatler* in 1709 followed by *The Spectator* in March 1711. At first the government viewed this intellectual freedom as a potential threat to the status quo and tried to restrict demand through the Stamp Act of 1712, amended in 1725, which imposed a tax of one penny on each copy sold.

But taxing newspapers was no barrier to free speech and radical opinion. An explosion of news media in the early eighteenth century occurred in spite of attempts by the government to gag the press. Loopholes in the legislation coupled with poor enforcement and an almost universal belief in the virtue of a free press created the conditions for a burgeoning newspaper industry. The coffee-houses in many cases provided the springboard for tyro journalists.

Over the next thirty years there were over 100 new titles launched in London, many of which could boast a national readership, including daily, weekly and monthly newspapers and digests.* From around twenty single leaf newspapers published in London in 1712,** by the end of the century London could claim slightly over 100 different daily, evening and weekly papers.***

To satisfy their customers' voracious appetite for news, coffee-houses subscribed to a number of papers which were kept at the public bar for customers to read. News articles prompted and informed discussion and debate within the coffee-house which in turn inspired journalists and helped shape their opinions. All information had a value particularly within the closed circle of the coffee-house. Many coffee-houses kept pens, ink and writing paper handy for customers' use. Any resident journalist or 'news writer' would not have had to

---

* Michael Harris, *London Newspapers in the Age of Walpole: A Study of the Origins of the Modern English Press*, London, Associated University Presses, 1987 Bibliography, p. 235
** Ibid., p. 19
*** Ibid., p. 235

look far for the tools of his trade. News was seen as more credible if it was associated with a high status coffee-house. This was especially the case if readers came from outside London. Articles bylined from a particular coffee-house lent credibility that its author was au fait with the latest London news.

But there is another fascinating link in the chain that connected coffee-houses with journalism and that is the fact that many London coffee-houses were also post offices for the internal London penny post.

This was of great value to customers especially from outside London since they could not only use the coffee-house as a convenient address for receiving mail when in London, but they could also send letters as part of the penny post launched in 1680. Under this system, letters or packets left at London coffee-houses would be collected and delivered by the General Post Office within the City and Westminster parishes. The penny post funnelled news from the provinces into London, and the coffee-houses acted as a vast clearing house for information – rather like today's social media.

The connection with London society gossip was warmly welcomed in the provinces, and many contemporary newspapers like *The Spectator* and the *Gentleman's Magazine* had a national reach after being founded as London-centric news-sheets.

Revolt of the Coffee-Men

The public realm created by journalism, although popular, came to be regarded by coffee-house proprietors as a threat to their business. They recognised the influence of the press and wanted to impose restrictions in order to protect the privacy of their customers. There was another objection too. Coffee-houses had been accustomed to spending the entrance fees collected to subscribe to an ever increasing number of publications to satisfy their customers' thirst for news, market intelligence, entertainment and society gossip. But the subscription costs ate into their profits.

In 1728 matters came to a head when a committee of enterprising coffee-shop owners proposed cancelling all of the newspapers they subscribed to and replacing them with a single publication appearing twice daily as a morning and an evening edition. They would encourage other London coffee-men to follow suit and collectively they would finance and run the paper, sharing an annual dividend from the profits of this publication. A meeting of subscribers held at Tom's Coffee-House in Wood Street on 30 November 1728 resulted in a short-lived publication, the *Coffee-House Morning Post*, which made a brief appearance during 1729. The details are contained in an anonymous pamphlet written by a 'Coffee-Man' entitled:

> The Case of the Coffee-men of London and Westminster, or an Account of the Impositions and Abuses put upon them and the whole Town by the present Set of News-Writers, With The Scheme of the Coffee-men for setting up News-papers of their own and some Account of their Proceedings thereupon.

Although the writer of the pamphlet chose to remain anonymous, the publication features prominently a circular letter written for distribution to coffee-houses throughout London and signed by eleven proprietors, mainly from the City and Cornhill. The signatories of the declaration included Thomas Wills of Tom's Coffee-House (then in Wood Street but later to relocate to Cornhill), Stephen Wiggan of Baker's Coffee-House, and John Morris of Garraway's Coffee-House, both located in Change Alley, and Thomas Jemson of Lloyd's Coffee-House, Lombard Street.

The publication is a highly significant development in the transition of the coffee-house from a public to a private space. Signing themselves 'Your most humble Servants', the coffee-house owners believed that restricting London's free press and setting up their own competing newspaper would put a stop to unscrupulous journalists willing to publish private conversations or secrets revealed in confidence. An unrestricted press, the coffee-men argued, threatened the unwritten rules of social conduct.

The pamphlet explains that journalists:

thrust themselves into Companies where they are not known; or plant themselves at a convenient distance to overhear what is said, in Order to pick up Matter for the Papers. By this Means, Gentlemen are often betrayed and embarrass'd in the Management of their private Interests and Concerns.*

In St James's, coffee-men were worried about scandal and felt it their duty to protect their clients' misdemeanours, crimes, vices or indiscretions from public scrutiny. An unfettered press was an affront to the coffee-house culture of polite society because it could disturb the newly developing social structures on which a club's financial stability depended. There is very little evidence that coffee-houses were plagued by snooping 'news-writers' or that they resented their links with the press which could generate beneficial publicity.

What coffee-men objected to most about these papers was the cost of subscription: ' ... most of 'em *Ten*, many *Fifteen* and some *Twenty* pounds a Year and upwards'. Our 'Coffee-man' believes the cost of subscribing to a wide range of newspapers to satisfy the demands or expectations of customers is taking away his profits. The newspaper publishers, he complains, 'thrust such a Number of Papers upon 'em the Week round, that the Charge of them is more than the Trade and Profits of one half of the Coffee-Men will allow'.**

A newspaper subscription was an overhead the proprietors could not fully recoup as they had to keep their entrance price in line with what other coffee-houses were charging. If they cancelled a subscription or raised the price of admission then customers could easily go

---

* The Case of the Coffee-Men or London and Westminster, Or an Account of the Impositions and Abuses put upon them and the whole Town by the Present set of News Writers, London, 1728, p. 6
** Ibid., p. 13

elsewhere. Besides, papers were full of advertisements aimed at customers, all gaining additional revenue for their publishers, a lucrative source of income in which coffee-men believed they should share.

In 1729 the newspaper proprietors hit back with a pamphlet of their own: *The Case Between the Proprietors of Newspapers and The Subscribing Coffee-Men Fairly Stated being Remarks on their Case Lately Publish'd*. This 'case' rested on the assertion that newspapers were an essential part of the coffee-house experience, that the subscription costs could be easily recouped through selling more coffee at a higher profit and by raising the price of admission:

> ... Gentlemen often meet to read the Publick Papers, and from the Topicks furnished by them descant on what they read, and fall into Conversations upon these Occasions, which made them consider the News-Papers as an agreeable Amusement, and entertainment for a vacant Hour, and in consideration thereof, call for a Dish or a Dram, which they know they pay for far above the intrinsic Value.[*]

The pamphlet went on to accuse coffee-men of being low bred, unintelligent and therefore unsuitable gatekeepers of information in what was emerging as a privileged public sphere. Customers, they argued, were better off trusting to the judgement of a professional news writer than to 'the dull Comprehension of an illiterate Coffee-man.'[**] It accused the coffee-men loftily as follows: 'Many of them are cast-off Valets, discarded Footmen etc who marrying their Fellow-Servants, turn into this Way of Business, purely because they can do nothing else; and would have no other Pretentions to it at all.'[***] In short, coffee-men were not to be trusted. The pamphlet could have been an exact description of one of the most famous of all early club proprietors, William Almack.

---

[*] The Case Between the Proprietors of Newspapers and the Subscribing Coffee-Men, Fairly Stated, London, 1729, p. 4
[**] Ibid., p. 7
[***] Ibid.

Coffee-House Politicians

The Hanoverian dynasty which succeeded to the throne of England in 1714 sparked a bitter rivalry between Tory Jacobites loyal to the Stuart monarchy and the Whigs who favoured the Hanoverian succession. The political rivalry between the opposing camps was played out in the coffee-houses of St James's. By the turn of the eighteenth century, coffee and chocolate-houses were differentiated according to political affiliation and social class. Emerging cliques were busy transforming their favoured haunts into private political or social spaces which excluded any individual not loyal to their cause. Whig supporters patronised the St James's Coffee-House while Tories favoured the Cocoa Tree and Ozinda's. The differences between Whigs and Tories gradually led to the exclusion of members of other political parties or to people who simply did not conform. Writing in 1732, the Scots traveller John Macky possessed a keen eye for the way coffee-houses tended towards exclusivity. Writing in 1732 he observed:

> I must not forget to tell you that the Parties have their different Places where, however, a stranger is well received; but a Whig will no more go to the Cocoa-Tree or Ozinda's than a Tory will be seen at the Coffee-House of St James's.[****]

The journalist Joseph Addison writing in *The Spectator* describes the atmosphere at the Whig-dominated St James's Coffee-House. He refers to the speculations of 'coffee-house politicians' on the death of the King of France:

> I found the whole outward room in a buzz of politics. The speculations were but very indifferent towards the door, but grew finer as you advanced to the upper end of the room, and so were very much improved by a knot of theorists who sat in the inner room,

---

[****] John Macky, *A Journey Through England*, Vol. 1, 5th edition, London, 1732, p. 191

within the steams of the coffee-pot, that I heard the whole of the Spanish monarchy disposed of, and all the line of Bourbon provided for in less than a quarter of an hour ...*

Despite the Whig Supremacy that lasted for half a century after a Whig government was first elected in 1721, many landed gentry whose ancestors had been granted land by Charles II and James II continued to support the Jacobite cause. Jacobites were regarded with the utmost suspicion, although few were radical enough to countenance a revolution.

This political division acted as a catalyst in the creation of private members' clubs. Customers of St James's Coffee-House, for example, formed the nucleus of the Whig stronghold Brooks's which moved from Pall Mall to 60 St James's Street in 1778. The Cocoa Tree converted to becoming a private club at some time between 1745 and 1746, while in 1733 White's created a private members' club which, in spite of the high stakes gaming allowed on the premises, was synonymous with the Tory party.

White's: From Coffee-House to Club

White's, the most exclusive of St James's members' clubs, began life in the late seventeenth century as a chocolate-house. Its history reflects the social and economic changes that marked the transition from coffee-house, through gambling hell, via fine dining to a modern members' club. However, from early times, there existed a darker enterprise, a back room where gentlemen wishing to indulge in high stakes card playing, paid for admission to what was in effect a private club room.

A haven of calm tranquillity and polite manners White's was not. Hard drinking and gambling was the order of the day. The bewigged denizens of this latter-day den of iniquity were transported by sedan chairs carried aloft by two footmen through filthy and noisy

---

* *The Spectator*, number 403, 12 June 1712

streets as described in 1716 by John Gay in his poem *Trivia*. His contemporary, the essayist Jonathan Swift notes that Robert Harley, Earl of Oxford ' ... never passed by White's Chocolate-House (the notorious rendezvous of infamous Sharpers and noble Cullies) without bestowing a curse upon that famous academy as the bane of half the English nobility.'[**]

By the early eighteenth century, White's had transformed itself from a public space serving drinking chocolate to a private gaming club. This was a far more profitable venture. Members were charged a shilling to sit down and play during the hours of daylight and half a crown ' ... by candlelight.'[***] According to the antiquarian John Timbs, ' ... professional gamblers who lived by dice and cards, provided they were free from the imputation of cheating, procured admissions to White's.'[*****]

All of this was a long way from the genteel pretensions of Francesco Bianchi, an Italian, and his wife Elizabetta, who established the original chocolate-house in 1693 at 70 St James's Street under the anglicised name of White. Several years earlier, the Bianchis had run a small dining house on the north side of Pall Mall opposite the site of the present Royal Automobile Club. As Clubland historian T.H.S. Escott informs us:

> ... he [Bianchi] gave new prominence to the specialities of his cuisine and cellar — ortolans a la Lucullus, macaroni prepared in the most alluring shape, and the choicest Italian vintages from the regal *monte pulciano* to the Florence wine, lately brought into fashion by Lord Bolingbroke.[*****]

[**] Ibid., p. 640

[***] John Timbs, *Club Life of London*, with anecdotes of the Clubs, Coffee Houses and Taverns of the Metropolis during the 17th, 18th and 19th centuries, 2 vols. London, Richard Bentley, 1866, p. 96

[****] Ibid., p. 96

[*****] T.H.S. Escott, *Club Makers and Club Members*, T. Fisher Unwin, London, 1914, p. 102

Soon, Bianchi set his sights on a more prestigious location and a more profitable line of business based on the newly fashionable drink, chocolate. Little is known about the Bianchis' Italian origins or why they came to set up a chocolate-house. But the evidence points strongly to the fact they were Venetians who would have been known to the many aristocratic young Englishmen on the Grand Tour.

Venice was the principal trading city in Europe involved in importing cocoa beans, and by the early seventeenth century its merchants had already developed the recipe for making fine drinking chocolate. Not only can Venice lay claim to some of the oldest established chocolate-houses in Europe, but it was also famous for its culture of gambling and masquerade balls that were part of its annual carnival. The wealthy and enterprising Bianchis were involved in both of these activities in London. It would have made clear sense to follow grand tourists like Lord Bolingbroke to St James's where there would be a huge demand for the luxurious and exotic drinking chocolate.

Bianchi, who had by now anglicised his name to Francis White, died in 1711, leaving his widow to carry on the business. Elizabeth remained actively involved until 1729 when she handed over the day-to-day running of the establishment to John Arthur who had joined the business as a servant in 1702. As Elizabeth's business manager, Arthur had been instrumental in acquiring leases to the two adjoining premises numbers 69 and 68 possibly to accommodate his 'casino', where the wealthiest patrons took turns to play the role of banker, holding the collective stake money and settling winnings at the end of play. In 1729 Arthur's Chocolate-House was established at 37–38 St James's Street. This business was run by John Arthur's son Robert. Under his ownership, the chocolate-house and the gambling club were split into two separate businesses. Then a notorious gambling hell, White's, evolved into the private members' club we know today.

Not long after Robert Arthur had bought the business from the widow White, disaster struck. In the early hours of 28 April 1733, White's burned down. Within three years it was back in business having been rebuilt on its old site. During this period, it had continued to operate from temporary premises at Gaunt's Coffee-House. Mr Arthur clearly took the fire as a warning that the club needed reform. The rebuilt White's would offer domestic comfort, coupled with privacy for members staying in Town. No one could become a member unless invited to submit to election by secret ballot. The management introduced a strict set of rules which would henceforth influence the way all St James's members' clubs were run. Thus was created, in effect, a self-governing code of conduct that was to be the model for all subsequent members' clubs.

Listed in Algernon Bourke's *The History of White's*, the club's rules were as follows:

That no one shall be admitted but by ballot

That nobody be proposed but when twelve members are present

That there be twelve members present when the person is balloted for, which is to be the day seven night after he is proposed, and one black ball is an exclusion for that time

That any person that is balloted for before ten a clock is not duly elected

That every member is to pay a guinea towards hiring a good cook

That no person be admitted to dinner or supper but what are members of the club

That every member that is in the room after ten a clock is to pay his reckoning at supper

That supper is to be on the table at ten a clock and the bill at twelve

That every member who is in the room after seven a clock and plays is to pay half a crown

That no person be proposed or balloted for but during the sitting of Parliament

Following the disastrous fire, White's was split into two distinct clubs, the 'Old Club' made up of gentlemen who had been members before the fire, and the 'Young Club' for members elected under the new set of rules. With a strong emphasis on the landed aristocracy, the eighty-two original members of White's Old Club included the Duke of Devonshire, the Earl of Cholmondeley, Major General Churchill, Bubb Doddington and Colley Cibber.

Over the following years, White's took on the character of a club for politicians. Writing from White's in 1745 to George Selwyn, Richard Rigby writes: 'I am waiting to hear the rattle of coaches from the House of Commons in order to dine at White's.'*

In 1781 the Old and New Clubs were amalgamated. White's now needed space to expand. Occupying the site of 37–38 St James's Street, White's original clubhouse was replaced in 1787 with a magnificent clubhouse built in stone in the Palladian style with Doric columns and a five-bay frontage designed by the architect James Wyatt. A magnificent barrel-vaulted coffee room on the first floor ran the full width of the building, and on the ground floor, facing the street, is the morning room with its famous bow window while to the rear is the billiard room. To underpin the club finances, the annual subscription was set at 10 guineas and the membership was set at 400. From the time of Tory prime minister, Pitt the Younger, White's became the senior club of the Tory party.

The history of White's reflects the journey from fizzing, rowdy coffee-house attracting the brightest and best intellectually, artistically and socially, in far from ideal surroundings, to the more measured and dignified St James's members' club offering a more sedate experience based on shared British values.

---

* Algernon Bourke, *The History of Whites*, London, 1892, p. 82

CHAPTER 3

THE RISE OF THE DANDY

Beaus their canes with Amber tipt produce,
Be theirs for empty Show, but thine for Use.
In gilded Chariots while they loll at Ease,
And lazily insure a life's Disease;
While softer Chairs the tawdry Load convey
To Court, to White's, Assemblies, or the Play.

John Gay *Trivia*

Despite the strong political affiliations of coffee-house patrons that spanned the social divides, the clubs of St James's reinforced class divisions and social hierarchy. The grand establishments founded from the mid-eighteenth century selected members for their power, influence and pedigree. This equated to aristocrats, generals, politicians, bishops, and a smattering of influential writers and artists.

John Gay's epic poem *Trivia* emphasises this through a scathing attack on the yawning chasm of London's class divide, and on the coarseness and profligacy of its idle rich carried in sedan chairs by straining chairmen through filthy and unlit streets 'To Court, to White's, Assemblies or the Play'.**

Club membership was inspired by loyalty to the two main political parties. Tory clubs like White's, Boodle's and the Cocoa Tree

---

** John Gay, *Trivia*

appealed to the old aristocracy. In contrast, the Whigs were members of Brooks's, a club which was both radical and progressive. Founder members included a group of young, extravagantly dressed aristocrats who had been on the Grand Tour. Known as 'Macaronis', these aesthetes were some of the forerunners of a later social grouping known as the dandies. The division between Whig and Tory and the contrasting lifestyles mirrored the political upheavals of the Hanoverian period.

Irrespective of their political affiliations, clubmen shared a common propensity for hard drinking and high stakes gambling. Sometimes duels were fought. Bankruptcies were not uncommon. There was a tendency, fuelled possibly by the ongoing European wars, to hold life cheap and take one's pleasures immediately and to excess in some cases.

Idle Pleasures

August establishments such as White's and Boodle's may have attracted gentlemen jockeying for power and position in politics, but they commonly had a faro table and a gaming room where whist and hazard could be played. A later generation of clubs from the Regency period like Crockford's and Watier's Club made no pretence of fostering political debate. They were gaming clubs, pure and simple.

During the long eighteenth century,* virtually all clubs encouraged betting, and the more bizarre the challenge the better. Bets were carefully recorded in ledgers, many of which still exist among club archives. At White's, for example, a bet was taken that a gentleman's manservant could breathe unaided under water for twelve hours. The bet was lost and the servant (predictably) drowned. Brooks's Betting Book records that in 1785 'Ld Cholmondeley has given two guineas to Ld Derby to receive 500 Gns (guineas) whenever his lordship fucks a woman in a balloon one thousand yards from the Earth.' The outcome of the bet is not recorded.

---

* The long eighteenth century stretches from Queen Anne's accession in 1702 to the end of William IV's reign in 1837

As well as offering opportunities for gambling and drinking, gentlemen's clubs fulfilled another important function. They provided home comforts for the landed gentry and members of parliament who had either moved to Town from their country estates in accordance with the London 'season' or were in London on business. Club life revolved around an early dinner when members would be waited on at table and served often excellent food and wine. The club also provided a ready-made social network.

From the late eighteenth century to the 1820s, clubs vied with each other in giving expensive masquerades and ridottos at grand mansions or hired assembly rooms.** Elizabeth White, the feisty widow and owner of White's in the early 1700s, used to make and supply masquerade costumes as well as sell tickets to these events. Being entertained by a club was expected to be a lavish experience. The historian Edward Gibbon speaks of a costumed ball given by members of Boodle's that cost 2,000 guineas. But this pales into insignificance beside one of the most extravagant entertainments of the Regency, the grand masquerade ball given by Watier's Club on 1 July 1814 to celebrate the defeat of Napoleon and his exile to Elba. A total of 1,700 guests were invited to a sit-down supper at Burlington House, Piccadilly followed by a masked ball. Among the guests mingling on the dance floor were Lord Byron, John Cam Hobhouse, society courtesan Harriette Wilson and Jane Austen's naval officer brother, Henry. Piccadilly was blocked by coaches from five in the afternoon to eight o'clock at night.

By the early nineteenth century, club membership had proliferated. Many people including the dandies described later in this chapter saw the club as a mark of status that provided access to important social networks. For this reason alone, many individuals were members of more than one club. This tendency persists to the present day: some individuals are members of seven clubs. Clubs remain a nexus of influence across many fields of endeavour.

** Masquerade ball in the Venetian fashion.

The Original Clubman

More than any other individual, William Almack can lay claim to creating London's Clubland. A serial entrepreneur, Almack founded four major clubs and several influential social networks during his years in Pall Mall and St James's Street. William Almack arrived in London in around 1754 with his new wife, determined to make his fortune. He had until recently been the Duke of Hamilton's valet and had married the Duchess's ladies' maid Elizabeth Cullen. The Scottish connection has led many historians to assume that Almack adopted an anglicised version of the Scottish surname McCall, but there is no evidence to support this, as Almack is a recognised Scottish surname. Whatever the case, the Almacks headed south armed with some useful introductions from their former employers and made straight for St James's.

William put his toe in the water by taking over the licence of an ale house at 49–50 Pall Mall. He moved onwards and upwards, acquiring the lease of the next-door property, and opened a gentlemen's club at number 51 Pall Mall in 1762. Originally called the 'Savoire Vivre', but soon after renamed in honour of its head waiter Edward Boodle, Boodle's is the second oldest surviving gentlemen's club in London. Membership of Boodle's was initially limited to 250 and the subscription fee fixed at 2 guineas. No high stakes gaming was permitted but card players were allowed a limited stake of 9 guineas per rubber or session at Whist. Boodle's was established in 1762. The title page of the original club constitution proudly proclaimed: 'WILLIAM ALMACK has taken the large new House West of his now dwelling House in Pall Mall for the sole use of a Society Established upon the following Rules.'*

Set up in opposition to the Tory-leaning White's, Boodle's attracted followers of William Pitt the younger, three times prime minister from 1782–1806. Describing himself neither as a Tory nor a Whig,

---

* Roger Fulford, *Boodles's 1762-1962: A Short History*, Eyre and Spottiswood, 1962, plate 1

Pitt's governments frequently took unpopular decisions such as raising taxes to fight the Napoleonic wars. In 1782 Boodle's moved to a new palatial clubhouse at 28 St James's Street, a building which it still inhabits.

Having developed a taste for the hospitality industry after making a start with Boodle's, William Almack decided to surrender his tavern licence and transform his public house into a private members' club. Known initially as Almack's Club, this opened in March 1764. Almack's Club had a far more tolerant approach to high stakes gambling and this no doubt helped attract aristocratic members including the Duke of Portland, the Duke of Roxburghe, John Crewe and the distinguished politician and second son of Lord Holland, Charles James Fox.

Almack's Club proved a money spinner. Leaving the day-to-day running of this club to his capable business manager William Brooks, Almack went on to create a new business venture known as Almack's Assembly Rooms in King Street, St James's. Raising the funds to employ an architect and builder and sparing no expense on fitting out a high-ceilinged ballroom, Almack's Assembly Rooms opened in 1765. It provided much material for twentieth-century novelists like Georgette Heyer, who exploited the changing social interactions through the marriage mart aspect of Almack's. The dress rules in particular paralleled the aspirations of the well-dressed gentleman like Brummell. With the Assembly Rooms, Almack had finally hit upon a winning formula to attract the beau monde. Unable to devote his attention to so many ventures, Almack sold the lease of his club to Brooks and a fellow manager Ellis in 1771. Almack was what would be referred to today as a serial entrepreneur.

Brooks's: The Story of a Whig Club

Founded in 1764, Brooks's went from strength to strength after its manager broke away from Almack to run the club separately and independently in 1776. High stakes gambling was, of course, an essential part of the club's attraction and the club's easy-going atmosphere attracted the leading celebrities and intellectuals of the day including David Garrick, Richard Brinsley Sheridan, Edmund Burke, Horace Walpole, and the anti-slavery campaigner William Wilberforce. Many of the original members were men of taste who had formed impressive libraries and collections of classical art and antiquities. The bibliophile Roxburghe Club, for example, was formed following the acquisition of the Duke of Roxburghe's library and is still in existence today.

William Brooks chose Henry Holland as architect for his new clubhouse in St James's Street, completed in 1778. Designed in the Palladian style, Holland's square, yellow-brick building is decorated with classical stone columns and balustrades. The classically inspired interiors and marble busts reflected the current taste for Roman architecture and became a style bible for numerous stately homes. Over the following years, Brooks's became the informal headquarters of the Whig party, and its major influence on British politics began in the main with one man, Charles James Fox. The most influential politician of his age, and a leading Whig, Fox was a supporter of radical causes such as the abolition of slavery and universal human rights. He was briefly foreign secretary under a Whig government in 1782.

From the outset, Brooks's was more of a gambling den than a political club. William Pitt, the younger, son of the Earl of Chatham and a future Tory prime minister, was a member for several years. He had even been proposed by Fox himself! But the two strong-willed parliamentarians fell out over their response to events across the Channel in France. In 1789, Fox, an avid supporter of the French revolution and its declaration of citizens' rights, was associated with a violent demonstration in St James's Street in which Pitt was forced to take refuge in White's. Followers of Fox, and members of Brooks's, were accused of aiding and abetting the affray which polarised politics. From then on, White's became staunchly Tory and Brooks's Whig. The cartoonist James Gillray, who lived in St James's Street with his lifelong partner, the print seller Hannah Humphrey, satirised, and no doubt exaggerated, the encounter with an image of a burly and irate Fox birching the bare back of Pitt the younger.

The young Whigs Fox introduced to the club formed an elite cadre known as 'Foxites' who dominated politics of the early nineteenth century. A later generation of members included the Whig prime ministers Earl Grey, who gave his name to his favourite blend of tea, Lord John Russell, Lord Melbourne, and Lord Palmerston. Ever keen to mix with the movers and shakers, the Prince of Wales joined Brooks's, where he fell under Fox's influence. Fox, however, had a serious character flaw: he was an inveterate gambler. Losing or winning vast sums in games that went on over several days and nights of uninterrupted play, Fox would often appear in public bleary eyed and dishevelled.

The Prince of Wales may not have understood the finer details of Whig politics, but he certainly shared Fox's enthusiasm for gambling at cards. This angered the king who was in any case disposed to object to anything his son got up to. To George III's disgust, the prince took to wearing the buff and blue Whig colours as a mark of his friendship with Fox. Despite taking a relaxed view of Fox's dissipated lifestyle, Brooks's had a strict code when it came to electing members. When the notorious duellist George Fitzgerald applied to join, he was blackballed. Never one to take no for an answer, 'Fighting Fitzgerald', as he was known, attempted to brazen it out. Mr Brooks tried in vain to placate the bully as he paced to and fro in the entrance lobby. As Timbs relates:

> ... many of the members were panic-struck, foreseeing a disagreeable finale to the farce that had been playing ... At length, the Earl of March, (afterwards Lord Queensberry) said aloud 'Try the effect of two balls: d-n his Irish impudence, if two balls don't take effect on him, I don't know what will.'[*]

Fitzgerald dashed upstairs to the principal room and confronted each and every member of the ballot committee demanding to know who had cast the black balls. No one was brave enough to look him in the

---

[*] John Timbs, p. 88.

face. Brooks died in 1782 and was succeeded as master of the club by a Mr Griffin who was master of the club until 1815.

The Dandies' Club

By the dawn of the nineteenth century, clubs were beginning to reflect changing fashions of a new generation. Despite their reputation, old established gaming clubs like White's and Boodle's were seen as too tame for the new fast set known as the 'dandies'. A new mood was on the move, led by Brummell, a middle class parvenu, and George, Prince of Wales. The prince, or 'Prinny' as he was popularly known, befriended progressive thinkers like Charles James Fox and David Garrick. He was determined to modernise the monarchy and encourage a less deferential and more meritocratic society. Ripples were felt throughout Clubland.

In 1807, after a dinner party hosted at the Brighton Pavilion, the Prince of Wales asked his guests, Beau Brummel, Henry Mildmay, Henry Pierrepoint, Sir Philip Francis and Sir Thomas Stepney what the food was like at the St James's clubs. Stepney replied describing ' … the eternal joints, or beef-steaks, the boiled fowl with oyster sauce, and an apple tart – this is what we have, sir at our clubs, and very monotonous fare it is.'[*] Deciding on the spot to create a club for connoisseurs of haute cuisine, the prince volunteered the services of his personal chef, Jean-Baptiste Watier, to front the enterprise. The gentlemen's club named in his honour would come to define Regency luxury and decadence. Lord Byron, a member of Watier's, dubbed it 'The Dandies Club'. Beau Brummel was enrolled as the club's president while the Carlton House steward, Madison, would be responsible for day to day management.

Watier's Club duly opened at 81 Piccadilly on the corner of Bolton Street. Never mind that the Napoleonic Wars were in full swing and

---

[*] John Timbs, *Club Life of London*, Richard Bentley, New Burlington Street, 1866, p. 320

Britain stood at imminent risk of a French invasion. Since the revolution of 1787 a steady stream of aristocratic émigrés was making its way across the Channel, among them a number of talented French chefs keen to place their culinary skills at the service of '*les rosbifs*'. Despite being volunteered by the prince to set a new standard in club cooking, Watier declined further involvement and suggested his colleague, Monsieur Labourie, under whose guidance impressive bills of fare reflected the pinnacle of French culinary art.

Indicative of the dishes on offer to the dandies is this menu devised by royal chef Charles Francatelli. It includes the following:

Quenelles of rabbit in consommé
Crimped turbot
Lobster sauce
Chickens à l'Allemande
Croustades of soft roes of mackerel à la Ravigotte
Turkey-poult
Ramequins en casse and
Iced pudding au Prince of Wales.**

Labourie's exquisite dishes were soon attracting the aristocratic set, but Watier's Club had another claim to fame. Billed at first as a musical society and glee club, the establishment was closely associated with a particularly dangerous and addictive card game, Macao, a version of *vingt-et-un* where stakes could rise swiftly and where fortunes could be won or lost at a single sitting. The Macao tables proved an irresistible attraction for wayward younger sons of the nobility, hardened rakes, dashing guards' officers and, inevitably, dandies of the 10th Light Dragoons, (the Prince of Wales' Own), a hussar regiment whose colonel-in-chief was none other than the prince himself.

The 10th was a vanity project, a position conferred on the wayward prince in 1793 by his over-controlling father, George III. It was small

---

** Charles Elmé Francatelli, *The Modern Cook: A Practical Guide to the Culinary Art*, Richard Bentley and Son, London, 1846, p. 507

compensation for having to play second fiddle to his younger brother Frederick, Duke of York, whose military ambitions were quickly rewarded by his appointment as Commander-in-Chief of the British Army. As heir to the throne the prince, frustrated by his father's persistent refusal to allow him a more active role, busied himself with such weighty matters as the cut of his men's uniforms, and taking parades and march-pasts. While the 10th might not have been the most disciplined fighting unit, its officers were certainly the best dressed.

Beau Brummel

The dashing George Bryan Brummel had begun his career as a cornet (junior officer) with the 10th Light Dragoons, and his relationship with the gregarious prince dates from soon after the regiment was formed. A full sixteen years younger than the prince, Beau Brummel and the heir to the throne forged a remarkable friendship. The prince was captivated by his young officer's charm and sophistication, and especially his sense of fashion. Brummel was the ideal which the prince, over-fond of exquisite food but with an ever-expanding girth, aspired to but could never quite match. This, then, was the presiding genius of Watier's Club.

While many of the prince's circle were famed for their courage and military prowess, Beau Brummel simply liked strutting about in a dashing uniform. The Prince of Wales' Own were distinguished by their dark blue hussar uniform with deep yellow facings, tight breeches and top boots. Sometimes referred to as 'inexpressibles', the hussar's breeches were immodest to say the least. Worn without underwear these skintight garments were laced tight at the back. As part of his dress uniform, Brummel also wore long pantaloons sometimes referred to as trousers or 'trowsers' which covered the entire leg and were fastened with a strap under the instep to maintain a clean line.

Brummel's flirtation with military life came to an abrupt end when the regiment was ordered north to Manchester late in 1798 to assist the local militia. Having reached the rank of captain, he wasted no time in selling out his commission to pursue a life of fashion, profligacy and gambling. His natural habitat was Watier's Club and White's where he and his cronies were frequently to be found seated in the large bay window overlooking St James's Street appraising any lady brave enough to pass by.

Successful gaming required nerve and an ability to dissemble, qualities which Brummel possessed in abundance. John Timbs in his book *Club Life of London* refers to the diarist Thomas Raikes as Watier's resident expert on Macao which he describes ironically as a 'very genteel game'. A soldier turned professional gambler, Beau Brummel's success at the card table enabled him to fund a lavish but precarious lifestyle as he alternated between Watier's Club and White's. Clubland chronicler John Timbs recounts an incident at Watier's when things went badly wrong for Brummel. Among the members was Bligh, a notorious madman:

> One evening at the Macao table when the play was very deep, Brummel, having lost a considerable stake, affected in his farcical way, a very tragic air and cried out, 'Waiter, bring me a flat candlestick and a pistol.' Upon which Bligh who was sitting opposite him produced two loaded pistols from his coat pocket, which he placed on the table and said, 'Mr Brummel, if you really are desirous to put an end to your existence, I am extremely happy to offer you the means without troubling the waiter.'[*]

Brummel's deep card play fuelled ill-feeling among his victims and slowly added to his list of enemies. 'George Harley Drummond, of the famous banking house at Charing Cross, only played once in his whole life at White's Club at whist, on which occasion he lost £20,000 to Brummel. This event caused him to retire from the banking house of which he was a partner.'[**]

---

[*] Ibid., p. 169
[**] John Timbs *Club Life of London*, Richard Bentley, New Burlington Street, 1866, p. 322

Defining the Dandy

The historian Thomas Carlyle famously defined the dandy as '... a man whose trade, office and existence consists in the wearing of clothes. Every faculty of his soul, spirit, purse and person is heroically consecrated to this one object.' To be a true dandy one needed to be in possession of a significant fortune, to spend it lavishly and be prepared to risk huge sums at the gaming table. What mattered most was being part of an exclusive clique closely identified with expensive tailoring, fastidious rituals of dress, and a casual disregard for morals. Dandies were typically drawn from a narrow aristocratic elite, treading a well-worn path from Eton or Harrow to a paid commission in an exclusive regiment. Aspiring middle class, Brummel ought not to have made the cut, but educated at Eton and having spent two terms honing his drinking, gambling and womanising talents at Oriel College Oxford, the Beau's profligacy and wit as well as his friendship with the prince cast him in the role of London's leader of fashion.

Unlike other dandies, Brummel was not noted for his wit – or even his looks. The Regency's most celebrated courtesan, Harriette Wilson gives us a pen portrait of him in her *Memoirs:*

> ... nobody could have mistaken him for anything like handsome ... he had by some accident, broken the bridge of his nose ... He possessed (also) a sort of quaint, dry humour, not amounting to anything like wit; indeed he said nothing which would bear repetition; but his affected manners and little absurdities amused for the moment.*

Whatever Brummel's personal shortcomings, the dandy style quickly caught on among a tight knit group who came to define the true

---

* Harriette Wilson, *The Memoirs of Harriette Wilson,* London, John Joseph Stockdale, 1825: this edition The Perfect Library, p. 35

St James's dandy. Writing in his memoirs some quarter of a century after the dandy phenomenon was at its height, the diarist and former dandy Captain Rees Gronow of the Grenadier Guards is quite specific:

> The dandies of society were Beau Brummel, the Duke of Argyle, The Lords Worcester, Alvanley and Foley, Henry Pierrepoint, John Mills, Bradshaw, Henry de Ros, Charles Standish, Edward Montagu, Hervey Aston, Dan McKinnon, George Dawson Damer, Lloyd (commonly called Rufus Lloyd) and others that have escaped my memory. They were great frequenters of White's Club, in St James's Street where, in the famous bay window, they mustered in force.[**]

To this list must be added some equally famous dandies: 'Golden Ball' Hughes, 'King' Allen and the Count d'Orsay.

Centred on St James's, Clubland helped create a thriving economy based on luxury goods and services as the area developed a reputation for smart tailoring, luxurious accessories, and extravagant entertainment. Within a few minutes' walk, the dandy could find gaming clubs, chocolate-houses, tailors and all the glove-makers, hatters, breeches makers and linen warehouses that supplied his needs. Together with the theatre, opera and assembly rooms, this tiny enclave of luxury could fill a dandy's day from a leisurely rise to falling into bed in the early hours of the morning. White's and Brooks's in St James's Street were a dandy's favourite evening haunt. And if a casual sexual liaison was sought, there were plenty of high-class brothels to be found nearby. Libertines like Brummel frequently availed themselves of the services of prostitutes, viewing marriage and children as an impediment.

[**] Captain Gronow, *Reminiscences of Captain Gronow Formerly of the Grenadier Guards and MP for Stafford*, Smith, Elder and Co., 63 Cornhill London, 1842, from p. 20

Wellington's War Heroes

The dandy's sybaritic lifestyle contrasted strongly with the bravery demanded when called upon to fight for king and country. The Regency buck was typically a junior officer who had seen action in the Napoleonic Wars. Gentlemen's clubs of this era were shaped by the need for diversion and an appetite for horseplay, practical jokes and showing off. Of the dandies listed by Captain Gronow, many were war heroes whose experiences of combat shaped an insouciance and a complete refusal to conform to the norms of civilian life. Dandyism was an act of defiance – a celebration, in effect, of having survived. Clubs were their natural habitat. As the Duke of Wellington observed: 'The Dandies fought splendidly in Spain.'

The young clubmen were a close-knit clique who eschewed serious conversation, preferring schoolboy pranks and banter, a part of which was nicknaming. Alexander Charles 'Teapot' Crawfurd (born 1794) served in the 10th Light Dragoons as a young ensign during the latter stages of the Peninsular War. An avid tea drinker, Crawfurd acquired his soubriquet at Eton from the small black teapot which he carried even in later life as a kind of mascot. Tall and strong, Crawfurd served with distinction at Orthès where he led the charge and went on to achieve the rank of Lieutenant Colonel. He was a favourite of the prince and the story goes that while on parade prior to embarkation for Spain, Prinny singled him out, saying: 'Go my boy and show the world what stuff you are made of. You possess strength, youth and courage; go and conquer!'* Crawfurd's brother was killed at Waterloo defending the farm at Hougoumont where the Guards were caught up in some of the heaviest fighting of the battle.

Another noted man about St James's where he confined himself to a daily walk between Crockford's and White's and from White's to

---

* Vol. 3, *Reminiscences of Captain Gronow Formerly of the Grenadier Guards and MP for Stafford*, Smith, Elder and Co., 63 Cornhill, London, 1842

Crockford's was the Irish peer Viscount Allen, known as 'King Allen'. Always resplendent in highly polished boots and top hat, as an ensign in the Guards, King Allen had led a detachment of troops across a ravine in the face of enemy fire. He was one of the sole survivors of this gallant action.

An officer and a gentleman, 'Poodle' Byng, a.k.a. the Honourable Frederick Gerald Byng was, like Crawfurd, a junior cavalry officer as well as being a favourite of Brummel's and the prince. He acquired his nickname from his crop of tight white curls and went on to have a distinguished career as a member of parliament. An altogether more substantial character and close friend of the prince was William, Lord Alvanley. He saw action with the 15th Hussars at the battles of Vittoria, Orthès and Toulouse for which he received the Peninsular War Medal with three clasps. Alvanley was renowned for his intelligence and dry wit and would often accompany the prince hunting or to Newmarket. A member of White's and Watier's, Alvanley lived well beyond his means and squandered his family's estates in reckless gaming. Alvanley was notoriously quick tempered and a man of unshakable habits, one of which was always finishing his dinner with a baked apricot tart. On learning from his cook that the anticipated fruit might not materialise, Alvanley despatched the man with a flea in his ear: 'Go to Gunter's and buy all the preserved apricots he has and don't bother me any more about the damned expense.'

Soldier and dandy Henry Frederick 'Kangaroo' Cooke served in the Coldstream Guards and earned his nickname from the marsupial discovered by Captain Cook on his voyages to Australia. Close friends insisted on calling him 'Kang'. 'Kangaroo' Cooke saw action at Minden and Toulouse, rising to the rank of lieutenant colonel and a position as the Duke of York's aide-de-camp from 1814–1827. He was equally at home in St James's as on the battlefield. Cooke is described by Mrs Arbuthnot, a confidante of Wellington's, as having 'mustachios like Blucher's' and, when in London, he could be spotted anywhere between Horseguards and his Bond Street tailor Weston.

The dandies' enjoyment of rowdy fun, together with their habit of nicknaming each other – in addition to Teapot, Kangaroo, and Poodle we also have 'Tiger' Somerset, 'Red Herring' Yarmouth, and Sir Lumley Skeffington, predictably dubbed 'Skiffy' Skeffington – captures the high spirits of an England post Waterloo, from which the threat of Napoleon is suddenly lifted. The dandies' foppish horse-play offers a foretaste of P.G. Wodehouse's fictitious Drone's Club. Bertie Wooster's feckless associates 'Barmy' Fotheringay-Phipps, 'Catsmeat' Potter-Pirbright, 'Stilton' Cheesewright, 'Bingo' Little, 'Boko' Fittleworth and 'Tuppy' Glossop might easily pass for trainee Regency rakes.

Hero and Practical Joker

Founder member of the Guards Club in 1810 along with Captain Rees Howell Gronow, Colonel Dan MacKinnon of the Coldstream Guards fought at the battles of Talavera and Toulouse in the Peninsular wars and was a hero of the Battle of Waterloo. MacKinnon held Hougoumont farm with a force of 250 Coldstream Guards and the first regiment of Grenadier Guards against repeated attacks by the French. Severely injured in the leg and with his troops suffering huge losses, McKinnon held on until the British line advanced to relieve him. He was carried off the battlefield to a hospital in Brussels in a stretcher.

Notwithstanding his heroics, MacKinnon was a dandy and a practical joker who on one occasion made the Duke of Wellington the butt of one of his japes:

> Lord Wellington was curious about visiting a convent near Lisbon and the lady abbess made no difficulty; MacKinnon on hearing this, contrived to get clandestinely within the sacred walls, ... at all events when Lord Wellington arrived Dan MacKinnon was to be seen among the nuns, dressed out in their sacred costume, with his head and his whiskers shaved, and as he possessed such good

features, he was declared to be one of the best looking among those chaste dames.*

Gronow describes MacKinnon as 'remarkable for his physical prowess'. His party piece was to:

> … amuse his friends by creeping over the furniture of a room like a monkey. It was very common for his friends to make bets with him; for example, that he would not be able to climb up to the ceiling of a room, or scramble over a certain house-top. Grimaldi, the famous clown, used to say, 'Colonel MacKinnon has only to put on the motley costume and he would totally eclipse me.'**

Dressing the Male Peacock

During the Napoleonic era, the tailors of St James's saw brisk business from cutting and making military uniforms, giving full rein to the male peacock. Out of uniform, the dandy patronised an army of tailors who played their part in creating the look. Tailors would have been busy as not only were there military uniforms to cut but also court dress and formal clothes for the courtiers and ambassadors of St James's Palace as well as the new 'London Season' fashions demanded by the nobility or *haut ton*.

Kent's Directory of 1792 lists a number of tailors and hatters operating in St James's Street. At number 6 was Messrs Lock, the hatters whose premises still exists today and whose shop window is barely altered. At number 4 was Crellin's the tailor. *Tallis' Elevation of the East and West side of St James's Street*, a topographical guide, shows number 14 displaying a sign which reads, 'Pike, Breeches Maker.' The tailoring firm of Brass and Pike was still operating in the late 1930s, having by that time moved to Savile Row. Two

---

* Ibid., Gronow
** Ibid., Gronow

more tailors, Willis and Nugee, occupied premises at numbers 18 and 20. And at number 33 was listed 'G. Walker, tailor and habit maker.'

Mr Walker appears to have been something of an innovator, having discovered the secret of making 'trousers'. His trade advertisement is worth quoting in full:

> Trousers on a New Principle. – Walker, 33 St James' Street, has discovered an entirely new principle of Cutting Trousers, and offers to furnish the Nobility, Gentry, and the Public, with this important article of dress, admirably adapted to the display of the figure, and at the same time affording such comfort in all exercises as to ensure the highest satisfaction to those who honour him with their orders ... G. W. begs to add, that he continues to supply Uniforms for officers of the Army and Navy, also Deputy Lieutenants' and Court Dresses in the most fashionable style and at moderate charges for Ready Money.*

Tailoring was not merely centralised to a few streets but was widely spread throughout St James's and neighbouring Mayfair. One of the most famous tailors of Regency London favoured by dandies like Brummel and Kangaroo Cooke was Westons of 34 Old Bond Street. Another of Brummel's preferred tailors was Schweitzer and Davidson of Cork Street. He also visited Savile Row, a small street, yet to reach its later status as the centre of London tailoring, where he patronised three establishments – Stultz, Staub, and Delacroix who made his coats. Constantly in debt to his tailors, Brummel would have had to bestow the favour of his custom liberally.

Brummel's taste in clothes set a new standard for tailoring. Trousers or doe skin breeches and waistcoat were set off by a cut-away coat in

---

* E. Beresford Chancellor, *Memorials of St James' Street*, London, Grant Richards, 1922, p. 46

black or navy blue. Brummel's taste in fine cloth, sober colours and clean simple lines was widely adopted by leading London tailors, and is the ancestor of the formal suit that is still worn today. Brummel's fastidious dressing evolved into a ritual. To acquire the art, other dandies would gather at Brummel's apartment in Chesterfield Street to watch him shave and dress.

Brummel wore the collars of his shirts high with the collar fold almost touching his ears. A dart of fabric removed at the back allowed some movement of the neck. To fix his collar in place, Brummel was presented with a triangle of fine Irish muslin, cut diagonally from a square yard and plainly seamed. This was folded over twice at its widest point and wrapped carefully around the neck. Brummel stood in front of a mirror keeping his chin in the air before he tied the tail ends in one of several manners that became signifiers themselves of allegiance and taste. *Neckclothiana,* an anonymous treatise offering to divulge the secret of tying a stock in the correct manner, was later published.

With head held high, the dandy wound the folded linen around his neck before lowering his head until resting on the topmost fold it could be tied in a perfect knot. The process was lengthy and involved great patience as well as trial and error and a ready supply of spotless linen just in case the first efforts were spoiled. 'No perfumes,' Brummel used to say, 'but very fine linen, plenty of it and country washing.'[**]

This style of swaddling the neck in a high collar and tightly wound stock was uncomfortable. But there is a plausible theory that the reason collars were worn so high was in deference to the Prince Regent who wore high collars to disguise an unsightly goitre. If true, then Brummel had adopted a tactful form of flattery.

[**] Harriette Wilson, *The Memoirs of Harriette Wilson*, John Joseph Stockdale, London, 1825, The Perfect Library edition, p. 35

But gambling debts and unpaid bills to his tailors mounted up, forcing Brummel to borrow huge sums at inflated interest which he had no hope of repaying. By now his friendship with the prince was cooling. George acceded to the throne following the Regency of 1811–1820 on the death of his father George III. The Prince Regent's involvement with Watier's Club lasted from 1807 to 1819, just before his accession to the throne in 1820. The association would have been a serious embarrassment at a time when a series of scandalous liaisons had already sealed George's reputation as a libertine.

Brummel's own downfall had taken place two years earlier. The ending of his friendship with the Prince Regent had come at a masquerade ball organised by Watier's Club at the Argyle Rooms located on what is now Regent Street. The Prince Regent had not been invited but had decided to come anyway, determined to snub Brummel once and for all. Ignored by the prince, Brummel famously inquired of Alvanley, 'Who's your fat friend?' The rest, as they say, is history. Denied credit, disgraced and now bankrupt, Brummel fled the country for France.

Last Throw of the Dice

Watier's Club continued under the ownership of Josiah Taylor. New life was breathed into the old clubhouse on Bolton Street after Taylor was joined by a new business partner, William Crockford, sometime tradesman, book maker and racehorse owner. Known as 'the Fishmonger', much of Crockford's wealth came from a successful family business, a fish seller's at the corner of Essex Street in the Strand. But Crockford and Taylor's partnership was not to last. Crockford had far bigger plans, namely to create London's biggest gambling casino. After about a year, Crockford left to form the club that is named after him, commissioning Wellington's architect Benjamin Wyatt to create a palatial clubhouse at 50 St James's Street, opposite White's.

Crockford's – not to be confused with the twentieth-century gambling club of the same name – opened in time for the Season of 1827. When opened, the glitzy club was invariably referred to by wags and humourists as 'Fishmonger's Hall' and descriptions of sharp practice at the gaming table were often laced with fishing puns. Describing an evening's play at Crockford's, the author of *The English Spy*, Charles M. Westmacott in the guise of the fictitious 'Bernard Blackmantle', indulged in plenty of fishing-related humour made at Crockford's expense such as sporting men having 'gone beyond their depth' and the club being a 'resort of *Greeks* and *gudgeons*'.*

Like Watier's Club in its heyday, Crockford's was renowned not only for its excessive gambling but also for the finest cuisine in London under its resident chef Charles Francatelli. Punters were encouraged to gamble beyond their means through games like *Rouge et Noir*, Roulette and French Hazard. It was the ruin of the former dandy 'King' Allen who fled to Dublin and it almost sapped the fortune of 'Golden Ball' Hughes. Hughes followed Brummel's example and headed for exile in France.

These so-called 'sportsmen' represented the pick of the elite London clubs as *The English Spy*'s Westmacott relates. 'By the strict rules of Fishmonger's Hall, the members of Brooks's, White's, Boodle's, the Cocoa Tree, Alfred and Travellers Clubs only are admissible; but this restriction is not always enforced particularly when there is the chance of a good bite.'**

In his latter years, 'Golden Ball's' fortunes were repaired by a railway company and a property speculator who together bought his last remaining asset, a country house at Oatlands, paying him a substantial sum. Hughes lived out his final days in comfort. Crockford personally underwrote the 'bank' to the tune of £5,000 a night. As the head of a gambling syndicate, Crockford could not cut his losses and stop play if it looked as though the bank could not

---

* Charles M. Westmacott, *The English Spy*, Methuen and C., London, A New Edition, 1907, p. 330
** *The English Spy*, Ibid., p. 334

meet its liabilities. Sometimes at the end of a hard night, he would be left with a mountain of IOUs, bankers' drafts, and mortgages. Despite the huge risks, Crockford retired in 1840, having amassed an immense fortune.

By this time, the tide of public opinion was turning against gambling. In 1844, a select committee of Parliament headed by Lord Palmerston was formed to tighten the laws around gambling and to licence private clubs. As part of this investigation, seventeen gaming-houses were raided by police on 7 May 1844. Crockford's somehow escaped the dragnet. Crockford's shut its doors for the last time in 1847. In less than a generation, and true to the moral strictures of the new Victorian age, Watier's had vanished and gentlemen's clubs had undergone a transformation from gambling hells to dining clubs. Despite this, gaming persisted and remained popular in St James's clubs throughout the nineteenth century though kept within bounds.

End of an Era

Many of the dandies either died young or fled into exile. But a substantial number of familiar faces reinvented themselves as senior army officers, diplomats or as politicians, where they happily fell into the role of Victorian elder statesmen.

Lord Alvanley was left to carry the torch for dandyism, a spendthrift and a member of White's to the very end. And while Wellington's 'fighting dandies' stepped gracefully into middle age, the dandy's libertine behaviour came to be exemplified by Lord 'Red Herring' Yarmouth who continued to flaunt a retinue of underage prostitutes, earning him immortality as the original for Thackeray's wicked Marquis of Steyne in the novel *Vanity Fair.*

Beau Brummel's fate was a life of poverty, obscurity and ill-health. His clothes were patched but he would occasionally toy with the seals, watches and snuff boxes which had been given him by female admirers in the days of his pomp. Brummel spent his final days virtually friendless at an asylum, l'Hôpital de Bon Sauveur in Caen, Normandy. He died on 30 March 1840 of syphilis, which he had contracted many years earlier.

CHAPTER 4

THE BEAU MONDE

To that Most Distinguished and Despotic
CONCLAVE
Composed of their High Mightinesses the
Lady Patronesses of the Balls at
ALMACK'S
The Rulers of Fashion, the Arbiters of Taste, the
Leaders of Ton, and the Makers of Manners, whose
Sovereign sway over 'the world' of London has
Long been established on the firmest basis

Title page dedication from *Almacks* by Marianne Spencer
Hudson 1827

Clubland may have been the preserve of gentlemen, but court etiquette and a social sphere that included balls, assemblies, theatre and the opera were shaped by ladies of fashion, those 'leaders of the *haut ton*'. St James's Palace was the official seat of the court where the monarch could grant audiences and confer honours. Bordering St James's Park, the palace was easily accessible to the public and one of a number of royal households that included Kensington Palace, Carlton House, Leicester House, home of Frederick Prince of Wales from 1730–1753, and Buckingham House, acquired by George III from the Duke of Buckingham in 1761 for his wife Queen Charlotte and known as 'the Queen's House'. Clustering around St James's, institutions evolved where gentlemen and ladies could engage in courtship, and where advantageous marriages might be arranged.

In the eighteenth century, Britain boasted 1,003 peers of the realm. These noble families together with wealthy merchants, bankers and professionals comprised what is often referred to as the 'Upper 10,000'. This fashionable elite was known as the beau monde or simply the *ton* – derived from the French *bon ton* meaning good form, and sometimes also referred to as the *haut ton*. This concentration of privilege survived over many centuries and is still evident today. As the courtier Percy Armytage was to recall at the beginning of the twentieth century, 'London Society was as compact socially as it was geographically. Everybody either knew or knew of everybody else.'* Life in St James's gave access to a world of privilege and influence.

The London Season

Beginning with the opening of Parliament in January and finishing when it went into summer recess, February to August marked the London season. During the London season, balls, entertainments, and court functions dominated the social life of St James's. The busiest part of the season was between Easter and early August. This marked the time when many aristocratic families left their country houses and departed for the capital. Some kept prestigious second homes in St James's in popular enclaves like St James's Square and its subsidiary streets, and brought with them a retinue of servants, while others rented a small house for the season or stayed at a hotel. At the top of the scale wealthy landowners like the dukes of Devonshire and Norfolk kept private palaces – Devonshire House on Piccadilly and Norfolk House, St James's Square.

---

* Percy Armytage, *By the Clock of St James's*, John Murray, London, 1927, p. 45

The seasonal influx of the landed gentry to St James's boosted the takings of tailors, mantua makers, shopkeepers, tradesmen, livery stables and providers of all kinds of luxury services. It was the long-awaited moment when small businesses could hike their prices in an effort to compensate for the lean months when trade was slack. 'Hotel keepers who, during the dead season have been comparatively poor, and consequently proportionately civil, now commence the bustle of their business, and with it the extent of their extortion and impertinence … '*

Along with a round of activities centred on the royal court, the London season included private balls given by noble families in their London mansions, public balls, for example, at the Argyll Rooms, and visits to the opera at the King's Theatre, Haymarket. The season ended as abruptly as it had begun with an exodus of carriages heading back to country estates and the start of the grouse shooting season which began on 12 August and, in the early autumn, fox hunting. With Parliament in recess, the political clubs of St James's were almost deserted.

Attendance at court where gentlemen and ladies would be presented to the monarch was an essential part of the London season. Being presented at court confirmed your membership of the beau monde. But some ceremonies were not exclusively confined to this unvarying social calendar and were more public. During the reign of King George II and Queen Caroline, 'Drawing Rooms' or informal receptions were held in the evening twice weekly throughout the year. Frederick Prince of Wales introduced a similar custom at Leicester House. It was an opportunity for subjects to see their monarch in the flesh.

A 'Drawing Room' was an eagerly anticipated event. Visitors would arrive at the appointed time where they were herded together and rushed through a series of rooms until they eventually came to the inner sanctum, or 'withdrawing room', where the royal family would be gathered. There, guests were obliged to file through the room, pausing briefly to be greeted by the king who as custom dictated saluted all ladies with a kiss on the cheek. The Queen only

---

* Charles White, *Almack's Revisited*, Saunders and Otley, London, 1828, p. 1

kissed earls' daughters or those of higher rank. Then, after a few words were exchanged, the audience was over and the gentleman and lady were ushered out. In the beginning, virtually anyone could attend a 'Drawing Room', the only condition being that individuals first had to submit their names to the Lord Chamberlain. 'Indeed from contemporary records it would almost seem that anyone decently dressed was admitted any evening to watch the Royal Family play cards!'[**]

Following the death of Queen Caroline, George II reverted to the old custom of receiving visitors in the morning. As the eighteenth century wore on, audiences became less frequent and more formal. Members of the beau monde were expected to wear court dress, embroidered tailcoats with knee breeches for the gentlemen and elaborately embroidered silk gowns and mantuas for the ladies.

Preferring the privacy of Kew Palace, Windsor Castle, and Buckingham House, a run-down mansion the king had bought for his wife in 1761, King George III and Queen Charlotte were infrequent visitors to the Court of St James's. Hospitality was instead delegated to the Prince of Wales who received visitors at his private palace, Carlton House. Obtaining an audience with the monarch could be a stressful and uncomfortable experience. The formalities and etiquette introduced by the Hanoverians included 'Drawing Room Teas' to which only ladies were invited. Former courtier to Queen Victoria, Percy Armytage, explains:

> Inside the Palace very few chairs were provided, practically everyone having to stand. Each of the rooms contained a sort of pen into which the ladies were herded; when the barrier of this enclosure was opened they made a wild rush to a similar pen in the next room. In the process, trains, lappets and feathers were torn, and it is said that ladies even clawed, scratched and beat each other to get in first.[***]

[**] Percy Armytage, *By the Clock of St James's*, John Murray, London, 1927, p. 117

[***] Ibid., p. 122

'Drawing Rooms' persisted right through the nineteenth century and into the twentieth century. It was a simple but effective way in which the monarch could connect with his or her subjects. The present Queen Elizabeth II terminated the practice of receiving debutantes at Court in 1958.

Debutantes

26 July was the focal point of the London season for the aristocratic mothers of daughters who had reached the age of 17. For on that date in 1780 King George III threw a ball for his wife Queen Charlotte to mark her birthday. Invitations were sent out to a select group of single gentlemen and young ladies of marriageable age.

The occasion was repeated each season. The ceremony was where daughters were formally presented at court as debutantes to mark their official coming of age or 'coming out' into society. Being 'out' meant a young lady could attend balls and usually only happened after her elder sisters were safely married. This audience with the monarch was traditionally held at the Court of St James's. Presentation at court required a strict dress code, and correct conduct and deportment. Debutantes had to be chaperoned. Once 'out', a young woman was free to participate in all the social events of the London season including the famous Queen Charlotte's Ball and escorted visits to the opera or the theatre.

Marriage *à la Mode*

Like many of the playwrights of his day, the artist and printmaker William Hogarth (1697–1764) satirised the beau monde's empty lifestyle and lack of moral compass. Painted in 1745, his series *Marriage à la Mode* traces the story of a loveless marriage which is arranged by an elderly but impoverished nobleman, Lord Squanderfield, between his son and the daughter of a wealthy businessman. By marrying him to money, the lord hopes his wayward son will repair the family fortunes. But it is not to be. Hogarth's paintings show the young couple's rapid descent into a life of high spending, gambling, infidelity and debauchery. The drama culminates in the husband discovering his wife in the arms of her lover who draws his sword and inflicts a fatal stab wound. In the final scene the countess poisons herself when she reads of her lover's imprisonment and execution.

Visiting London for the season was essential if a parent belonging to the beau monde had a son or daughter of marriageable age. Virtually all marriages within the beau monde were arranged or negotiated by the parents of the prospective bride and groom, providing a rich field for modern historical novelists. Romance rarely played a part. An arranged marriage could combine the property and estates of two aristocratic families, thereby ensuring a continuity of wealth and power. Or it could be a bargain by which a penniless male heir might marry into money thus rescuing the family estate.

A father's consent to a proposed match was essential. But the 1755 Marriage Act which applied to England allowed a young woman to marry without the permission of her parents if she was over the age of 21. Young women had to be especially careful when agreeing to enter into matrimony, as under law a wife's money and property became her husband's to dispose of as he saw fit.

Introductions between the sexes were carefully managed. Chaperoned at all times, a young lady would only be allowed to be alone with a young man if he had come to propose marriage – with the father's consent. No correspondence could be entered into between a couple until the young lady was engaged to be married. One further complicating factor was that a young man could only court a girl who was 'out', that is allowed into society and to attend balls. The age at which a young lady was considered to be 'out' varied and could be anything from the age of 16 upwards. Younger siblings would be kept at home.

Social encounters which might lead to marriage took place in assembly rooms where the sexes could be supervised. Intimate conversations were rarely possible even while dancing. It was considered bad form for a young lady to dance with the same partner more than twice in an evening; ideally she should ensure that her dance card was filled in with the names of eligible partners who booked dances in advance.

Almack's

Ambitious club-owner William Almack was closely associated with two St James's clubs, Boodle's and Brooks's when he launched an even more ambitious venture, a grand ballroom and reception space known as Almack's Assembly Rooms. In 1764 Almack had secured a site on the south side of King Street which links the aristocratic St James's Square with the fashionable St James's Street. No expense was spared. Designed and built by Robert Mylne, the large and impressive three-storey assembly rooms were opened on 12 February 1765. Almack's reputation as an exclusive marriage mart had yet to be forged. It was a club that admitted both sexes, with men allowed to propose and elect female members who in turn had the same rights to nominate suitable men.

At the outset, the assembly rooms boasted a gambling casino and late night opening hours. But Almack was quick to realise that organising society balls was the key to attracting and retaining the *ton*. What Beau Nash had achieved in popularising the Assembly Rooms at Bath, Almack would bring to St James's. Dancing and dining in genteel surroundings would attract society ladies from across the country, ambitious to find suitable partners for their daughters. With eligible suitors thin on the ground in rural towns, the London season promised a plentiful supply of young Guards officers and elder sons of the aristocracy.

Almack duly invested in fitting out a luxurious ballroom. A contemporary account describes a:

large ball-room ... about one hundred feet in length by forty feet in width; it is chastely decorated with gilt columns and pilasters, classic medallions, mirrors etc, and is lit with upwards of five hundred wax lights in five cut glass lustres.*

A small orchestra would play from a raised balcony at one end of the room. A typical ball at Almack's could accommodate around 500 to 600 people, and accordingly numbers of subscribers were limited to between 700 and 800. The refreshments were frugal. No alcohol was served, only tea and soft drinks including a weak lemonade known as orgeat, and ratafia almond biscuits.

To ensure exclusivity, Almack enlisted the support of a group of patronesses: society ladies with impressive credentials and a network of contacts that included all of the great and the good. Between them these formidable ladies would vet the subscription list, ensuring that young ladies of *ton* would meet only the wealthiest and most eligible bachelors. Young men and chaperoned young ladies would sit down to supper served by Mr and Mrs Almack, after which introductions could be effected. The dancing that followed was a mixture of Scottish reels and English country dances. Dance cards would be filled in with the names of eligible partners and the socialising came under the combined scrutiny of patronesses, and of course the ladies' chaperones. It was possible for a girl of good breeding to find herself a dancing partner and a husband. The patronesses controlled the subscription list and hence were able to confer favours or to cut people who might give offence. Subscribers were invited to pay 10 guineas for the season comprising twelve balls on alternate Wednesdays. Only those who passed a rigorous vetting procedure were allowed admission. 'No lady patroness can give a subscription or a ticket to any lady she does not visit, or to a gentleman who is not introduced to her by a lady whose name is upon her visiting list.'**

William Almack died in 1792 at which point James Willis, formerly landlord of the Thatched House Tavern in St James's Street, took over as general manager. For a time Willis traded under the name of

---

* John Timbs, *Curiosities of London*, David Bogue, London, 1855, p. 3
** Ibid., p. 3

Almack's but his descendants who ran the business in an unbroken succession up to 1887 changed its name to Willis' Rooms. The glory days of Almack's were during the Regency when it was said that Beau Brummel advised the patronesses over which gentlemen should be on the invitation list. Almack's assemblies were drawn from the very cream of English society.

The 'Lady Patronesses'

Almack's was governed by patronesses drawn from the very highest rank in society. Their role was to ensure invitations were only issued to gentlemen of genuine fortune and to young ladies of impeccable pedigree. Young ladies and their families could be confident they would not be troubled by the attentions of penniless adventurers, for every guest was thoroughly vetted. During the Regency period there were six or seven patronesses at any one time. Patronesses included the Marchioness of Londonderry, Lady Castlereagh, Lady Cowper, the Duchess of Beaufort, Lady Tankerville, and the Princess de Lieven, the Russian ambassador's consort.

The popular misconception is that the patronesses were elderly grandes dames. This is not so. Emily, Lady Cowper, was just 18 when she became a patroness in 1805. Princess de Lieven was 26 and the newly wed Lady Tankerville was a youthful 30. Born Corisande de Grammont, Lady Tankerville had been sent by her mother to England to escape the horrors of the French Revolution. These women were well connected and politically influential. Born Emily Lamb, sister of a later Whig prime minister Lord Melbourne, Lady Cowper remarried on the death of her husband, the much lionised politician Lord Palmerston.

Sarah, Lady Jersey

The most celebrated and best known of all the Almack's patronesses was the formidable Sarah Sophia Child-Villiers, Lady Jersey. Known as the 'Queen of London Society', Lady Jersey, like her fellow 'despots' had decided tastes as to what constituted masculine eligibility, and very few men passed muster. Polite manners, social graces and a handsome appearance were considered as important as a healthy bank balance. The dandy and club-man Captain Gronow writes:

> … one can hardly conceive the importance attached to getting admission to Almack's, the seventh heaven of the fashionable world. Of the three hundred officers of the Foot Guards, not more than half a dozen were honoured with vouchers of admission to this exclusive temple of the *beau monde.**

Sarah, Lady Jersey – not to be confused with her notorious mother-in-law Frances, Countess of Jersey whose torrid affair with the Prince of Wales had scandalised London society – was determined that strict propriety between the sexes should be observed. Independently wealthy, Lady Jersey had inherited Osterley House from her grandfather Robert Child, head of the banking dynasty, and on his death became a senior partner of Child's Bank, thus wielding considerable influence in the world of business as in fashionable circles. Captain Gronow in his *Reminiscences* described her as a '… theatrical tragedy queen; and while attempting the sublime, frequently made herself simply ridiculous.'** Quick, intelligent and with a strong sense of humour, Lady Jersey ruled with a rod of iron. She was known familiarly as 'Silence' on account of her habit of talking non-stop.

Gentlemen were required to abide by a strict dress code which meant wearing knee breeches, white cravat and chapeau bras – a formal bi-corn hat. The rules were applied without fear or favour. In August 1814, fresh from defeating Napoleon in the Peninsular War, the Duke of Wellington was regarded as the saviour of the nation. A ball was thrown in his honour at Burlington House and the whole

---

* Captain Rees Howell Gronow, *Celebrities of London and Paris*, Smith Elder and Co, London, 1866, p. 35
** Ibid., p. 36

of London society was at his feet. Lady Jersey was unimpressed. When the duke sought admission to Almack's wearing the newly fashionable trousers, he was turned away. The episode is recalled in Charles White's *Almack's Revisited*:

> 'How is he dressed?' demanded her ladyship, frowning. 'In longs, my Lady,' was the answer. 'In longs! How highly improper!' rejoined the patroness. 'What, tight?' 'No, my Lady; loose.' 'Loose! How indecent!'*

Following the Allies' final victory at the battle of Waterloo in 1815, Almack's was at last open to European influences. With the ranks of eligible men swelled by Wellington's war heroes, Lady Jersey introduced a French dance, the quadrille. Immortalised as Zenobia in Benjamin Disraeli's novel, *Endymion,* 'Queen Sarah' reigned supreme at Almack's from 1807 until 1835. Meanwhile the waltz had made it across the Channel championed by Countess Esterhazy and Baroness Lieven.

Danced in England for the very first time in 1812 at Almack's Assembly Rooms, the waltz quickly caught on despite being considered risqué on account of the close physical contact between the dancers. The waltz as danced today has become much more staid than its Regency counterpart. To the duennas, the most worrying aspect of this new dance was its intimacy. In a country dance, there is much eye and body contact, but this is of short duration as the moves require alternating with new partners. In the waltz, the eye contact is continuous and unflinching and, according to Byron, so is the body contact:

> Waltz -- Waltz alone -- both legs and arms demands,
> Liberal of feet, and lavish of her hands;
> Hands which may freely range in public sight
> Where ne'er before --- but --- pray 'put out the light.'
> Methinks the glare of yonder chandelier
> Shines much too far --- or I am much too near;

---

* C. White, *Almack's Revisited,* London, Saunders and Otley, 1828, p. 383

And true, though strange --- Waltz whispers this remark,
'My slippery steps are safest in the dark!'**

From this description, it is clear that this is a dance strikingly different from the jigs and reels customarily danced at Almack's. For the Upper Ten Thousand, who spent an inordinate amount of time curbing and concealing their sons' and daughters' sexual urges, this was a disturbing new development and only acceptable because endorsed by the lady patronesses.

By Royal Command – Opera at the Haymarket

Aside from its gentlemen's clubs, St James's was known for music, opera and the theatre, all of which were associated with the royal court and with royal patronage. The celebrated composer George Frideric Handel had been appointed choirmaster and composer at the Chapel Royal, St James's Palace in the Spring of 1723. Henry Purcell had been organist at the Chapel in the 1680s.

Handel's position at the heart of the royal household cemented a strong relationship between the German composer and the Hanoverian court which began in 1717 with Handel's 'Water Music', composed for an outdoor performance on a royal barge sailing down the Thames for George I. Handel went on to write the choral music for the coronation of George II, including the famous anthem 'Zadok the Priest'.

Written with an Italian libretto for an Italian star cast, Handel's opera *Rinaldo* premiered at the King's Theatre Haymarket in 1711. Star billing went to the castrato Nicolo Grimaldi, 'Nicolini'. *Rinaldo* was the first of a string of more than twenty-five baroque operas composed by Handel for the King's Theatre.

** J.W. Lake, *The Works of Lord Byron, Including the Suppressed Poems by George Gordon Byron Baron Byron*, Henry Adams, Philadelphia, 1829, p. 503

Handel's rivals in popularity were the Italian composers Attilo Ariosti and Giovanni Bononcini whose work was received rapturously by the beau monde. Between them these composers kept up with a seemingly insatiable demand for Italian opera. Handel's response in 1719 was to form an opera company, the Royal Academy of Music. Royal patronage had begun under the reign of Queen Anne when the theatre designed by architect and playwright John Vanbrugh in 1705 had been named the Queen's Theatre in her honour. It was later renamed the King's Theatre on the accession of George I. Dedicated to staging operas during the London season, winter months saw the King's Theatre transformed into a ballroom by boarding over the orchestra pit. Masquerade balls promoted by the Swiss entrepreneur John James Heidegger drew in the crowds and kept the theatre's finances in good shape. From 1729 to 1734 Handel joined forces with Heidegger with the two men acting as joint managers.

The King's Theatre burnt to the ground in 1789, but was rebuilt twice: once by John Nash before being renamed the Italian Opera House in 1830. Staging an opera was an expensive undertaking as composers like Handel wrote their operas for individual star performers who then had to be lured from the continent with the promise of eye-watering sums of money. When the Italian soprano Francesca Cuzzoni arrived in England in 1722 to play the lead in Handel's opera *Ottone* she was paid £2,000 for the season, soon topped by the £2,500 offered to her rival Faustina Bordoni the following year.

Duets performed by these talented prime donne drew large audiences and each had their loyal following. Some noblemen were reported to be paying up to 50 guineas for a seat at Cuzzoni's benefit concert despite the fact that she was described by the diarist Fanny Burney as being '... short and squat with a doughy cross face but fine complexion.' Competition sparked intense rivalry and the ill feeling between the two divas finally came to a head. Egged on by jeering factions in the audience the two women started pulling each other's headdresses and trading blows during a performance of Bononcini's opera *Astianate* on 6 June 1727. To make matters worse the fracas on stage was witnessed by Princess Caroline. The curtain came down and the performance and the rest of the opera season were cancelled.

Quite apart from the astronomical salaries awarded to the stars, a baroque opera required elaborate staging and costumes which all added to the cost. A visit to the opera was an expensive luxury only the wealthiest could afford. While a pit seat could be had for half a guinea, boxes for the opera could only be purchased by an annual subscription of 20 guineas per person and was available for the entire season.

Due to the subscription system, a box at the opera was the pre-rogative of only the wealthy few. A tightly knit section of the beau monde visited the opera to meet each other and to be seen. Relaxed rules allowed patrons to wander about the theatre at will during the performance. By thus excluding people of the 'middling sort', the King's Theatre operated, in effect, as a private club with its own set of rules and customs.

Going to see a play was more affordable and more rowdy than a visit to the opera. *The Man of Pleasure's Pocket Book* 1780 lists the cost of a single box ticket at the Theatre Royal at 5s while a seat in the pit was priced at 3s. Standing immediately opposite the King's Theatre was a small brick-built playhouse, known as 'The Little Theatre in the Haymarket'. Dating from 1720, the theatre specialised in acerbic political satire, a reason that led to it being shut down under the 1737 Licensing Act. It survived in hand to mouth fashion by acquiring a succession of temporary licences that enabled it to compete with the Theatre Royal Covent Garden and the Drury Lane Theatre where a new generation of actors including David Garrick and Peg Woffington held sway.

The Little Theatre was more than any other associated with one man, the playwright, mimic and gossip Samuel Foote. A discharged bankrupt, Foote's first play, *Diversions of the Morning,* performed in 1747 was an instant success. A scurrilous satire on the acting fraternity, all the main parts were played by Foote himself in a series of cameos. Foote subsequently advertised his riotous solo shows in which he would do impressions of the rich and famous as 'Tea Parties'. The expression to 'give tea' became a polite euphemism for giving offence and Foote was thereafter known as the 'Tea Party Man'. During the next two decades, Foote received regular star billing.

Taking over as manager of the Little Theatre in 1762, Foote was finally able to buy the theatre outright from its previous owner in 1766. Leveraging his influence with the king's brother, the Duke of York, Foote secured a royal patent. On 25 June 1766 George III signed a document stating 'Our Will and Pleasure are that you Samuel Foote Esq, do … gather … together a Company of Comedians to Act (at the Haymarket) between the Fifteenth Day of May and the Fifteenth Day of September in Every Year.'* What was once the Little Theatre was now the Theatre Royal, Haymarket.

By the end of the first season Foote had acquired a site next door and set about building a much larger and vastly improved theatre. With the capacity to seat 1,000 people, Foote's Theatre Royal opened in May 1767. The present theatre designed by John Nash dates from 1820. Always a controversial figure, Foote trod a fine line between outraging public morals and courting the aristocracy. But in 1776 Foote's luck ran out. While a guest at an aristocratic hunting party at Seaton Delaval he was thrown from a horse, smashing his leg below the knee, an injury which required amputation. Later that same year and after being fitted with a wooden leg, Foote was arrested for a homosexual assault on a footman. The case came to court but Foote was acquitted. He died the following year.

Going to see a play or an opera was an essential part of the London Season and a performance would be even more of an attraction if the royal family were expected. A royal box was kept at the King's Theatre and the Theatre Royal, Haymarket for their visit and every effort was made to ensure the comfort and safety of the royal party. This included an armed guard.

---

* BL Add MSSS 36133 quoted by Ian Kelly, *Mr Foote's Other Leg*, Picador, London, 2012, p. 240

Guarding the beau monde at play was an onerous task. In the early eighteenth century it was customary for a force of up to eighty soldiers led by an officer to police major public gatherings in St James's while an opera performance would be protected by a detachment of one corporal and four men. But in 1771 Field Marshal Tyrawley instigated a defence spending review:

> It is Field Marshal Tyrawley's orders that for the future no Guards will be sent to any publick or private exhibitions excepting the Opera House and two Playhouses unless by a particular order from the King and this to be a standing order.[**]

Pleasure Gardens

There were also certain locations where both sexes could mingle and where introductions, some of which might lead to marriage, might be discreetly arranged. Popularised by the Prince of Wales who was a regular visitor, a visit to one of the private pleasure gardens like Ranelagh or Vauxhall was high on the list of entertainments available during the season. The prince even had his own pavilion built at Vauxhall where he could watch the proceedings. Here one might dance in the open air to an orchestra, see jugglers or witness a balloon ascent. But the whole idea of the concept of a pleasure garden where people could promenade marked a step change from the polite sociability of public open spaces like St James's Park. Here, between an avenue of trees flanking a canal, fashionable couples or families might take a stroll. A popular rendezvous was an open-air tea garden and a stall where people could buy fresh cow's milk served by a dairymaid from the park's resident herd for a penny a cup.

[**] Percy Armytage, *By the Clock of St James's*, John Murray, London, 1927, p. 152

The Temple of Hymen

In June 1781 Scotsman James Graham launched the Temple of Hymen at Schomberg House in Pall Mall, in a suite of rooms designed to house the newly built Celestial Bed. This 'wonder-working edifice' was 12 by 9ft (3.7 by 2.7m), '... canopied by a dome covered in musical automata, fresh flowers, and a pair of live turtle doves'. Stimulating oriental fragrances and 'aethereal' gases were released from a reservoir inside the dome. A tilting inner frame put couples in the best position to conceive, and their movements set off music from organ pipes which breathed out 'celestial sounds', whose intensity increased with the ardour of the bed's occupants. The electrified, magnetic creation was insulated by forty glass pillars. At the head of the bed, above a moving clockwork tableau celebrating Hymen the god of marriage, and sparkling with electricity, were the words: 'Be fruitful, multiply and replenish the earth!'

This rather charming and somewhat naïve approach to securing the succession offers an intimate view of the apparently heartless focus on advantageous marriages required to preserve family interests. However, the beau monde was primarily devoted to the preservation of property and the social order, in the face of the terrifying events of the Napoleonic Wars that were driving rapid and far-reaching political change. Within this context, parents had to control the libidos and the possibly disastrous marital preferences of their offspring in order to secure the financial health of their estates and family. Establishments like Almack's – truly the first club for women – were key to this endeavour. At the same time, members' clubs, largely for the senior male members of the *haut ton*, flourished as never before. Not wholly surprising, given the strictures of the lady patronesses.

CHAPTER 5

A LOOKING GLASS WORLD

Every cove that put in an appearance was quite welcome,
colour or country considered no obstacle …
The group was motley indeed – Lascars, blacks,
jack-tars, coal-heavers, dustmen, women of colour, old and young,
and a sprinkling of the remnants of once fine girls, and all jigging
together.

Description of 'All Max' from Pierce Egan's *Life in London*

The popular impression of eighteenth-century St James's is of a
wealthy and privileged enclave surrounding a royal palace – a world
inhabited by courtiers and noble men and women. But take a closer
look behind the grand town houses and venture into the back alleyways and you will see a different St James's, a district that is home to
a wide social spectrum. In among the many respectable tradespeople
and hard-working shopkeepers, publicans and coffee-house proprietors were the inevitable hucksters, con men, and prostitutes looking
to prey on the wealthy and impressionable. This half world is a looking glass reflection of the surface of Clubland, with some individuals
freely moving between the two worlds.

   This was a world beyond the looking glass – an economy built
around satisfying the pleasures of the idle aristocracy and the ambitious middle class. Painted in 1734 and reproduced as a set of satirical

engravings, William Hogarth's *A Rake's Progress* depicts the fall of Tom Rakewell, a young aristocrat addicted to gambling, prostitutes and unaffordable excess. In St James's Street on his way to White's, Rakewell is taken by bailiffs from his sedan chair, arrested for debt and sent to the Fleet Prison. He later loses his mind and is committed to a lunatic asylum, Bethlehem Hospital, an institution near Liverpool Street where visitors could pay a small fee to gawp at the deranged inmates.

Satire and St James's seem to have gone hand in hand because almost a century later the cartoonist James Gillray, who lived with the print-seller Mrs Humphrey above her shop in St James's Street, portrayed comic scenes of venality involving the Prince Regent, his lovers and many instances of political intrigue gone badly wrong. Stinging satire revealed that power and position was all too often accompanied by its mirror image, vice and venality. Reputation was a fragile commodity. Many of the beau monde lived on credit but once an individual had been publicly discredited, their debts could be called in at a moment's notice. Failure to pay gave your creditors the right to send you to one of London's much feared debtors' prisons, even for a relatively minor sum. In London's Clubland, respectability came at a high price.

Gambling Hells

In 1753 crowds flocked to see a play entitled, *The Polite Gamester; or the Humours of Whist: A dramatick satyr as acted every day at White's and other coffee-houses and assemblies.* Written by an anonymous author, the play makes a savage attack on the vice of high stakes gaming. In it there is a scene set in White's Old Club in which a 'young man has been bubbled out of his fortune' at a game of whist by a card sharper, Professor Whiston. But is the gambling satirised in the play taking place within the club where it is a private matter regulated by private rules, or is it taking place in the public coffee room? In which case, this behaviour is of public concern and potentially a threat to law and order as many gaming debts ended in duels fought with sword or pistol.

The formation of White's, later the Old Club, dates from 1733, a few years before the famous fire which burned the Chocolate-House to the ground. At different times three institutions occupied the site of White's: the Chocolate-House, the Old Club and the New Club. The Old Club was formed for the most part of the aristocratic gamesters who had patronised the Chocolate-House. The New Club was formed from entirely new members, subject to election according to rules set out by Mr Arthur and key members of the Old Club. In plate 6 of *A Rake's Progress*, 'Scene in a Gambling House', Hogarth takes us inside White's Chocolate-House, to a back parlour known as 'Hell', a private room where gentlemen mixed with card sharps and criminals and where huge sums were won and lost. Rakewell can be seen at the centre of the gambling room unaware that an overturned candle has set fire to curtains. The players are either so drunk or so transfixed by the gaming tables they failed to notice the blaze until it is too late to save the building. The *Gentleman's Magazine* reports that:

> White's Chocolate-House near the Palace in St James's Street kept by Mr Arthur and two adjoining houses were consumed by a sudden fire. Young Mr Arthur's wife leapt out a window up 2 pairs of Stairs upon a feather Bed without much hurt.[*]

Associated with rakes was a particular type of gentlemen's club dedicated solely to gaming and which attracted criminal types such as card sharpers. Some of the more notorious clubs were fronts for extreme forms of gambling. The privacy and discretion afforded by such premises ensured activities and individuals were kept safe from the prying eyes of the law. Vast fortunes were often gambled away.

Gambling fever started early. According to Steinmetz:[**]

---

[*] The *Gentleman's Magazine*, 28 April, 1733

[**] Andrew Steinmetz, *The Gaming Table: Its votaries and victims*, London, 1870

A boy ... is sent to school to be initiated. In the course of a few years he acquires a profound knowledge of the science of gambling, and before he leaves the University he is perfectly fitted for a member of the gaming clubs into which he is elected before he takes his seat in either house of Parliament ... Scarcely is the hopeful youth enrolled among these honourable associates than he is introduced to Jews, to annuity brokers, and to the long train of money lenders. They take care to answer his pecuniary calls, and the greater part of the night and morning is consumed at the club. To his creditors and tradesmen, instead of paying his bills, he offers a bond or annuity. He rises just in time enough to ride to Kensington Gardens; returns to dress, dines late; and then attends to party of gamblers, as he had done the night before.

Charles James Fox, the second son of Lord Holland, was the most notorious gambler of Regency England. His father had to settle debts of a stupendous £140,000. Fox routinely lost (and won) enormous sums of money in a wide range of ways, often gambling continuously for days at a time. On one occasion he gambled from Tuesday evening until late on the following Friday – taking one evening off to address the House of Commons. He initially lost £12,000 on Tuesday but recouped that by Wednesday afternoon, though losing £11,000 just before going to the House. After the debate he went to White's, drank all night and then returned to Almack's where he won £6,000. He took his carriage to Newmarket later in the day and promptly dropped £10,000 on the horses.

Fast forward to the early 1800s and gambling is, if anything, even more of a problem among this aristocratic elite. Created by the Prince Regent in 1807 and with Beau Brummel installed as its president, Watier's Club in Bolton Street, Piccadilly was a renowned gambling hell. Watier's was synonymous with a dangerous and addictive card game called Macao in which stakes could rise swiftly and where fortunes could be won or lost at a single sitting. Players are dealt five cards from the pack. Leading from the right of the dealer a player tries to lay down a run of cards from the same suit. The next player follows on by building the suit or if this is not possible must lay a joker or an ace. When a player is down to a single card he must shout 'Macao!' The winner is the player who ends up with no cards. Players can withhold cards in order to frustrate their opponents and get a higher score.

The Macao tables proved an irresistible attraction for wayward younger sons of the nobility, hardened rakes, and dashing guards' officers. Successful gaming required nerve and an ability to dissemble: qualities which Beau Brummel possessed in abundance. John Timbs in his book *Club Life of London* refers to the diarist Thomas Raikes as Watier's resident expert on Macao which he describes ironically as a 'very genteel game'. In the adrenaline fuelled atmosphere of Watier's gaming room, gentility was in short supply:

> Upon one occasion, Jack Bouverie, brother of Lord Heytesbury was losing large sums, and became very irritable. Raikes with bad taste, laughed at Bouverie; upon which Bouverie threw his play-bowl with the few counters it contained at Raikes' head; unfortunately it struck him and made the City dandy angry, but no serious results followed this open insult.*

Gaming clubs came and went in quick succession. Two of the most notorious 'gambling hells' were Graham's Clubhouse, 'a great place for whist', according to Lord Bentinck, and a den known simply as Number Five, Pickering Place. This latter was an anonymous establishment whose specialism, according to a contemporary trade card, was 'Rouge and Roulette, French and English Hazard'.

Hellgate

The most famous rake of his day (1769–1793) was the hellraising Richard Barry, 7th Earl of Barrymore, an old Etonian who

---

* John Timbs, *Club Life of London*, Richard Bentley, New Burlington Street, 1866, p. 320

squandered his considerable fortune on ladies of the night. In an age noted for excess, Barrymore was in a league of his own as a gambler and womaniser. He died unmarried aged 23. Appropriating the title, 'Lady Barrymore', his youthful paramour, the 18-year-old daughter of a sedan chair porter, went on to build an impressive career as a prostitute and promoter of women's bare-knuckle fighting.

The four Barry siblings were a class act in terms of hell raising of various types. Barry himself was known as 'Hellgate', his sister Caroline was dubbed 'Billingsgate' because she swore like a fish-wife while his brother Henry, born with a club foot, was known as 'Cripplegate' in those politically incorrect times. The youngest brother, Augustus, incredibly became a minister of the church. He was the most inveterate gambler among them and was given the nickname 'Newgate'. This was because Newgate was the only prison he had not been sent to.

A Harlot's Progress

The procuress Elizabeth 'Mother' Needham heads an impressive cast list of eighteenth-century bawds who plied their trade in St James's. Mother Needham was often to be found at the White Horse or the White Bear, busy coaching inns at Piccadilly, on the prowl for unac-companied country girls recently arrived in London. She would then lure them to her establishment at Park Place, St James's, where they would be plied with food, drink and a bed for the night before being forced to pay for the hospitality by being offered for sex.

The turnover of young women trapped in this way was high: one in five women in London was a prostitute. At the time, it was believed that making love to an 11-year-old virgin offered a cure for syphilis. Mother Needham is depicted in a scene from Hogarth's *A Harlot's Progress* on the lookout for girls travelling alone and unaccompanied. Syphilis was rife in Georgian London and although incurable, there were plenty of quack doctors whose patent remedies including face patches and mercury paste were painful but ineffectual against a disease that would lead to physical side effects and madness. Ned Ward's 'No Nose Club' from his satire, *A Compleat and Humorous Account of all the Remarkable Clubs and Societies in the City of London and Westminster,* poked fun at men and women maimed by the side effects of tertiary syphilis. Ward observed, 'that abundance of both Sexes had sacrificed their Noses to the God *Priapus*, and had unluckily fallen into the Aegyptian fashion of flat Faces.'*

Girls could be bought at auction, as an advertisement from the *Rambler* magazine reveals: 'TO BE SOLD by Inch of Candle at Mrs Kelly's Rooms several orphan girls under sixteen imported from the Countrey & never shewn before.' Mother Needham treated her girls like slaves and once in her clutches, the notorious Madam forced them to pay for their board and keep and even pay her for the clothes they stood up in while they plied their trade of prostitution. Mother Needham was finally convicted on 20 April 1731 for keeping a disorderly house. She was fined 1s, made to stand twice in the pillories at Park Place, St James's and at New Palace Yard. Finally she was requested to pay sureties for her good behaviour for three years. Writing of her exposure to the pillory, the *Grub Street Journal* said she was 'roughly handled by the populace. She was so ill-used that she died the next day'.

Another brothel keeper was a Scottish lady, Jane Douglas, who by the age of 17, was earning her living as a prostitute in St James's. Establishing herself as a brothel keeper, Douglas's stock of young women was celebrated by the playwright John Gay for their 'elegance, sweetness of disposition and sexual expertise'** at a house in St James's where she entertained 'Princes, Peers and Men of the Highest Rank ... And also Women of the highest Rank ... Who came incognito.'***

---

* Ned Ward, *A Compleat and Humorous Account of all the Remarkable Clubs and Societies in the City of London and Westminster,* printed for J. Wren, London, 1756, p. 24

** John Gay

*** John Gay quoted in *The Nocturnal revels or the history of King's Place and other modern nunneries,* Vol. 2, 1779 by 'a monk of St. Francis'

Aristocratic marriage was based on property and succession rather than mutual physical attraction. While it was relatively easy for men to satisfy their sexual appetites, it was slightly more difficult, although not impossible, for their wives to follow suit:

> I have purchased very extensive premises ... entered by means of shops devoted entirely to such trades as are exclusively resorted to by ladies ... I have erected a most elegant temple, in the centre of which are large saloons, entirely surrounded by boudoirs, most elegantly and commodiously fitted up. In these saloons, according to their classes, are to be seen the finest men of their species I can procure ... and all kept in a high state of excitement by good living and idleness ... *

Frustrated wives could visit this establishment in Old Bond Street and select as many men as they desired. The brothel was run as a club by subscription which allowed each woman to have any number of men they chose, either for an hour or two or overnight. Discretion was assured. Women would either make love in the dark or wear a mask to protect their identity if they preferred.

Lower-class brothels or bagnios known as 'cock and hen' houses often masqueraded as coffee-houses. An example of this is illustrated by George Cruickshank's cartoon *Tom and Jerry Visit a Coffee-shop near the Olympic Pavilion in Drury Lane*. This 'coffee-shop' is crammed with a bawdy crowd of men and women clad in petticoats engaging in some kind of Bacchanalian orgy. Most 'cock and hen' houses were to be found in Covent Garden and Soho. *Harris's List of Covent Garden Ladies*, a directory of prostitutes published annually from 1757 through to 1795 and thought to be the work of Grub Street hack Sam Derrick shows the trade to be focused on a handful of streets such as Newman Street and Queen Anne Street. The seedy publication lists young women by name, cataloguing their physical attributes

---

* Mary Wilson, *The Voluptuarian Cabinet*, London, 1824, quoted in Linnane ibid., p. 85

in much the same way as an online restaurant review. For example 'Mrs B-ooks, next to the Pawnbroker in Newman Street' who is described as being 'tolerably well-made, with well-formed projecting bubbies, that defy the result of any manual pressure'.** Few freelance prostitutes could afford to rent a room in St James's where most of the sex trade took place in upper class brothels. But one entry for the year 1761 lists a Mrs Whiting, alias Sketch, of Bury Street, St James's. The list's author writes tactfully: 'This young lady is rather too short; though she makes ample amends for that deficiency in her complexion which is clear and fine.'***

High-class brothels patronised by gentlemen were hard to distinguish from their more respectable neighbours. Commonly referred to as 'nunneries', they were managed by an experienced older woman or 'abbess'. These establishments co-existed with the gentlemen's clubs of St James's and many high-class brothels were to be found conveniently close by among the alleyways and courtyards leading off King Street and Bury Street. It was said that no woman other than a courtesan or demi-rep could be seen south of Bury Street.

The Demi-Monde

The looking glass world of St James's was a deception. While the beau monde kept up appearances and social ritual, there existed a parallel society where polite values were turned on their head. This was the domain of the demi-rep or courtesan. Educated, fashionable and at home in the upper reaches of male-dominated society, these independent women were sought as much for their company as their sexual favours. The closest equivalent to the courtesan is a geisha or 'accomplished person', an alluring young lady brought up to entertain and enslave male admirers with her refined talents.

** *Harris' List of Covent Garden Ladies from Hallie Rubenhold, Sex in the City in Georgian England,* Tempus, Stroud, 2005, p. 91
*** Ibid p. 133

The courtesan kept a small household – commonly a female servant or live-in companion, their lifestyle heavily subsidised by one or
more wealthy aristocrats who were prepared to pay dearly for their
company. She was expected to act as the gentleman's London escort,
a role which could involve accompanying him to balls, the theatre
or the opera, while his wife and family were safely tucked away back
home in the country.

Undisputed doyenne of the demi-monde, Harriette Wilson
took London society by storm. The daughter of John and Amelia
Dubouchet, her father a Swiss clockmaker, Harriette's birth on
22 February 1786 is recorded in the parish register of St George
Hanover Square. Changing her name to Wilson at an early age,
possibly to avoid bringing shame on her family, Harriette was pro-
miscuous in her affections. An accomplished writer, Wilson kept a
diary in which she listed all of her many amatory entanglements with
the cream of English society. The diary was later reworked as *The
Memoirs of Harriette Wilson*. Published by John Stockdale, it shocked
and titillated in equal measure, becoming an overnight bestseller.

Harriette opens her saga in true 'bodice-ripper' tradition:

> I shall not say why or how I became at the age of fifteen, the mis-
> tress of the Earl of Craven. Whether it was love or the severity of
> my father, the depravity of my own heart or the winning arts of my
> noble lord which induced me to leave my paternal roof and place
> myself under his protection, does not now much signify …[*]

The young Harriette, then installed at a house in Brighton, succeeded
in driving Lord Craven into a frenzy of sexual jealousy when she took
up with Lord Melbourne's son, Fred Lamb. Moving onwards and
upwards she offered companionship to a succession of lovers including
Fred Bentinck, the Duke of Argyle, and Lord Ponsonby with whom
she professed to be in love, despite his married status. Harriette writes:

---

[*] Harriette Wilson, *The Memoirs of Harriette Wilson,* John Joseph Stockdale,
London 1825. This edition The Perfect Library, 1909, p. 7

Lord Ponsonby and myself met every evening, for more than a week. We were never tired of conversing with each other … We seldom contrived to separate before five or six o'clock in the morning and Ponsonby generally came to me as soon as it was dark. Nor did we always wait for the evening to see each other, though respect for Lady Ponsonby made us ever … avoid all risk … [**]

But it was the wayward Duke of Wellington who was to be Harriette's calling card to the upper reaches of society and her chief claim to fame. In around 1805 she recalls the duke 'one sultry evening, ordered his coachman to set him down at the White Horse Cellar in Piccadilly, whence he sallied forth to No 2 or 3 Berkeley Street',[***] a high-class brothel. Rapping on the door he accosts the Madam, a Mrs Porter. Never one for small talk the duke gets straight to the point: "'There is a beautiful girl just come out," said his grace, without answering her question, "a very fine creature; they call her Harriette."'[****]

Wellington is duly directed to Wilson's house in Somer's Town where she commanded her servant to dismiss him but not without extracting a large banknote. Wellington returns, pleads his case and is grudgingly admitted. The conversation is stilted and Harriette baits the hero of the Peninsular War with casual insults to which he replies by professing his undying devotion. She writes: 'Wellington was now my constant visitor – a most unentertaining one, Heaven knows! And, in the evenings when he wore his broad red ribbon, he looked very like a rat catcher.'[*****] The historian should not, perhaps, place too much trust in Harriette's *Memoirs* as her account may have been exaggerated for dramatic effect or written in retribution for past insults. But taken as a whole it holds up a mirror to the insouciance and sexual permissiveness of the upper classes at that time.

[**] Harriette Wilson, *The Memoirs of Harriette Wilson,* John Joseph Stockdale, London 1825. This edition The Perfect Library, p. 69

[***] Ibid., p. 41

[****] Ibid., p. 41

[*****] Ibid, p. 47

The public soon learned of and laughed at the duke's misconduct as a series of scurrilous cartoons emerged lampooning the duke as 'the rat-catcher'. It is interesting to note that before publishing her *Memoirs*, Harriette Wilson attempted to blackmail the duke, suggesting that if he paid her a cash sum she would remove all references to his infidelities from her forthcoming book. Wellington is famously reported to have replied: 'Write and be damned!'

Masquerade

Opportunities for gentlemen and ladies to meet and form relationships outside of marriage were limited. But illicit romance or the thrill of flirtation could be kindled through a visit to that highly popular entertainment, the masquerade ball. The origin of the masquerade or masked ball goes back a long way but St James's events were based on the seventeenth-century Venetian *Carnevale* with its extravagant masks and costumes. The term masquerade means to assume a false identity, and gentlemen and ladies of the *ton* shed their inhibitions as harlequins, shepherdesses, milkmaids, clowns, or allegorical figures. Cross-dressing was common. If they wanted to be discreet, ladies wore an ankle length hooded silk cape known as a domino. Or they could come au naturel like Elizabeth Chudleigh, Duchess of Kingston, who created a sensation in 1749 by appearing as Iphigenia naked beneath a diaphanous veil with only a garland to cover her modesty. An apocryphal story has it that when presented to George II, the monarch asked whether he might be permitted to touch her breast, at which point the quick-thinking Ms Chudleigh replied that she 'knew something softer' and lifting the king's hand she placed it on his head.

The winter season was masquerade time, where a dimly lit ballroom, masks and costumes enabled late-night partygoers to give free rein to sexual fantasies. The masquerade was open to anyone who could afford to buy a ticket and aristocrats mingled freely with *demimondaines*, prostitutes and con men. The leading organiser was a Swiss entrepreneur of dubious reputation, 'Count' John James Heidegger. Heidegger had arrived in London in 1708 sent by a relative to negotiate a business transaction. The deal fell through and Heidegger gravitated towards the opera where he gained rapid success organising spectacular scenes and effects. From 1710 onwards 'Count' Heidegger promoted masquerade balls at the King's Theatre, a successful venture that was to net him around £5,000 a year, a respectable position in society, and ultimately the role of joint manager with none other than George Frideric Handel.

King's Theatre masquerades ran throughout the eighteenth century. Mrs White, proprietor of White's Chocolate-House, sold tickets for Mr Heidegger's balls as well as hiring out costumes. The ball would include a supper, and dancing would commence as late as 1.00 a.m. according to a report which appeared under the title 'Masquerade Intelligence' in the *Gazeteer and New Daily Advertiser* of 5 March 1783. Between 600 and 700 party-goers were present, including the Prince of Wales, while celebrated demi-reps like Mary Robinson and Grace Dalrymple Eliot who flirted shamelessly with Lord Cholmondeley, wore costumes 'admirably calculated to display their charms and to fascinate desiring youth'.*

A report in the *Morning Herald* of 24 May 1786 describes another King's Theatre masquerade in disparaging terms. The ball was:

> equal in insignificant dullness to what we have seen before. Harlequins without wit, clowns known only by the stupidity that is their natural characteristic; nosegay girls, men turned into women and vice versa, equally distinguishable by their impudence, together with a world of characters badly supported throughout …

Following on from Heidegger was the characterful Teresa Cornelys, an Austrian opera singer, wealthy widow and former lover of Casanova who was the father of her daughter. After an eventful but peripatetic

---

* 'Masquerade Intelligence' in the *Gazeteer and New Daily Advertiser* of 5 March 1783

life around the royal courts of Europe, Cornelys arrived in London in 1760 determined to make a name for herself. Renting Carlisle House, Soho Square, she proceeded to remodel the mansion as a venue for fashionable card parties and masquerade balls. Introduced into London society by Elizabeth Chudleigh, whose bare-breasted Iphigenia was still the talk of the town, Madame Cornelys opened for business in 1761. Cornelys invested heavily in elegant furnishings for Carlisle House and hired the best musicians available including J.C. Bach and Stephen Storace, brother of the celebrated operatic soprano Nancy Storace, star of Mozart's opera *The Marriage of Figaro* and the composer's intimate friend. Heavily oversubscribed, Madam Cornelys's masquerades were held twice a month in winter and were an instant hit with fashionable women of the day.

The Cyprian's Ball

From the late eighteenth century to the 1820s, gentlemen's clubs vied with each other in giving expensive masquerades and *ridottos*, entertainments with music and dancing. Well-connected courtesans played an important role in hosting these events. In 1818, for example, the many times married Augusta Corri, together with four other 'celebrated courtesans', organised a 'Venetian Carnival' at the Argyll Rooms attended by members of Watier's Club. When the invitations were sent out, the *haut ton* were abundantly represented including the rake Lord Petersham. Popularly referred to as 'The Cyprians' Ball', no wives or girlfriends were admitted. 'Cyprian' indicates a licentious person, especially a prostitute or dancer, presumably derived from the orgiastic worship of Aphrodite on Cyprus. Peddler of tittle-tattle Charles Molloy Westmacott, under his nom de plume Bernard Blackmantle, reveals in his social satire *The English Spy*:

> Never were the revels of Terpsichore kept up with more spirit, or graced with a more choice collection of beautiful, ripe, and wanton fair ones. Nor was there any lack of distinguished personages of

the other sex; almost all the leading roués of the day being present, from Lord P★★★★★★★★★★ to Tom B★★★★★★, including many of the highest note in the peerage, court calendar and army list.*

Gender Identity

Masquerade balls contributed to an overall willingness to explore new sexual identities but they were also entertainments for the upper classes. Within the shady world of the Georgian sex trade there was plenty of encouragement to cater for unusual sexual tastes of both men and women. Molly Houses, or brothels for cross-dressing men, revealed a new willingness to question gender roles, as an increasing number of individuals sought to redefine their sexuality. Ned Ward in his *Compleat and Humorous Account* treats the reader to a description of a typical Molly House whose inhabitants:

> … rather fancy themselves Women, imitating all the little Vanities that custom has reconciled to the female Sex, affecting to speak, walk, tattle, courtesy, cry, scold and a mimick of all manner of Effeminacy … that they may tempt one another, by such immodest Freedoms to commit those hideous Bestialities that ought for ever to be without a name.**

But it was not just men who broke with convention. There were well-documented cases of Georgian women masquerading as men such as the cross-dressing soldiers Susannah Cope, Christian Davies, Mary Ann Talbot and Hannah Snell who took the name of James Gray after she had been deserted by her husband. Snell alias Gray

---

* Bernard Blackmantle, *The English Spy*, Vol. II, Sherwood, Gilbert and Piper, London, 1826, p. 36

** Ned Ward, *A Compleat and Humorous Account of all the Remarkable Clubs and Societies in the City of London and Westminster*, printed for J. Wren, London, 1756, p. 265

'enlisted in Col. Guise's Regiment of Foot and marched with that Regiment to Carlisle, in the Time of the Rebellion in Scotland'.*

Arrested for Debt

Hogarth's moral tale of *A Rake's Progress* is no exaggeration. Fortunes could be won and lost in an instant as the huge financial crash that followed the South Sea Bubble proved in 1720 when many City traders were made bankrupt almost overnight. Family estates mortgaged to the hilt were rarely enough to support a lifestyle that included high stakes gambling and keeping up with the latest fashions.

Madame Cornelys had built a thriving business organising masquerade balls. But her heady career had generated many enemies happy to see her fail. When Cornelys finally overreached herself and fell foul of the law, her enemies closed in. The cause of her downfall was in 1771 when she presented an opera, *Artaxerxes* by Thomas Arne without obtaining a royal licence. Fined heavily, Cornelys was soon on a downward spiral. Sent to the Fleet Prison, a jail for debtors in Farringdon, Cornelys had all of her assets seized to pay off her debts. Carlisle House, her grand home, was sold and its contents auctioned, buying her temporary freedom. But cut off from her former patrons and unable to stage masquerades or assemblies, Cornelys slid in and out of bankruptcy, finally dying in the Fleet Prison on 19 August 1797 aged 74.

The cartoonist James Gillray also trod a precarious path. Hugely popular, his savage portrayals of royalty and politicians like George III, the Prince of Wales, and Charles James Fox courted legal retribution. Even the tolerant Prince of Wales was forced to threaten court action to get one particularly objectionable cartoon withdrawn. Part of Gillray's success owed itself to the support and encouragement of his

---

* *The Female Soldier Or, The Surprising Life and Adventures of Hannah Snell born in the City of Worcester,* Printed and Sold by R. Walker, the corner of Elliot's Court in the Little Old Bailey, London, 1750, Title Page

partner Hannah Humphrey, a print-seller of St James's Street. Gillray's biggest problem was his health. By 1808 and losing his eyesight, he went to Margate to convalesce. The quality of his work greatly diminished and he abandoned printmaking altogether. In 1811 with his health deteriorating and having taken to drink, Gillray attempted suicide by throwing himself out of the top floor window of Humphrey's shop. He survived. A severe invalid, the bedridden Gillray was nursed by Hannah. He died in 1818 and is buried in St James's churchyard.

There were many such prisons in eighteenth-century London, institutions which had grown up over time to contain anyone from out-and-out fraudsters to respectable individuals in temporary financial straits. The Fleet, the Marshalsea, and the King's Bench prisons were overcrowded hell holes where prisoners would be systematically set to arduous labour to pay for their incarceration. Prisoners with modest means might be able to afford meagre lodgings within the prison but those with no means whatever would be stripped of their dignity and even their clothes.

Creditors or tradesmen owed even the smallest unpaid bill could if they wished obtain a court order from the local magistrate who would then send in the bailiffs. In a strictly cash economy with a handful of banks serving the needs of a wealthy elite, there was nowhere to go but prison where, if you were physically fit or skilled in some way, you could be put to work to repay the debt.

Under an iniquitous system condoned by Robert Walpole's Whig government, the governorship of a debtor's prison was a sinecure that could be bought and sold. Governors recouped the money it had cost them to secure their position by systematically exploiting prisoners and putting them to work. Debtors would start their imprisonment owing money for the legal costs of executing the warrant for their arrest. If this went unpaid the interest would quickly mount until the debt became so mountainous it could never be repaid. In this way debt could mean life imprisonment in squalid unsanitary conditions and an early death.

Debtor's prisons remained a national scandal until Victorian legislation forced their reform and ultimate closure. The whole iniquitous system is researched and described in the context of the Marshalsea in Jerry White's *Mansions of Misery*. The Marshalsea could be described as a club for the chronically impecunious, as graphically illustrated by Charles Dickens in *Little Dorrit*.

In 1742 the Irish poet and adventuress Laetitia Pilkington (1708– 1750) was arrested over an unpaid debt of just £2 at her lodgings in St James's Street opposite White's. She had arrived in London from Dublin a few years earlier, recently divorced and reliant solely on her unflagging energy and her wit to scrape a precarious living as a courtesan–cum–hack writer. A short poem dedicated to a group of gentlemen at White's who saw her at her window and raised their wine glasses runs thus:

> Your rosy Wine
> Looks bright and fine;
> But yet it does not chear me:
> The Cause I guess
> Is surely this:
> The bottle is not near me.[*]

In response, the members of White's despatched a servant to take her a glass of red wine so that she could toast them. Pilkington's friendship circle included the influential playwright Colley Cibber and the novelist Samuel Richardson. Jonathan Swift who had once been a good friend in Ireland snubbed her after her divorce, label- ling Pilkington, 'Her Serene Highness of Lillyput'. The diminutive Pilkington – she was less than 4ft tall – was promptly despatched to the infamous Marshalsea on Borough High Street, Southwark where, upon arrival, her fellow prisoners demanded a bribe or 'garnish' to provide her with a meagre bed and lodgings. When it was found that she had no money about her, Pilkington writes, 'a Parcel of Wretches seized me and sung a song about Garnish, and were going to pull

---

[*] Norma Clarke, *Queen of the Wits: A Life of Laetitia Pilkington,* Faber, London, 2008

my clothes off.'** She wrote appealing to Colley Cibber who had evidently loaned her money in the past. He organised a subscription among her friends and in a matter of a few weeks the debt was repaid and her release secured.

Conditions at the Marshalsea evidently distressed the Irish poet since before leaving prison she was persuaded to pen a letter pleading for legislation to end the iniquities she had witnessed. Some small amendments to an earlier Act were forthcoming. The reform was agonisingly slow, finally culminating in a new Insolvent Debtor's Act of 1824. The debtors' prisons including the Marshalsea did not finally close until 1842. Recalling her efforts, Pilkington wrote:

> I may praise God that I was under him, the happy Instrument of Good to numbers of my wretched Fellow Creatures since by one pathetic Memorial I wrote for them, the sorrowful, Sighing of the Prisoners reached the Hearts of the Legislative Powers.***

Tom and Jerry

In 1820 a publishing sensation hit Britain. Written by Irish sporting journalist, boxing enthusiast and man of letters Pierce Egan, *Life in London* was a celebration of the racy life of two would-be Regency bucks, Corinthian Tom and the Hon. Jerry Hawthorn esq. – Tom and Jerry. Cousins newly arrived from rural Somerset, Tom and Jerry are introduced to London's low life by a disreputable Oxford don, Bob Logic. As Tom and Jerry discover, there were many dubious entertainments and distractions for the wealthy but gullible young men who frequented St James's and who offered easy pickings for an army of prostitutes, bullies, thieves and card sharpers. Corinthian Tom who takes his name from a class of individual regarded as the highest of the

---

** Jerry White, *Mansions of Misery: A Biography of the Marshalsea Debtors' Prison*, The Bodley Head, London, 2016, p. 147
*** Jerry White, ibid, p. 164

Regency beau monde is partnered by a girlfriend Corinthian Kate, a vacuous young lady out to impress with her veneer of social accomplishments. The name Corinthian was in popular usage and is derived from the ornate capitol of the classical Greek style of column popular in Regency architecture. London's low life was represented as the plain foot of the column. By extension, brothels and bawdy houses were sometimes called 'Corinths' because they were frequented by the likes of Bob Logic.

Tom and Jerry sample the contrasting delights London has to offer including getting fitted for a suit of clothes, spending the night drinking 'blue ruin' at a gin shop or sluicing house, visiting the opera, enjoying a masquerade supper, ogling the ladies in their carriages on Rotten Row, watching a fight between a bull mastiff and the celebrated Italian monkey Jacco Maccacco at the Westminster Pit and dancing at Almack's. Innocents abroad, the two gentlemen are observers of debauchery unlike their mentor Bob Logic who is an active participant.

With Egan's keen journalistic eye for detail we can be assured that *Life in London* is an accurate representation of street life in Regency London. Vice is never far from the surface of things, albeit dressed up in outward respectability. To take one incident observed while out riding on Rotten Row:

> 'What lovely girls!' exclaimed HAWTHORN; 'I suppose that is the Mamma and her three daughters. I declare I was quite struck with their pleasant countenances. You seem an old acquaintance of theirs.' LOGIC said, laughing outright, 'Yes, yes; they are good natured enough if you will furnish the means.'[*]

Bob Logic goes on to describe the girls as nuns (prostitutes) while their mother is 'a female of great notoriety designated the Abbess of ... '

Our pair ascend and descend the social scale visiting a coal heaver's pub in the East End dubbed 'All Max' where Bob Logic falls heavily for the charms of African Sall and Flash Nancy, breaking off to spend

---

[*] Pierce Egan, *Life in London*

the night in their company before finally getting arrested the next day by bailiffs executing a warrant for the repayment of a debt. He winds up in the Fleet Prison. On one last evening, Tom and Jerry while away the time with a 'turn or two in Bond Street – a stroll through Piccadilly – a look in at Tattersall's – a ramble through Pall Mall – and a strut on the *Corinthian Path* (Regent Street)'** before heading for an evening's entertainment at Vauxhall Pleasure Gardens.

Egan's *Life in London* popularised the use of flash slang, a street language seen here in print for the first time. Horses were called 'prads'. 'Flash coves' or 'swells' were types of dandy; those keen on sport, particularly boxing, were referred to as 'the fancy'; money was termed 'blunt' or 'rhino' and some of the many words for gin included 'daffy', 'lush', 'Mr Lushington' and 'Max'. The book may have shocked or amused those unaccustomed to London ways but the streetwise reader revelled in seeing the slang they or their servants might use in gin shops, coffee-houses, inns and stables appearing for the first time in black and white.

Such was the craze for Tom and Jerry that publishers started cashing in on the demand for lexicons of street slang. Many readers would have needed a glossary to cope with Egan's colourful jargon. Take his description of a crowd scene, for example:

> With that admired sort of LIFE in London, all jostling against each other in the park with the utmost sang froid, The NOBLEMAN and the Yokel – the DIVINE and the 'Family Man' – the PLAYER and the Poet ... the DANDY and the Gentleman – the out-and-out SWELL and the Groom – the real SPORTSMAN and the Black Leg – the HEAVY TODDLERS and the Operators – the dashing BUM TRAP and the Shy Cove ... ***

A 'BUM TRAP' for example, is a sheriff's officer who arrests debtors. A contemporary dictionary of Regency slang shows the expression in context: 'Ware hawke! the bum traps are fly to our

---

** Ibid.

*** Pierce Egan, *Life in London*, p. 193

panney'. Or in modern parlance, 'Keep a good look out, the bailiffs know where our house is.'

The book reflects Pierce Egan's rackety existence as a hack writer who contributed a regular sporting column for *Bell's Weekly Dispatch* and as a printer and publisher of cheap reprints. The title page of one of Egan's productions carries the imprint: 'Printed by and for P. Egan, 29 Great Marlborough Street.' Egan supplemented his hack writing with work as a fight promoter – a field of endeavour where his knowledge of the ring was second to none. Egan describes bare-knuckle boxing matches fought for prize money – typically a purse of 10 guineas – which represented a percentage of ticket sales. However, a fight between celebrated champions like Tom Cribb or Bill Richmond (the 'Black Terror') might draw far larger crowds and on at least two occasions the prize money was reportedly as high as £100. Illustrated by the brothers George and Robert Cruikshank, *Life in London* was a true collaboration. Containing verse, music and coloured illustration, the work appeared in monthly parts, and ran to many sell-out editions. *Life in London* spawned dozens of imitators and was even dramatised for the stage, remaining popular well into the late nineteenth century.

The Four Horse Club, the Daffy Club, and the Pugilistic Club

The sudden popularity of low pursuits such as gin drinking, bare-knuckle fighting and carriage driving among upper-class men led to the formation of several ad hoc clubs, including the Four Horse Club, the Daffy Club and the Pugilistic Club. The Four Horse Club comprised aristocratic amateurs who gained a certain kudos from driving carriages four-in-hand known as 'drags' along public turnpike roads. Driving four-in-hand requires great skill and a great understanding of horses which had to be selected for strength and stamina and carefully paired to pull at the same speed. Club members were clearly confident enough to pit their knowledge and skill against that of experienced professionals. Members of this fraternity drove at a sedate pace but their passengers would often hang out of the drag blowing bugles to the consternation of other road users. At one time the club conducted a regular outing to Windsor, starting at about midday from Piccadilly. 'Between twelve and twenty coaches left, lined up in single file and maintaining a rhythmic trot.'*

Named after the flash slang for gin, the Daffy Club had no fixed premises but members met at the Castle Public House in Holborn run by a former boxer Jem Soares. Boxing and gin consumption seemed to go hand in hand. Sporting gentlemen referred to in contemporary slang as 'the Fancy' would travel long distances to watch and gamble on the outcome of prize fights. This loose network of boxing aficionados was referred to as the Pugilistic Club.

The best evidence we have for how fights were staged comes from Pierce Egan who published in 1814 his famous panorama, a continuous strip of pictures wound round a spindle and enclosed within a cylindrical wooden box small enough to be carried in a coat pocket. Intended as an entertaining comic strip, Egan's panorama was titled, 'The Road to a Fight or Going to a Fight at Moulsey Hurst or a Picture of the Fancy'. Drawn by Robert Cruikshank, the colour plate depicts a procession of assorted horse-drawn vehicles from swells in their high flyers and phaetons followed by a motley assortment of carts and gigs driven by boxing fans including 'the Bermondsey boys and the Tothill Fields costermongers'** on their way from Hyde Park Corner to Moulsey Hurst to see the fight between Jack Randall and West Country Dick. Prize fights were open-air all-ticket events which mostly took place on commons outside London which afforded ample space to set up a ring and accommodate thousands of spectators. Here wealthy – often aristocratic – fight promoters would organise betting syndicates and offer prize money of up to 100 guineas, where the protagonists were famous. Smaller events could be staged indoors at suitable arenas such as the Fives Court in St

---

* From the website www.janeausten.co.uk
** Robert Cruikshank illustrated

Martin's Street, Leicester Fields and Gentleman John Jackson's rooms in Bond Street.

The elevation of pugilism to a sport starts with Jack Broughton, considered by many including Egan to be the father of English boxing. He opened Broughton's New Amphitheatre in Oxford Road, now Hanway Street, which opened on 10 March 1743. It closed down in 1750 after Broughton, the reigning champion of England, was defeated by Jack Slack the 'Hounslow Butcher'. In its day, Broughton's amphitheatre not only staged fights but was also an academy where pugilists would learn and practise the finer points of 'milling' or sparring under the tuition of Broughton himself or one of his associates. Broughton had devised a set of rules of conduct for boxing which he published in a pamphlet dated 10 August 1743. The rules established that the fight would be contained within a roped-off boxing ring, 16 to 18ft square with posts at each corner. Pugilists must be stripped to the waist. Boxers could have up to two 'seconds', helpers whose job it was to prepare their man for the ring and to tend his injuries or call time when their man was defeated. The fight was divided into a series of bouts or rounds. Stress was laid on the art of boxing, parrying blows, neat footwork and feinting – avoiding blows. Broughton's rules stipulated that:

> no boxer or his second was to enter the ring before the start of the fight or 'set to' had been signalled. At this point, everybody was to leave the stage. Two umpires were present outside the ring to oversee fair conduct.[*]

There was no time limit for matches and there are records of fights lasting for over two hours. However, a fight customarily concluded with one of the pugilists either knocked unconscious or being so badly beaten that his second would drag him out of the ring and signal defeat. If a second failed to 'bring his man to the side of the square within the space of half a minute' he was deemed to have lost the fight.

---

[*] Pierce Egan, *Boxiana,* Vol. 1 reprint, Elibron Classics, London, 2006, p. 51

These rules of conduct seem barbaric to modern sensibilities, but Broughton's rules remained standard for almost a century until they were superseded in 1838 by the London Prize Ring Rules. These were the rules observed by well-known fighters of the period including Jack Slack, 'the Hounslow Butcher', 'Gentleman' John Jackson, Tom Johnson and Tom Cribb. Many pugilists like the black bare-knuckle fighter, US born former slave Bill Richmond, lived locally. Richmond, who earned enough through his fighting career to buy a public house, the Horse and Dolphin near Leicester Fields, is buried in St James's Gardens, Euston, an overflow cemetery for St James's Piccadilly.

Nor was boxing confined only to the men. There were a few fearsome women pugilists like Elizabeth Stokes, who in 1728 fought Ann Field of Stoke Newington for a purse of £10. The ladies' sport achieved further notoriety through the activities of a prostitute, Mary Anne Pearce, who had been at one time Lord Barrymore's mistress. Known as 'Lady Barrymore' or the 'Boxing Baroness', Pearce was said to strip down to her shift when she wanted a fight. More often than not, however, her fighting came in the form of a drunken affray at a gin house.

Pugilism or bare-knuckle fighting attracted huge audiences drawn from across the social spectrum. Public houses run by famous boxers such as 'Gentleman' John Jackson, founder of the Metropolitan Ring Society, and Tom Cribb whose pub which bears his name still exists in Panton Street, Haymarket, provided supplementary 'entertainment' to the gambling which took place at many gentlemen's clubs and an extra opportunity to gamble. The craze for pugilism and honour fighting reflect the sense of entitlement enjoyed by members of gentlemen's clubs. In contrast to revolutionary France where mob rule supplanted the rule of law, pugilism was regarded as a quintessential expression of English fair play. It was widely admired as evidence of a free and fair society.

Clubland extended its tentacles throughout society, including the looking glass world. The club-man who liked to gamble, enjoyed spectator sports, drink, and women found himself mixing with some of the rougher elements to be found in London's West End. Wealth was the driver of an alternative economy; any gentleman of means could readily find someone to assist him in procuring his guilty pleasures.

Activities like pugilism and driving carriages four-in-hand were part of a lively and vibrant counterculture. Men sharing a common interest naturally gravitated towards clubs. The racy slang of the Regency Buck defined a generation of self-indulgent club-men.

CHAPTER 6

PALACES OF POWER

There were many men of note in the room.
There was a Foreign Minister, a member of the Cabinet,
Two ex-members of the Cabinet, a great poet,
an exceedingly able editor, two earls, two members
of the Royal Academy, the president of a learned society, a celebrated
professor – and it was expected that Royalty might come in at any
minute, and blow a few clouds of smoke.

Anthony Trollope, from *Phineas Redux*

As the nineteenth century dawned, an emerging middle class began
to explore areas of common interest and engage in political debate.
The concept of masculinity was redefined to embrace new forms
of civilised behaviour, fashion and recreation. Through joining an
exclusive members' club, a man might be regarded as a gentleman.
The status brought with it an aspiration to learning and culture as
well as a declaration of political affiliation and, as we can see from
the opening quotation from Anthony Trollope, the opportunity to
network with the highest and most powerful in the land.

During the eighteenth century, club membership was mostly
confined to the wealthy aristocratic elite. But London was growing
rapidly. In 1700 the capital's population stood at less than 600,000.

In 1801, the date of the first official census, it had risen to 900,000, and by 1831 it had almost doubled to 1,654,994. The rapid growth of London and the building boom that followed the end of the Napoleonic Wars saw increases in trade and the rise of a new professional class. But while the peace dividend brought wealth for the few it also resulted in growing inequality. The vast bulk of Britain's labouring classes were impoverished by the repressive Corn Laws and struggled to put food on the table. During this period, clubs expanded their membership to include some of these rising men, blurring the boundaries between intellect, artistic skills, scientific knowledge and breeding. At the same time, new kinds of clubs were born, narrowing the divide to some extent.

Athens Re-Imagined

John Wilson Croker, an exemplar of the new breed of club-man, deserves far wider recognition than the mere footnote afforded him by history. Elected in 1807 as MP for Downpatrick, the young Dublin barrister rose to one of the highest and most influential roles in government. As Secretary of the Admiralty, Croker served in four successive Tory administrations from 1809 to 1830, during which he helped establish the Royal Navy as the formidable fighting force it was to become after Trafalgar. A personal friend and confidant of the Duke of Wellington, whose support as secretary for Ireland helped launch his parliamentary career, Croker had an even greater claim to fame – his friendship with Lord Elgin and his passion for classical Greek art and architecture. When Lord Elgin proposed acquiring the Parthenon frieze from Greece's Turkish rulers, it was Croker who smoothed the way for a government grant, arguing forcefully and persuasively in the *Quarterly Review* the case for their removal to Britain. And for good measure, as head of the Admiralty, Croker instructed the senior naval officer in the eastern Mediterranean to purchase on his behalf any other Greek antiquities that might come his way.

This, then, was the presiding genius behind the Athenaeum. Founded in 1824 and dedicated to the Greek goddess of wisdom, Pallas Athene, the club was to become a temple to culture, science and the arts, especially poetry and literature. And despite its founder being a Tory, the club would be apolitical. Croker was disparaging of what he saw as the malign influence of the fashionable St James's coffee-houses, their exploitation of the lower classes through pugilism and prostitution, and the gambling which took place in some of the older clubs. With nothing but his ambition and his intellect to recommend him, Croker placed a high value on the improving power of knowledge, as his meteoric rise to become part of the political establishment testified. Like the coffee-house debating societies a century earlier, the Athenaeum was conceived as a vehicle for self-improvement. It is interesting to note that the name Athenaeum was not unique to this London institution. It was at the time a generic name for a library of learned books. There were already two Athenaeums – in Liverpool and in Boston, Massachusetts.

Seeking the support of president of the Royal Society Sir Humphry Davy, an institution of which he himself was a member, Croker outlined his ambition to found a club that would unite the arts and sciences:

I will take this opportunity of repeating the proposition I have before made to you about a Club for literary and scientific men, and followers of the fine arts. The fashionable and military clubs not only absorb a great portion of society, but have spoiled all the Coffee-Houses and Taverns, so that the Artist, or mere literary man, neither of whom are members of the established clubs, are in a much worse situation, both comparatively and positively, than they were.[*]

---

[*] Letter from John Wilson Croker to Sir Humphry Davy sent from The Admiralty, 12 March 1823. Source – The Athenaeum Club General Committee Minutes 1824–1826

The two men agreed that 'no one should be eligible except gentlemen who have either published some literary or professional work or a paper in the Philosophical Transactions of the Royal Society.'* Membership was to be initially restricted to 500 to be drawn from eminent academics, politicians, lawyers, churchmen, artists, and writers. Bishops and clergymen continue to be well represented. The Royal Academy, Society of Antiquaries, and the College of Physicians – heavy guns of the intellectual and artistic establishment – lent their backing. The club's instant popularity combined with the pressing need to raise finance saw the original cap on membership lifted, and by 1830, the Athenaeum's intake had doubled.

Forming a club whose influential members could discuss and debate the foremost scientific theories and philosophical ideas of the day would generate new avenues for discovery and lead science and thought in new directions. The late Georgian period when the Athenaeum was conceived was an era of discovery and exploration. The Admiralty and the Royal Society, both based at Somerset House, worked closely together on scientific discovery such as establishing longitude and latitude, producing a nautical almanac, and instigating the quest for the North-West Passage. Sir Humphry Davy, famous for designing the miner's safety lamp, became the Athenaeum's first chairman, while the pioneering physicist Michael Faraday of the Royal Institution was elected as the club's first secretary.

To be a member of the Athenaeum was a great honour as only those pre-eminent in their chosen field were proposed. Joshua Reynolds, William Blake, Robert Peel and Sir Walter Scott were among the list of prominent men invited to join. The original subscription of 6 guineas per annum, the equivalent to £350 in today's money, gave members access to a large and impressive library and a burgeoning art collection.

---

* *Armchair Athenians: Essays from Athenaeum Life,* The Athenaeum, London, 2001, p. 160

View of Pall Mall in the reign of Queen Anne – from *Old and New London*.

St James's Square in the early eighteenth century – from *Old and New London*.

The formidable Sarah Sophia Child Villiers, Lady Jersey, a portrait by Alfred Chalon – by kind permission of the Bonham family.

Carlton House, an engraving from *c.* 1800 – from *Old and New London*.

Beau Brummel: an engraving taken from a miniature portrait – from *Old and New London*.

The first Quadrille to be danced at Almack's. Sarah, Lady Jersey is second from the left – from *Old and New London*.

The Reform Club from a watercolour by George Belton Moore – by kind permission of the Reform Club.

The Duke of Wellington's funeral procession marches past the Pall Mall clubs. It was the largest event ever seen in London. *The Illustrated London News* – reproduced from an original source.

Alexis Soyer adds the finishing touches to a sauce in the kitchen of the Reform Club – by kind permission of the Reform Club.

Lizzie Le Blond, alpine pioneer – by permission of The Martin and Osa Johnson Safari Museum.

The 'library boy' fetches a hefty volume at the Reform Club. An engraving – by kind permission of the Reform Club.

Kitchen staff preparing dinner at the Reform Club *c.* 1900 – by kind permission of the Reform Club.

REFORM CLUB : AWAITING ELECTION RESULTS.

Awaiting election results at the Reform Club (early twentieth century) – by kind permission of the Reform Club.

The Lew Stone Orchestra at the Monseigneur Restaurant. Vocalist Al Bowlly can be seen singing into a microphone with guitar front left – by kind permission of Ray Pallett/ Memory Lane.

Diners wait to take to the dance floor at the Monseigneur Restaurant – by kind permission of Ray Pallett/ Memory Lane.

The Athenaeum was built partly on the site of the recently demolished Carlton House. Fronting onto the newly named Waterloo Place, the focus of which is the Duke of York's Column at the top of a flights of stairs leading down to the Mall and St James's Park, Decimus Burton's grand clubhouse forms an impressive grouping of stately buildings which include the United Service Club, the Travellers Club and the Reform Club.

These lofty ideals are reflected in the architecture. The Athenaeum's palatial clubhouse designed by Decimus Burton and completed in 1830 would become a showcase for Britain's peacetime achievements in science, industry and the arts. It was said at the time that rather than waste money on building an ice house to chill champagne, Croker insisted the money be spent commissioning the sculptor John Henning to design a Parthenaic frieze to surround the building. This gave rise to a satirical couplet:

I'm John Wilson Croker
I do as I please,
They asked for an Ice House,
I give you – a Frieze.**

Model Institutions

Britain's industrial cities spawned a new class of wealthy entrepreneurs and merchants who saw clubs as a way of building contacts, promoting trade and raising finance. Founded in 1797, the Liverpool Athenaeum is the only one of six Liverpool gentlemen's clubs to have survived intact to the present day. The spectacular growth of Liverpool as a trading port during the late eighteenth century saw its population triple between 1760 and 1801 to 77,000. In addition to a burgeoning merchant class was an expanding professional class

---

** Quoted in Michael Wheeler, *A History of the Athenaeum 2017*. Also on http://www.athenaeumclub.co.uk/

that included lawyers, doctors and clergymen. The club's inaugural prospectus notes:

> It has often been a matter of surprise … that in a town of such commercial and national importance as Liverpool, the conveniences and accommodation for the acquisition of knowledge, both local and general, both ancient and modern, should be so imperfect as they confessedly are.[*]

The term 'athenaeum' refers to a library or seat of learning, and the club's well-stocked library which included nautical charts of America and the Caribbean as well as official census returns was an invaluable resource for the many Liverpool merchants engaged in overseas trade. The club's resources were strengthened by subscriptions to all the leading local and national newspapers and magazines. Liverpool's clubmen were as well-versed in the issues of the day as any coffee-house denizen of St James's. The enthusiasm for club life also extended to Britain's other major cities which established parallel institutions such as the Manchester Reform Club, the Ulster Reform Club, the New Club Edinburgh and the St James's Club, Manchester.

The idea of the club as a learned society was exported to the United States via the trans-Atlantic cotton trade between Liverpool and America's eastern seaboard. The Boston Athenaeum, a circulating library, lecture hall and art gallery, was established in the US city in 1826 as a membership institution for wealthy Bostonians. There is also a Portsmouth Athenaeum in Portsmouth, New Hampshire.

A Grand Vision

The end of the Napoleonic Wars in 1815 saw a transformation in London's West End as the peace dividend sparked a boom in confidence

---

[*] *The Athenaeum Liverpool, 1797–1997*, p. 3

and speculation. The Prince Regent's vision of a revived London had begun in 1811 when a short-lived credit boom and the promise of long leases encouraged investors to participate in an ambitious property development. The plan was to build a new village in what was then one of the outskirts of London. This *rus in urbe*, the first garden suburb, featured carefully laid out terraced streets and crescents of high status, stuccoed houses as well as a number of grand villas set within the picturesque and tranquil landscape of Regent's Park. The architect and developer was John Nash, who at the time held the government post of Surveyor of Woods and Forests. Nash's close relationship with the Prince Regent was a key to attracting architects like the young Decimus Burton who designed the Regent's Park villas. Integral to this vision was a grand route cutting through the West End and connecting Regent's Park with Waterloo Place and St James's. The guards' barracks at Albany Street and the Wellington Barracks at St James's Park were a part of this ambitious scheme.

A massive undertaking, Regent Street was built in stages between 1817 and 1823. Nash's classical styled development of Regent Street and Waterloo Place provided a series of stunning architectural set pieces. These included the Italian Opera House which replaced the old King's Theatre on Haymarket, and the Quadrant, a colonnade of shops with a pedestrian terrace at the Piccadilly end of Regent Street. The finished scheme amply fulfilled the Prince Regent's ambition to rival the grand boulevards of Paris. The prince persuaded Parliament to approve funds to begin a major project to remodel the minor royal residence Buckingham House into a palace, doubling its size and creating a unified classical frontage. At the same time he sought approval for the demolition of Carlton House, a palace he now regarded as inconvenient and unfit for purpose. The demolition of Carlton House in 1824 created the opportunity to remodel Waterloo Place and build two new developments, Carlton House Terrace and Carlton Gardens.

Pall Mall, the imposing route towards St James's Palace, offered the Department of Woods and Forests (subsequently Crown Estates) the opportunity to encourage the building of the large palatial clubhouses. In effect the clubs collaborated in creating a unified architectural vision in the form of a grand vista linking Charing Cross with St James's Palace. On the east side of what is now Lower Regent Street, Nash built a magnificent double residence for himself and his relative John Edwards. Trafalgar Square was laid out partly on the site of the old stable block for Carlton House, so creating a focus for the subsequent development of the Strand.

Nash took pains to ensure his development functioned smoothly. At this time London was entirely dependent on horse-drawn transport. Stabling for horses was provided by Carlton Mews, a massive underground structure designed by John Nash and built in 1832. With a cobbled floor and bays divided by slender cast-iron columns and iron balconies leading to accommodation for the many grooms and ostlers, Carlton Mews serviced Carlton House Terrace and the clubs on Pall Mall. Sadly demolished in 1969 to make way for the British Council headquarters in Spring Gardens the mews, had it survived, would have provided the missing part of the jigsaw of Clubland history. The sole surviving link to the vital role horses played are the two granite horse mounting blocks sited on the pavements outside the Athenaeum and the United Service Club (now the Institute of Directors). A bronze plaque simply states 'This Horse Block was erected at the Desire of the Duke of Wellington, 1830.' Taken as a whole, Nash's major remodelling of the West End opened the way for a boom in club building in Pall Mall and St James's Square. St James's became the heart of London's Clubland.

High Ideals

The new generation of clubs reflected high ideals and aspiration. In the post Napoleonic era, clubhouses became grander and more imposing. The demolition of the Prince Regent's palace, Carlton House, in 1824 created a vacant site ideally suited to major development. Ninety-nine-year leases were to be made available from the Crown, prompting newly formed clubs to set about raising funds through the financial markets to commission architects and builders. Some debentures and stocks were bought as an investment by members. The building costs could be enormous. Situated at 104 Pall Mall, the Reform, one of the grandest of all the clubhouses, cost a total of £84,000 including architects' fees of £4,000.* Added to this would be the ongoing cost of annual ground rent, staff costs and maintenance, all of which had to be covered by members' annual subscription.

Sited on the corner of Pall Mall and Waterloo Place, John Nash built the magnificent United Service Club between 1826 and 1828. Standing opposite, Decimus Burton's palatial Athenaeum was completed in 1831, seven years after the club was founded. Its grand opening on 1 January was marked by an inaugural dinner. Next door to the Athenaeum, architect Charles Barry was supervising the construction of the Travellers Club, a project that was finally finished in 1832. A little further up Pall Mall, the Carlton Club which had been founded in 1832 opened its grand clubhouse in 1837. Following his commission for the Travellers Club, Charles Barry went on to design an even more impressive Italianate palazzo for the Reform Club which opened in 1841.

The architectural vision behind Clubland was now a solid reality. The Guards Club and the Oxford and Cambridge followed. Within the space of two decades Pall Mall was flanked by imposing clubhouses. Larger, grander, the new generation of clubs were markedly different from what had gone before. While most of the eighteenth-century clubs had grown up organically from coffee-houses and gambling dens – White's occupied what was essentially a large private mansion – the new clubs were owned by their members under articles of incorporation. This gave clubs the ability to raise finance and to develop sustainable business models.

---

* George Woodbridge, *The Reform Club 1836-1978: A History from the Club's Records*, The Reform Club, London, 1978, p. 62

The game changer had been the Union Club founded in 1805 by a group of Anglo-Irish peers including the Duke of Wellington in response to the Union of Great Britain and Ireland and the dissolution of the old Irish parliament. This was the first club to be owned by its members, a co-operative venture under which members were shareholders and an elected management committee was responsible for financial decisions, membership and fees. Expanding rapidly, the Union Club moved from its original rented premises in Pall Mall before moving to St James's Square and finally to a new clubhouse in Trafalgar Square in 1824 where the club negotiated a long lease.

Taken as a whole, this new generation of clubs laid the foundation for a meritocratic governing class. Members' clubs extended membership to the rising political and middle classes and 'new money' that was to become the backbone of the Victorian era. Despite reflecting Britain's new perception of itself as an emerging world power, high-minded institutions like the Athenaeum and the Reform co-existed with the louche sporting and gambling clubs and the bastions of aristocratic privilege located just a stone's throw away in St James's Street.

Shifting the axis of London's Clubland to Pall Mall held obvious advantages. The clubs were close to the seat of royal power, the Court of St James's, where foreign ambassadors were received and audiences with the monarch were granted. Just as important were Clubland's strong links with Parliament, the Civil Service, the military, the established Church and the Inns of Court, much of it through the influence of Arthur Wellesley, the Duke of Wellington.

Wellington's Clubland

A vast amount has been written about Arthur Wellesley's successful campaigns in the Peninsular War and his defeat of Napoleon at the battle of Waterloo. But there was another side to Britain's military hero. In peacetime, the Duke of Wellington switched his very considerable energies to seeking and wielding political power and he saw clubs as the ideal power base from which to build his support.

Few other individuals were more active in promoting the concept of Clubland. In all, he was a member of no fewer than nine clubs.

Wellington helped launch the Union Club in 1805 for his fellow Anglo-Irish peers and members of Parliament following the dissolution of the Irish Parliament. Like Pitt before him, Wellington was a member of White's which threw a banquet for him in 1814 after his initial defeat of Napoleon, doubtless to deliver a firm riposte to Brooks's whose members had supported Napoleon. Wellington was a strong and pragmatic Tory, and he saw in the old aristocracy of Brooks's a dangerous libertarianism which if unchecked could result in revolution along the lines of France.

The focus of Wellington's campaigning zeal for gentlemen's clubs was the new generation of clubs springing up on Pall Mall. The Iron Duke's support and advice was crucial for club formation and helped legitimise institutions which might otherwise have struggled to establish themselves on a firm footing. The clubs in turn provided him with a ready-made political platform and a loyal following. In 1816, Wellington helped secure the backing of the Prime Minister Lord Liverpool for the establishment of the United Service Club in Pall Mall for senior officers of the British Army and the Royal Navy who had served in the Napoleonic Wars. Subsequently, Wellington's involvement in re-inventing Clubland took him in some interesting and unusual directions. As a general and administrator for the East India Company, Wellington developed a close working relationship with his clerk, Benjamin Dean Wyatt, architect son of the celebrated James Wyatt who had supervised the building of White's.

When the nation showed its gratitude to the victor of Waterloo, Wellington asked Benjamin Wyatt to find him a suitable site and having settled on Stratfield Saye in Hampshire, commissioned him as its architect. Having proved his credentials beyond any doubt, Wellington then gave Wyatt the job of altering and adapting his London home Apsley House for entertaining on a grand scale. Wellington's patronage helped Benjamin Wyatt secure the commission to design the new Crockford's Club in St James's Street.

Wellington was a founder member of the Travellers Club the Athenaeum, which had been launched by his political protégé J. W. Croker, and Crockford's gambling club. The Duke 'seldom played at all and never played deep'* but he enjoyed meeting his officers and doubtless appreciated his protégé's architecture and resident chef Charles Francatelli's French cuisine. Together with General Sir John Malcolm, Wellington was a founder member of the Oriental Club. When approached to support a group of high-ranking officers from the East India Company's army in 1824, the Duke's advice was clear: 'Have a club of your own,' and 'Buy the freehold.' On the strength of this, Wellington was invited to be the club's first president. His involvement stemmed from his early career within the British East India army.

Wellington's motivation in seeking out and joining clubs stems from the need to wield power and influence and to win converts to his brand of conservatism. But his involvement with the Carlton Club, which he helped found in 1832 in response to the Great Reform Act, was a major political statement. Some sources date Wellington's decision to launch a political club to the first years of his Premiership in 1828 when he led a group of influential Conservative allies including Sir Robert Peel and the Marquess of Salisbury. Despite his role in establishing the Carlton Club, Wellington came to hate it, possibly on account of a public snub he received from Peel while at the Carlton. He was rarely seen within the building and wrote in later life, 'Never write a letter to your mistress, and never join the Carlton Club.' **

Wellington may have seen the gentlemen's club as a diversion from his career as a Parliamentarian. But nevertheless, political clubs provided a counterweight to Parliament, helping consolidate power in the hands of the ruling elite. The duke's affinity for clubs was entirely in character for, as prime minister, Wellington was known for his

---

* T.H.S. Escott, *Club Makers and Club Members*, T. Fisher Unwin, London, 1914, p. 204
** Tom Girtin, *The Abominable Clubman*, Hutchinson, London, 1964, p. 136

brusque command and control, managerial style and for attempting to overrule political consensus. He regarded his cabinet in the same way that he did his general staff on the battlefield. He is reported as despairing after a bruising political encounter with colleagues who disagreed with his decisions: 'An extraordinary affair. I gave them their orders and they wanted to stay and discuss them.' In spite of his autocratic leadership style, clubs became sanctuaries removed from the political sphere where Wellington could build support informally and in relaxed surroundings. The Duke was a highly sociable individual who was at his most comfortable among the masculine comradeship of the officers' mess.

Prime minister from 1828 to 1830 and for little less than a month in 1834, the Duke of Wellington was staunchly Conservative. In particular he was against reform of the electoral system under which MPs were sponsored by powerful landed interests, the so-called 'rotten boroughs'. Swimming against the tide of progress, Wellington was voted down and the process of reform was taken up by the Whig/Liberal opposition.

Fighting reform propelled Wellington into the realms of academia. He saw salvation in a new London college aligned to King William IV's position as head of the Church of England. As prime minister, Wellington took the chair at the opening of King's College on 21 June 1828. MPs accused the Duke of jettisoning his pro-Protestant stance by supporting the Catholic Emancipation bill. Winchilsea challenged Wellington to a duel which was duly fought with pistols and seconds in Battersea Fields. Winchilsea did not fire a shot; Wellington deliberately fired wide with the result that he received an apology which he graciously accepted. Appointed Chancellor of Oxford University in 1835, Wellington finally joined the United Universities Club, a role in which he was able to bring his patriotic common sense to bear, despite Tories being out of power and Wellington himself being widely derided in the wake of the Great Reform Act.

Wellington's death in 1852 saw the great military leader's total rehabilitation. His reputation necessitated a grand state funeral. A massive bronze funeral carriage bearing the coffin drawn by twelve horses was followed by Wellington's groom leading his riderless horse with the duke's boots reversed in the stirrups. This was followed by a procession of massed soldiery at a slow march. Around a million people are said to have lined the streets as the solemn cortege made its way from Horse Guards, up the Mall to Constitution Hill, before turning right past Apsley House, and proceeding along Piccadilly and Pall Mall and on to St Paul's Cathedral. In Pall Mall, clubmen and their guests watched from black draped, two- and three-tier wooden viewing platforms outside the United Service Club, the Athenaeum, and the Travellers Club.

St James's and the Military

St James's is closely associated with the military and in particular the Brigade of Guards. Originally the guards and the horse guards fulfilled the function of a royal bodyguard sent out to protect the king when he appeared in public. Any public excursions by the king from St James's Palace would have involved a heavily armed cavalry escort. The Prince Regent's grand vision for a ceremonial street also formed a nexus between three substantial military establishments, the Albany barracks near Regent's Park, Wellington Barracks at St James's Park and Horse Guards at Whitehall. With the army close at hand should an emergency arise, the king could feel secure.

Today, the changing of the guard is marked by a ceremonial march of the guards from Wellington Barracks to Buckingham Palace or following the Mall, St James's Palace. But St James's connections with the army run much deeper than military or royal pageant. St James's was first to hear the news of Napoleon's defeat at the battle of Waterloo. Dispatched by Wellington on 19 June 1815, Major Henry Percy had landed at Broadstairs by packet boat and had been driven at top speed with three captured French eagle standards and a report destined for the Prince Regent. On the evening of 21 June, the Prince Regent, prime minister Lord

Liverpool and foreign secretary Lord Castlereagh were attending a private dinner at number 16 St James's Square, the house of Mr and Mrs Boehm, when Major Percy's post chaise and four with the Napoleonic eagles hanging out of the window tore into the square. Thus it was that the victory at Waterloo was announced to the public from the balcony of the house. The prince was reported to be saddened at the heavy toll of officers and men who had fallen on the battlefield. The event was one of those rare make-or-break moments in history. In the run-up to the battle of Waterloo, there had been a run on the pound as foreign investors speculated against the currency. If the battle had gone the other way and Napoleon had won, a British defeat could have been the precursor to a French invasion. As it was, financiers confident in the Iron Duke made a killing of their own overnight.

Erected in 1827 and dedicated to the commander-in-chief of the British Army during the Napoleonic Wars, the Duke of York's Column in Waterloo Place is a powerful symbol of the Hanoverian dynasty's close association with the military. Second son of George III, the Duke of York and Albany turned out to be a gifted administrator and army reformer and is credited with professionalising the British Army through the formation of the Sandhurst Military Academy. The Duke of York, however, fell from grace in 1809, when his mistress Mary Anne Clarke was discovered to have sold commissions behind his back to raise money to run his extravagant household. The duke was relieved of his duties. Despite the scandal, all was forgiven two years later when the duke was exonerated by Parliament. He was at the helm for the historic Battle of Waterloo won by his field-marshal Wellington and when he died in 1827, he was accorded full military honours. Beside this symbolic link between army and royalty, there was another tangible connection with St James's when in 1858 the War Office acquired a former royal residence Cumberland House, Pall Mall, which functioned as its headquarters until 1911.

The location of the old War Office explains the association between Waterloo Place and the Crimean War. At the junction of Pall Mall and

Waterloo Place, the Guards' Crimean War Memorial commemorates Britain and France's disastrous war with Russia, won at the cost of many British casualties, many of whom died not as a result of wounds sustained in battle but of fever and dysentery caused by lack of sanitation. The nurse Florence Nightingale revolutionised medical care for the injured and led efforts to improve basic hygiene. The centrepiece of this memorial flanked by four bronze guardsmen in the military uniform of the period is a statue of the man most associated with the Crimean War, Sidney Herbert, Secretary for War. Herbert's statue was originally placed outside the War Office in Pall Mall in 1861. But in 1914, it was moved, together with a companion statue of Florence Nightingale, to its present site.

Opposite the Guards' Crimean War Memorial is Cox's Bank, the army's bank where officers traditionally received their pay. Cox's Bank reserves were underwritten by the Treasury.

Military Clubs

Up until the Duke of Wellington's moves to promote the gentlemen's club as a civilising institution, no clubs existed specifically for military officers. It is not hard to see why army or naval officers were regarded as 'un-clubbable', a word coined by Dr Samuel Johnson for inclusion in his first dictionary. The army's reputation had been tainted by lurid stories of gambling, drunken excess, unpaid mess bills and occasionally duelling. With the core of its membership drawn from the Prince Regent's own regiment, the 10th Hussars, Watier's Club had caused a scandal through the fortunes won and lost at the card game Macao. Crockford's also attracted the youthful and spendthrift military dandies and junior officers, many of whom were second sons of aristocratic families.

The army and the navy both recruited men from a wide social spectrum, and officers generally had to pay for a commission. The pressure to keep up appearances could see young men without the security of a private income run up huge mess bills. Many ex-soldiers effectively left the services destitute. Wellington had decided what was needed was the professionalisation of the armed forces where men of the 'middling sort' could be promoted on merit. Clubs were the first step in this direction. Having seen off Napoleon's threatened invasion, the army and navy were welcomed with open arms in London's Clubland. The first move towards providing for the comforts of officers was the Guards Club founded in 1810. Following the example of the Union Club, it was one of the first clubs in London to be owned by the members themselves.

Three Guards officers, Captain Rees Howell Gronow, Jack Talbot and that well-known acrobatic dandy Colonel Dan MacKinnon established the Guards Club at the St James's Coffee-House at number 88 St James's Street opposite Lock's the hatter. The link between coffee-houses and club formation remained as strong as it was a century earlier. The establishment provided exactly the kind of relaxing and informal atmosphere where officers home on leave or waiting to be posted could enjoy decent hospitality. In fact, not long afterwards St James's Coffee-House became the St James's Club in 1840. Meanwhile, the Guards Club acquired premises at 49 St James's Street, opposite White's, finally moving to a newly commissioned clubhouse at 70 Pall Mall in 1849. A distinguished roster of members included the Dukes of York and Cambridge, both field marshals of the British Army. The Guards Club finally moved to a purpose-built clubhouse at 70 Pall Mall in May 1849.

The Guards Club inspired a slew of peripatetic clubs which held reunions for brother officers in the coffee-houses in and around St James's. The final days of the Napoleonic Wars saw the formation of the General Military Club, the Royal Military, the Flanders and Peninsular Club and even a Royal Navy Club. But senior army officers felt what was needed was a single overarching club complete with rules governing eligibility for membership and a code of conduct that would put members on a par with other high status members' clubs. Three weeks before the battle of Waterloo, Lt General Sir Thomas Graham, Lord Lynedoch, called eighty senior army officers to a meeting at the Thatched House Tavern, St James's, to plan what would subsequently be called the United Service Club. Overcoming opposition from the prime minister, Lord Liverpool, who feared that a military club might form a junto that might at some point threaten Parliamentary democracy, Lord Lynedoch and the club's embryo committee set about raising the funds needed to lease a suitable building. They were fortified by a letter from the Duke of Wellington approving the scheme.

Early in 1816, the United Service Club also known as 'The Senior' opened in Albemarle Street with Wellington, Fitzroy Somerset, Lord Combermere and Nelson's Captain Hardy among the first members. Fitzroy Somerset, as heir to the hereditary title Lord Raglan, went on to achieve notoriety by being held responsible for the Charge of the Light Brigade at Balaclava. Moving briefly to Charles Street, the club finally moved to Pall Mall in 1827 to a fine clubhouse designed by John Nash and built at a cost of £49,000.

Nor was this the only major general service club. With an Empire to defend, Britain's armed forces were in the ascendant and in 1837 the Army and Navy Club or 'the Rag' was founded with a grand clubhouse further down Pall Mall, so called because member Captain Duff described the food as 'a rag and famine affair'. This was followed by a Junior United Service Club, and another umbrella body, the Naval and Military Club, was formed in 1862. This fast expanding club quickly outgrew its Clifford Street clubhouse, and from there moved to Hanover Square before settling at 99 Piccadilly in the palatial former home of Lord Palmerston.

Political Powerhouses

Political clubs had always been a feature of St James's. But it had been clear for some time that White's and Brooks's, regarded by many as little more than aristocratic gambling clubs, needed bolstering to build support for Tory and Whig politics. The political ambitions of the 'middling sort' provided a new stage for members' clubs to re-invent themselves for a new era. Matters came to a head with the

Great Reform Act of 1832, the first step in overhauling Britain's out-dated and corrupt electoral system. Passed by a narrow majority in Parliament, the Act extended the franchise to more voters and revised electoral boundaries in recognition of the developing industrial pow-erhouse cities of Manchester, Leeds, Liverpool and Birmingham. This movement is reflected in the formation of the Carlton Club and the Reform Club.

Founded in the year of the Great Reform Act of 1832, the Carlton Club on the corner of Pall Mall and Carlton Gardens is widely regarded as the Conservative party's rallying cry to oppose further reform of the electoral system. The club would help further the careers of a new generation of Conservative MPs. But to be a member of the Carlton did not necessarily mean you were a Conservative. Prospective applicants merely had to demonstrate broad sympathy with Conservative principles. It all depended on who had proposed and seconded your application. The Liberal, William Gladstone, was a member – not of the Reform or of Brooks's – but of the Carlton. He resigned in 1860 when it became apparent that continued mem-bership would compromise his principles. Greater political alignment was secured in 1864 by the formation of a new club, the Junior Carlton, which made membership of the Conservative Party a pre-condition for joining.

The history of the Reform Club tells a different story. At the time of the Great Reform Act, the Whig party was divided into two camps, Radicals and Whigs. The two strands of thought were soon to unite under a common banner of Liberals or Whig Liberals as they were known during a transition period. The years following the Napoleonic Wars should have seen peace and prosperity. Instead, a series of disastrous harvests made worse by the Corn Laws imposed a punitive tax on imported grain between 1815 before they were finally repealed in 1846. Rioting and discontent were met with repression from a government fearful of a revolution similar to what had occurred in France. Radical politicians lobbied for extending voting rights beyond the wealthy land-owning elite. The Peterloo Massacre of 1819, when fifteen people were killed and hundreds of protesters were injured after mounted militia charged into crowds at a political rally in St Peter's Fields, Manchester, was a vain attempt to stem the tide of radical dissent.

In 1835 a small group of Radical MPs led by Sir William Molesworth, Joseph Parkes and Joseph Hume formed the Westminster Reform Club. Membership of this ginger group may have been small but the organisers were soon calling for a much larger club open to anyone keen to espouse the radical agenda outside Parliament. Their ambition was realised through the formation of the Reform Club.

The wealthy Liberal Whip William Ellice MP for Coventry, one of the club's founder members, was a late convert to the cause. Known as 'Bear Ellice' on account of his directorship of the Hudson Bay Company, this wealthy and influential MP was eventually convinced by Molesworth and his fellow committee members. So much so, that early meetings of the Reform Club were held in Ellice's house, 14 Carlton House Terrace. A recent study of the Reform Club's membership list drawn up in 1836 reveals that over a quarter of the list was composed of members of Parliament. 270 members were MPs out of a total of 998, the highest parliamentary intake ever recorded.[*] Anyone elected to Parliament as a Liberal was fast-tracked for membership of the Reform. The Reform Club's diverse membership also included merchants and industrialists, journalists, academics and financiers, landowners and members of the clergy. Besides this, the club attracted some prominent novelists. Thackeray was a member, and the American novelist Henry James took rooms in the club and made it his London home for more than a decade.

As they had done in the past for the landed aristocracy, political clubs fulfilled the function of being a home away from home for MPs while Parliament was sitting. Some even took permanent rooms, giving the club as their address. The clubs themselves assisted members' careers by

---

[*] Seth Alexander Thevoz, *Club Government: How the Early Victorian World was Ruled from London Clubs*, I.B. Tauris, London and New York, 2018, p. 69

bringing them into contact with influential patrons and on occasion assisted by contributing towards election expenses.

Anthony Trollope, in his novel *Phineas Finn,* part of the Palliser series, describes Clubland as an essential adjunct to the inner workings of the two main political parties. The social evolution of Clubland is present as an important part of the action, with the Duke of St Bungay representing the old guard and Plantagenet Palliser the 'new men' associating with talented but perhaps impecunious politicians like Phineas Finn. They personify the social shift that Clubland underwent during this period. A member of the Reform Club and therefore identifying with radical Whig politicians, a young Irish barrister Phineas Finn is introduced to a vacant seat in an Irish pocket borough by the party's secretary and power-broker Barrington Erle. Finn is duly elected. Finn, however, has set his sights successfully and is elected to Brooks's which was where all of the senior Whig/ Liberal appointments were decided in smoke-filled rooms. As one of the oldest established 'political' clubs, Brooks's influence was disproportionate to its size.

At the time of the passing of the Great Reform Act, all sixteen members of Earl Grey's Cabinet were members of Brooks's. This influence persisted. In 1852, thirteen out of fifteen members of Lord John Russell's Cabinet were from Brooks's, while in 1886 around half of Gladstone's Cabinet were members. In the early years of the twentieth century, half of Sir Henry Campbell-Bannerman and H.H. Asquith's Liberal governments were Brooks's men. Few other clubs were able to lay claim to such influence. The role of clubs in deciding who is nominated as a candidate for office and the selection of cabinet ministers has been described as 'club government'. Research into club membership among the political class conducted by Seth Alexander Thevoz reveals that between 1832 and 1868 around nine in ten MPs were members of a political club.** As a footnote, it should be added that Trollope,

---

** Seth Alexander Thevoz, *Club Government: How the Early Victorian World was Ruled from London Clubs,* I.B. Tauris, London and New York, 2018, Graph 2.2, p. 56

a member of the Athenaeum, based his fictional protagonist Phineas Finn closely on his club's founder, the thrusting Irish MP J.W. Croker.

Clubland's Masterchef

An essential ingredient to the success of any Victorian political club was its chef. With the celebrated Palanque providing cordon bleu menus at the Carlton and his rival Comte tempting jaded palates at Brooks's, the Reform faced stiff competition. It was thanks to the recruitment of Lord Chesterfield's chef Alexis Soyer that the Reform was able to outdo both clubs. Hired on the club's launch in 1837, Soyer's reign was to last thirteen years. The rising star of the culinary world, the French chef was celebrated for creations like *cotelettes Reform*, lean cooked ham mixed with breadcrumbs and his *sauce à la Reform*, finely chopped herbs mixed with preserved tomato, consommé and redcurrant jelly.

In command of the Reform's vast subterranean kitchens, Soyer was an innovator. The first chef to cook using gas, he invented a miniature stove for warming dishes at the table, a steam cooker or bain–marie, and a soup kitchen for feeding the poor. Publishing his first book in 1846, *The Gastronomic Regenerator*, the improvements and economies of his cooking methods enabled club members to dine in style. Soyer reduced the price of the *carte du jour* to 4 or 5s, cheaper and of far better quality than anything offered by coffee-houses or hotels. A wit, and a dandy out of the kitchen, Soyer habitually wore 'a light green frock coat, a crimson waistcoat with blue buttons, trousers with a large check pattern, boots with tips of shiny leather, a gold embroidered cap and a gilt cane'.[*]

After leaving the Reform in 1850, Soyer continued to exercise a powerful influence on British cooking. Seconded to the War Office during the Crimean War, Soyer set about reforming the British Army's catering and food supply chain. The result was a new type of field kitchen based on a portable oven which enabled army cooks to

---

[*] Cecil Woodham-Smith, 'The Man Who Invented Modern Cooking', *Harper's Magazine*, Vol. 217, December 1958, p. 33

prepare nutritious and healthy meals that could be prepared in the field to feed hungry troops in battle. The Soyer oven was used in the Crimean war, as were supplies of tinned food which preserved basic ingredients like bully beef and soup.

Below Stairs

In order to provide for the needs of its members, the nineteenth-century gentlemen's club employed a veritable army of cooks, servants, stewards, cleaners and administrators both above and below stairs. In an age before labour-saving appliances and modern heating and lighting, all tasks had to be carried out by hand, out of sight of members and with the minimum of fuss. Similar in organisation and hierarchy to a stately home, a club had hundreds of very demanding members, some of whom occupied the highest positions of state. In addition, many clubs offered accommodation in the form of upstairs chambers or bedrooms, an operation which required a separate but parallel set of tasks and duties such as booking, valeting, changing the linen and emptying chamber pots under the beds. All of this came under the responsibility of the club's chamberlain. Services had to be available day and night from breakfast through lunch and dinner and often late into the night. Many members attended the club after dining at home to smoke, play at billiards or cards or simply to relax over a glass or two of port.

Dating from 1921, the Reform Club's oldest staff ledger records the people employed at the club, their pay and their responsibilities during the early years of the twentieth century. Staffing and duties would have been broadly comparable to the 1840s. However, in the years immediately following the Great War, women outnumbered male servants at the Reform Club. Out of around 150 staff, ninety (60 per cent) were women. At the top of the clubhouse were around thirty bedrooms for members wishing to stay overnight or longer. Above stairs was the domain of the club steward, the most senior of the staff and in charge of all household servants including the cooks, waiters, maids and cleaners. His primary role, as today, was to meet and greet and act as a 'front of house' manager. He directly supervised the exclusively male hall porters and night porters, the waiters who served food and drinks to members, the butler who ironed and folded the newspapers, as well as the clerks who tallied up members' bills.

Below stairs were the servants' quarters, the wine cellar, laundry room, linen store, still room, and a plate room where silver and silver plate were kept under lock and key. As in stately homes, there was usually a servants' dining hall. Above stairs, members would have been greeted by the club steward, who in the club's heyday might have cranked a bell in the porter's lodge marked 'Lord Melbourne' or 'Lord Russell' to summon the grandees from their port and cigars to attend to important matters of state.

Further into the club were the coffee room waiters who served dinner assisted by a small team of wine waiters, all under the watchful eye of the head waiter Frank Hunter. Hired on 16 April 1896 and the longest serving employee, Hunter was paid £2 10s a week. The club employed three 'page girls' to run errands and a 'library boy' whose duties would have involved tidying up after members and returning books to their place on the library shelves. Twenty-five staff worked in the kitchens under the supervision of the resident chef, Jean-Baptiste Aubry. A team of four comprising a pastry cook, larder cook, sauce cook and roast cook assisted with the food preparation. There were additionally two 'carvers', a scullery man and four 'platemen'. Women were restricted to preparing fish, vegetables and pastry, and the Reform employed a kitchen maid, fish maid, pastry maid, vegetable maid, second vegetable maid, stillroom maid, and scullery maid. M. Aubry earned a salary of 4 guineas while a fish maid, clearly a skilled job, was paid £2 2s 6d, close to the wages of the head waiter. Most of the other women were paid around £1 10s. Maids, mostly young unmarried girls who lived in the servants' quarters also had food and board provided. Such earnings compare well with the minimum wage cited in Maud Pember Reeve's highly regarded study of

poverty in Lambeth, south London, *Round About a Pound a Week,*
published for the Fabian Society in 1913. A household income of
£1 a week was needed to provide a bare subsistence for an entire
family: enough to rent a room and put a meagre amount of food
on the table.

Clubmen

Throughout the nineteenth century and into the twentieth, Clubland
was essentially an all-male preserve, catering for the solid upper
middle and professional classes for whom membership was essential to climbing the social ladder or becoming established in one's
chosen career. To be a member of a club with its set of rules governing social conduct was to be accepted as a gentleman. Furthermore,
Clubland's conviviality, its reputation for fine dining and amiability
cemented bonds of friendship and trust. There were exceptions of
course: Ferdinand Lopez, the crooked financier in Trollope's political
novels, for example, was a recognisable type.

Clubland attracted politicians, civil servants, courtiers, diplomats,
bishops, senior army and naval officers. Membership was de rigeur
above a certain level in society and many individuals were members
of several clubs as each one offered distinct advantages and social
networks. Being a clubman conferred a sense of identity. It meant
that you were a member of a certain tribe. It was an outward sign of
success and acceptance into society. With its retinue of servants and
administrators, the members' club was a relaxing place for entertaining colleagues or a retreat if a man simply wanted to read the
newspapers in peace or enjoy a quiet drink. Visiting one's club was
an accepted part of the social ritual of London life and, for some at
least, offered a welcome retreat from family life. The eminent journalist George Augustus Sala, a member of the Reform, describes the
Victorian clubman who for an annual subscription of 10 guineas:

… has a joint–stock proprietorship in all this splendour; in the lofty halls, and vestibules; in the library, coffee rooms, newspaper and card–rooms; … in the kitchen, fitted with every means and appliance, every refinement of culinary splendour, and from whence are supplied to him at cost prices dishes that would make Lucullus wild with envy.[*]

Specialist clubs were established to cater for particular professions or social groupings. For instance, university educated men could belong to the United University Club or the Oxford and Cambridge; statesmen, diplomats and career soldiers might be found in the Travellers Club, while politicians could show their allegiance to a political party by joining the Reform Club for Whig/Liberals or its Tory counterpart, the Carlton Club. There was even a club for expatriate Scots, the Caledonian.

Clubland created an elite cadre at the heart of an already exclusive society. The flipside of being elected to a club was the disgrace that could result from being expelled from your club. Expulsion was a rare sanction applied only in extreme cases of dishonourable conduct and of breaking specific club rules. The process involved a quasi–legal hearing and an extraordinary meeting of the club's committee. The social disgrace could break a career, prevent an individual from obtaining credit, and lead to the individual being ostracised by polite society. When Colonel Dawkins, a member of the Travellers Club, published a pamphlet titled *A Farce and a Villainy* impugning the reputation of four fellow club members, all members of the military including the Duke of Cambridge and Lieutenant Stephenson in 1875, he was reprimanded. The membership committee met to consider:

---

[*] George Augustus Sala, *Twice Round the Clock or the Hours of the Day and Night in London*, edition John and Robert Maxwell, London, c.1880, p. 210

Having regard to Rule 28, whether or not it is injurious to the character and interests of the Club that a member of our body should print and circulate such a document and apply expressions of such a nature to four members of the Travellers who are universally esteemed as men of honour.**

The unhappy sequel of the story is that Dawkins contested his expulsion in the High Court and lost, bankrupting himself in the process.

Influential Women

Despite Clubland's focus on male sociability, women of the upper middle classes and aristocracy wielded a powerful influence on political decision-making through hosting the salons, dinner parties and country house parties frequently attended by cabinet ministers and their wives. Much of nineteenth-century politics was conducted out of the public eye in intimate conversations between friends, sometimes in the clubs, sometimes at aristocratic house parties, where privacy could be respected.

In addition to the patronesses of Almack's and Willis' Rooms such as Lady Palmerston, Lady Waldegrave and Lady Jersey, influential salons were also run by society hostesses such as Lady Holland, Lady Charleville and Lady Cork. These aristocratic women wielded considerable soft power in their choice of dinner guests, knitting together the confused strands of nineteenth-century politics. Seth Alexander Thevoz writes, 'The cosmopolitanism of salon spaces was made possible by the bond of aristocracy and the absence of formal membership.'***

** Sir Almeric Fitzroy, *History of the Travellers Club*, George Allen and Unwin, 1927, p. 88

*** Seth Alexander Thevoz, *Club Government: How the Early Victorian World was Ruled from London Clubs*, I.B. Tauris, London and New York, 2018, p. 130

One of the most colourful society hostesses was Lady Blessington, whose youthful beauty, ample décolletage and unaffected Irish charm ensured a glittering guest list for her dinners at 10 St James's Square. Leading politicians such as Lord Palmerston, Viscount Castlereagh, George Canning, Lord Grey and George Brougham often graced the Blessingtons' dinner table. Respectable society ladies politely declined because they suspected Lady Blessington was not quite all she seemed. They were right. Marguerite Blessington, born Margaret Power, from the village of Knockbrit, Co. Tipperary, had been sold into wedlock at the age of 15 by her drunken and impoverished father. It was further known that a substantial sum of money changed hands when she was subsequently bought by the Earl of Blessington, a spendthrift whose extravagant lifestyle was supported by the toil of the poverty-stricken tenants of his estates in Ireland.

But the real cause of Lady Blessington's social ostracism sprang from the couple's scandalous *ménage à trois* which included the young dandy Alfred, Count d'Orsay, a man thought to be her lover. In the summer of 1822, the Blessingtons and Count d'Orsay commenced a grand tour of France and Italy. The tour lengthened into a long exile during which the party settled for a time in Rome, Florence and Genoa, where they spent several months in the company of Lord Byron, an intense literary experience which the Countess subsequently turned into a bestselling memoir. In 1829 the Earl of Blessington died, leaving his vast estate to his daughter Harriet on the condition that she marry Count d'Orsay. Cut off from her former income, Lady Blessington returned to England where she sold the lease of her St James's Square house and downsized to a smaller establishment just off Park Lane. Scandal piled upon scandal when the newly wed Harriet ran away from d'Orsay who, in short order, squandered his remaining wealth on horse racing and fine clothes. Incurring a powerful enemy in the shape of that guardian of public morality Sarah, Lady Jersey, Marguerite Blessington's days as a political hostess never recovered. A portrait of the Countess painted by society artist Thomas Lawrence now hangs in the Wallace Collection.

Clubs provided space, privacy, ready-made social networks, the possibility of political influence and opportunity of all types: financial and political. During the nineteenth century they were indeed 'palaces of power'. The following anecdote gives a flavour of the mixture of the formal and informal power networks. Two members of the Guards Club, given reciprocal dining rights at the United Universities Club, remarked within earshot of an elderly gentleman sitting reading the paper in a comfortable armchair, 'Golly, these middle-class fellows really know how to do themselves well.' The paper was slowly lowered to reveal the aquiline features of the Duke of Wellington glaring back at them.

CHAPTER 7

A WINDOW ON
THE WORLD

Whether he dined or lunched, it was the Club's kitchens, the
Club's larder, pantry, fish stores, and dairy that supplied his table
with their savoury provisions; it was the Club's waiters, solemn
faced men in dress-coats, with molleton under the soles of their
shoes, who served his food on special china, upon admirable Saxon
napery; it was out of the Club's matchless glasses that he drank his
sherry, his port, or his claret flavoured with cinnamon and capil-
laire; and it was the ice of the Club, imported at great expense from
the American lakes, that kept his beverages in a satisfactory state
of coolness.

Jules Verne, *Around the World in Eighty Days*

The nineteenth century began with Britain starting to feel confident about its place in the world order, brokering peace treaties
and alliances that shaped the continent of Europe and the wider
world. The latter half of the nineteenth century saw the popularity
of clubs and their luxury at its absolute zenith. During this period,
there were around 400 clubs in London's West End, as the boundaries of Clubland extended into Westminster, Mayfair and Covent
Garden. Club membership was the *sine qua non* of the upwardly
mobile Victorian gentleman whose social position would have
necessitated him belonging to several clubs, each reflecting a dif-

ferent aspect of his personal or professional life. The proliferation of clubs coincides with the growth of British influence overseas and the rise of Britain's Empire. Taken from Jules Verne's classic novel *Around the World in Eighty Days*, the quotation that opens this chapter charts the epic journey of a fictitious Phileas Fogg. Connoisseur of French cuisine and fine wines, Reform clubman Fogg wagers that he can circumnavigate the world in eighty days. He wins. Modern railway networks, steam ships and even balloon travel had shrunk the globe, bringing distant and exotic lands within reach of the adventurous traveller.

This optimism is reflected in the type of club being formed as well as in a more outward-looking approach on the part of existing clubs. A new spirit of internationalism was being born. There were other factors at play closer to hand. By the late nineteenth century, Piccadilly's theatres, restaurants, shops and bustling night-life had shifted society's centre of gravity towards the West End. At the junction of five major roads – Regent Street, Piccadilly, Lower Regent Street, Coventry Street and Shaftesbury Avenue, Piccadilly Circus started to assume all the characteristics of a major shopping and entertainment district. Erected between 1892 and 1893 in memory of the energetic social reformer the Earl of Shaftesbury, and topped by a winged statue of Eros, Piccadilly's Shaftesbury Memorial Fountain came to symbolise the spirit of London's West End and its gravitational attraction for Londoners and foreign visitors alike.

A Diplomatic Mission

The Travellers Club was founded in 1819 by Viscount Castlereagh, Britain's foreign secretary during the Congress of Vienna which redrew the map of Europe after Napoleon had been defeated at Waterloo. Not formally associated with any one political party, the Travellers Club helped underpin Britain's foreign policy by enabling British diplomats to offer hospitality to visiting ambassadors. It was a grand setting where confidential talks or state banquets could take place. Adopting the head of Ulysses as its crest, the Travellers Club stipulated that membership was only open to men who had travelled at least 500 miles from London. The club welcomed statesmen, military commanders and individuals with strong overseas connections. Lord Elgin was a member and donated to the club a plaster cast of the famous Parthenon frieze he secured for the nation from Greece's Turkish overlords. Urgent diplomatic meetings were convened, with much diplomatic negotiation taking place in the club, to hammer out post-Napoleonic European alliances. The first grand reception at the club was hosted by Tory foreign secretary Lord Castlereagh who, in May 1820, invited a delegation including Count Maurice Lewenhaupt, Count Rostropchin, Prince Lichtenstein, Prince Villa Franca and Baron von Werden.

Foreign dignitaries and crown princes were given honorary membership. Between 1830 and 1834 the ambassador and statesman Prince Talleyrand, an honorary member, was a frequent guest of the club as France's accredited representative at the Court of St James's. Later in the century, the Prince of Wales was elected as a member while the decision to invite his wife Princess Alexandra led to the building of a special room for the reception of ladies in 1863. This is the first recorded example of clubs admitting women as guests. Membership for women would have to wait until the last half of the twentieth century.

Hub of Empire

The growth of Britain's empire proved a spur for the creation of a new type of club designed to meet the needs of soldiers, merchants, and administrators entering the colonial service. Clubs drew people together in a common enterprise. They created social spaces where individuals could meet and interact and where relationships and networks were formed which could assist people's careers. To discover their history we need to retrace our steps.

The Oriental Club in Hanover Square was founded by General Sir John Malcolm, an old India hand, in 1824. The Duke of Wellington was its first president. With an initial membership of 400, the Oriental was an expensive and exclusive club where high-ranking servants of the East India Company could meet and discuss business in congenial surroundings while home on leave. Curries were served and tea merchant Messrs Twinings produced for members an exclusive Oriental Club tea. In fact, some early brands of packaged food traded on the club's reputation such as Captain White's Fish and Chicken Curry and Mulligatawny Paste, 'exclusively used at the Oriental Club'.*

Officers in the service of the East India Company's private militia made up 45 per cent of the club's members but it also included administrators and wealthy merchants. Viceroys and governors of India such as Warren Hastings and Earl Cornwallis graced the establishment as portraits which line the clubhouse walls testified. But a rival club was about to be launched. In February 1849 a group of army officers met at the British Hotel in Cockspur Street in what was the inaugural meeting of East India United Service Club. Intended as a counterweight to the Oriental, the East India's aim was to offer hospitality at affordable prices to a wide cross-section of the East India Company employees, including clerks, lawyers, doctors and commissioned naval and army officers. An article which appeared in the *East India Army Magazine* asserted that: 'The proposal for starting an Indian Service Club in the great Metropolis originated at the Cape amongst the "Hindus", as the Indians on leave there are irreverently termed.'** Number 16 St James's Square, the very house where the news of Napoleon's defeat had been received by the Prince Regent, was acquired as the clubhouse, a building the East India Club occupies to this day.

---

* Barbara Black, *A Room of His Own: A Literary-Cultural Study of Victorian Clubland*, Ohio University Press, 2012, p. 72
** Denys Forrest, *A Foursome in St James's: The Story of the East India Devonshire*, Sports and Public Schools Club, London, 1982, p. 3

Refurbished in lavish style, with a coffee room, a billiard room and a smoking room, the East India United Service Club opened with an inaugural dinner on 1 January 1850. The club was an instant success and was to prove a serious threat to the Oriental which turned down an offer to merge with its rival. The result was that the Oriental Club was to broaden its appeal to the merchants, manufacturers and industrialists who traded with the East. The switch in emphasis from military to trade facilitated a knowledge and understanding of overseas markets that Britain needed in order to reap the benefits of its burgeoning Empire. Meanwhile the history of the East India Club took a different turn. With the dissolution of the East India Company in 1858, the club provided an exclusive, albeit non-political counterweight to the grand clubs lining Pall Mall.

Politics and International Affairs

The prime ministers who came to power after the Great Reform Act were emboldened by this apparent constitutional settlement. Lord Melbourne, a favourite confidant of the young Queen Victoria, exemplified a Whig rather than radical Liberal mindset. His successor, the Conservative Robert Peel, was a reformer. He in turn was followed by the Whigs Lord John Russell and Lord Palmerston before the Conservative prime minister, Lord Derby took over.

But it was the expansionist foreign policies pursued by Lord Palmerston that cemented Britain's power and global reach. Nothing illustrates this gunboat diplomacy better than the Don Pacifico Affair of 1847–1850. Don Pacifico, the Portugese consul in Athens, had been caught up in a wave of anti-semitic violence during which synagogues were burned down and Jews, including Don Pacifico, were stripped of their position and property. But Don Pacifico had been born in Gibraltar and was therefore a British subject. Palmerston decided to act at the request of the Rothschild family as, in addition to Don Pacifico's humiliation, the Greek government were defaulting

Palace of Power: the Reform Club, Pall Mall (by kind permission of the Reform Club).

St James's Palace gatehouse (photo Stephen Hoare).

St James's Park from an eighteenth-century print (author's collection).

The gaming room at White's from *A Rake's Progress* by William Hogarth. The cast of characters includes gamester, highwaymen, card sharps and money lenders. In the foreground a player who has just lost heavily has torn off his wig and is cursing his ill luck. Meanwhile the night watchman with his lantern has just entered the room to warn the building is on fire. From a contemporary engraving.

White's (photo Stephen Hoare).

Brooks's (photo Stephen Hoare).

Boodle's club house, St James's Street (photo Stephen Hoare).

Travellers Club: plaster cast of the Venus de Medici stands on the landing of the grand staircase flanked by oil portraits of former Chairmen (by kind permission of the Travellers Club/Libanus Press).

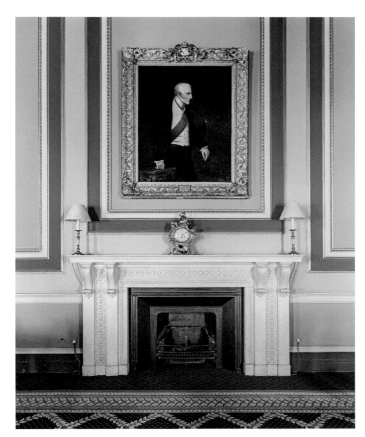

One of the many portraits of Wellington adorning the walls of the Pall Mall clubs. This portrait by Alfred d'Orsay hangs in the coffee room of the Travellers Club (by kind permission of the Travellers Club/Libanus Press).

Midnight, Tom and Jerry at a coffee shop near the Olympic – from *Life in London* by Pierce Egan, illustration by I.R. Cruikshank – reproduced from an original copy.

Exterior of the Reform Club (by kind permission of the Reform Club).

The Athenaeum (photo by Stephen Hoare).

The Travellers Club from the garden (by kind permission of the Travellers Club/Libanus Press).

An original ballot box: white or black balls posted into the hole denoted whether a candidate was accepted or declined (by kind permission of the Travellers Club).

Lord Castlereagh, founder of the Travellers Club (by kind permission of the Travellers Club).

The old In and Out Club, Half Moon Street, Piccadilly prior to redevelopment (photo Stephen Hoare).

The coffee room at the Reform Club (by kind permission of the Reform Club).

on loans made by the British. In December 1849 Palmerston sent a naval task force under Admiral Sir William Parker to seize and detain Greek naval vessels. Mission accomplished, the Greeks backed down and paid Britain and Don Pacifico a hefty sum in damages. The Reform Club threw a splendid banquet for the triumphant Lord Palmerston on 28 July 1850 and invited Sir Robert Peel to deliver an oration in his honour.

Clubs like the Reform were helping shape the political landscape. The mid- to late-nineteenth century saw frequent changes of government. At the helm of those parties were two very different leaders: the austere Liberal William Gladstone and his charismatic Tory counterpart, Benjamin Disraeli. Party politics appear confused as both parties at different times espoused similar causes. What mattered more than orthodoxy was the personal style of the two leaders as they jockeyed for power.

Opinion was divided over a series of highly contentious issues such as the disestablishment of the Church of England and Home Rule for Ireland. As one prime minister was defeated and resigned so the other was summoned to power and had to form a government. In all, Gladstone was prime minister four times while Disraeli was twice tasked with forming a government.

The power struggles between the two parties were played out in the main political clubs, the Carlton and the Reform, White's and Brooks's. Members of the Carlton and White's supported Disraeli's strong foreign policy which boosted free trade, sought to counter Russia's influence in the Balkans and aimed to protect Britain's Imperial ambitions in Africa and India. One of Disraeli's greatest achievements was buying a controlling interest in the Suez Canal from the Khedive of Egypt in 1875 following a share purchase brokered by Rothschild's Bank on behalf of the British government. This provided Britain with a permanent, secure and much shorter sea route to India. Liberals of the Reform and Brooks's were focussed more on social justice, Parliamentary reform and improving conditions for workers, an objective which was also shared by the Conservatives.

Diplomacy

To support Britain's foreign policy, certain clubs played a key role in furthering diplomacy. The Travellers Club and the Reform Club hosted dinners for visiting dignitaries, heads of state and distinguished exiles and granted honorary membership to important foreign diplomats. Honorary members of the Travellers included, over the years, the French ambassador Prince Talleyrand, the Russian statesman Prince Galitzine, His Excellency Auli Effendi, Turkish ambassador, secretary to the US Legation in London, Benjamin Rush, and the first Japanese representative to Britain in 1862. His successor ministers Kato Takaaki and Yamaza Enjiro became fully fledged members of the Travellers Club in 1873.

Meanwhile, the Reform hosted the King of the Belgians who visited in 1869. Like the Travellers, the Reform Club cultivated links with the United States of America. The northern states had just won the Civil War when in June 1877 the club gave a special dinner in honour of former US president General Ulysses S. Grant hosted by Lord Granville. Grant, who was making a short stay in London as part of a European tour, was offered honorary membership of the club after his rousing after-dinner speech. Many Americans were present including George Boker, the American minister to Russia. The American political connections with the Reform Club have remained strong ever since. In 1919 Franklin D. Roosevelt, then a senator, was elected as a temporary member of the Reform Club for a month during his stay in London. Winston Churchill was a member at the time.

Political Division

In view of the pervasive influence of Clubland in shaping the political landscape, it is odd that neither Gladstone nor Disraeli set much store by clubs themselves. Oddly enough, Gladstone started his political career as a member of the Carlton Club, only resigning in 1860 as his Liberal sympathies became clearer. He joined the Reform at the insistence of the Liberal chief whip in 1868 only to quit in 1874 at the end of a spell in office. He was rarely seen at the club. Disraeli had a similarly semi-detached and unenthusiastic attitude to clubs, starting out as a member of the Westminster Reform Club before joining the Carlton Club. He had set his heart on being elected as a member of White's but was turned down.

But politics could divide other clubs too. Military clubs like the United Service Club were strongly supportive of a bigger army and navy and for sending troops in support of Disraeli's muscular foreign policy which gave rise to the Afghan and Zulu wars. Religious affairs could also prove contentious. When politicians turned their attentions on the archaic structure of Church of England endowments, there was strong dissent within the Athenaeum and the United University Club, both of which had high numbers of bishops and clerics among their membership.

In the last year of his life, MP and veteran of the Peterloo Massacre Henry 'Orator' Hunt had campaigned vociferously for the Great Reform Act not merely to offer votes for women but also to open the door for women MPs. Many members of the Reform Club followed Hunt in promoting universal suffrage as further reform bills were debated in Parliament. During the debate of the 1867 Reform Bill, John Stuart Mill suggested replacing the word 'man' in the legislation with the more inclusive 'person'. William Woodall, Jacob Bright and Sir Willoughby Dickinson, once known as 'the forgotten hero of Women's Suffrage', showed that the Reform Club was among the most sympathetic to the women's cause.

An even more divisive issue was Home Rule for Ireland which promised self-determination and the improvement of tenants' rights. Championed by Prime Minister William Gladstone, the Government of Ireland Bill of 1886 split the Liberal party and was narrowly defeated in Parliament by a combination of Tories and dissenting Liberals, ending Gladstone's long-running prime ministerial career. The Irish Home Rule debacle ended the cosy relationship between the party and its two main supporters, the Reform

Club and Brooks's. The future belonged to a new and more closely aligned National Liberal Club which had been first mooted as far back as 1882. Championed by the 'grand old man' of politics, Gladstone, the Liberal party issued 40,000 shares at £5 per share to finance their project for building the club. Designed by architect Alfred Waterhouse, the magnificent gothic clubhouse building, One Whitehall Place, was completed in 1887, the year of Queen Victoria's Golden Jubilee.

The creation of the National Liberal Club diluted the numbers of Liberal MPs at the Reform Club, leaving it as an institution whose broadly progressive social agenda has since attracted left wing economists, academics and senior civil servants. The club's political role was to revive after the entry of the Labour Party into the British political arena championed by Keir Hardie and George Lansbury. Lacking a political club of their own, a new generation of Labour politicians including Sir William Beveridge, Hugh Gaitskell and Hugh Dalton found a home at the Reform Club.

Fred Burnaby: Heroic Adventurer

Carlton Club member Captain Frederick Gustavus Burnaby of the Royal Household Cavalry (the Blues) had political ambitions way beyond his already action-packed military career. Painted in around 1870, Tissot's famous portrait of the smartly dressed old Harrovian officer, cigarette in hand, in relaxed pose sums up the confidence of the late Victorian age of Empire. Soldier, balloonist, *Times* correspondent, adventurer, spy, and friend of the Prince of Wales, Burnaby was a larger than life character whose exploits read like a *Boy's Own* adventure story. They belong to an age of optimism and opportunity. At 6ft 4in tall and weighing 20 stone, Burnaby was immensely strong. He excelled at fencing, riding and boxing and in addition was fluent in five foreign languages including Russian and Arabic.

In 1874 Captain Burnaby took leave of absence and, with his soldier servant George Radford, travelled on horseback deep into

Russia's eastern empire to sound out friendly tribal chiefs and to observe whether or not the Russians presented a threat to India's north-west frontier. Wearing furs and native costume, the two soldiers survived freezing blizzards as they travelled through the Steppes in winter gathering valuable intelligence. On their safe return to England, Burnaby wrote an account of his travels, *A Ride to Khiva*. Three years later Burnaby managed to get himself seconded as an observer to the Russo-Turkish war where he wrote despatches for the *Times* newspaper and a best-selling book, *Travels in Asia Minor*.

Burnaby was equally at home with ballooning, then an extremely dangerous enterprise. While many aeronauts were killed in ballooning accidents, he persevered and became one of the first to fly solo from England to France on 23 March 1882. Setting off from Dover on a favourable wind, the gas-filled balloon was blown off course, leaving him stranded over the Channel for over an hour until the wind picked up and carried him westwards to make landfall near Dieppe in Normandy.

Like many men of his generation, Burnaby was a member of several clubs including the London Fencing Club, the Junior Carlton and the Carlton Club. A committed Conservative, Burnaby's politics were driven by what he saw as the Gladstone-led Liberal government's failure to pursue an expansionist foreign policy and to intervene decisively to support Turkey against Russian aggression. In 1880 Burnaby stood as Conservative candidate in Birmingham, coming within a whisker of defeating the Liberal incumbent Joseph Chamberlain. His membership of the Carlton Club was instrumental in providing him with a local agent and the grassroots support he needed to begin campaigning.

Over the next four years Burnaby applied himself to soldiering and enjoyed a rapid promotion to Colonel of the Household Cavalry (the Blues), all the while continuing to campaign vigorously for the Conservatives. Together with Lord Randolph Churchill he founded the Primrose League to secure grassroots support for Disraeli and the Conservative party.

Then in 1884 came news that General Gordon had been besieged by the Mahdi at Khartoum. Burnaby volunteered to join an expedition to relieve Khartoum and end slavery in the region. Trekking up the Nile with a column of British soldiers and a Camel Corps, Burnaby was keen to see action. He was speared through the throat and died fighting at the battle of Abu Klea in the Soudan in January 1885. Gladstone's government concluded a dishonourable truce with the fanatical Mahdi.

Twenty years later a junior cavalry officer and war correspondent called Winston Churchill took part in the battle of Omdurman that finally led to the defeat of the Mahdi. It is tempting to think that the young Churchill when he was a scholar at Harrow would have known about Fred Burnaby's exploits and how closely he was intertwined with his father Lord Randolph's own political career.

Lizzie Le Blond: Alpine Pioneer

It might be thought that women had no interest in forming or joining clubs. This is not so. One notable aristocratic Irishwoman was not prepared to accept the stereotype. She formed a highly influential club. Related to the Bentinck family Dukes of Portland, Elizabeth Hawkins-Whitshed of Killincarrick, Co. Wicklow had married Colonel Fred Burnaby at the age of 18. Shortly after their marriage she was sent by her husband to the Alpine resort of Chamonix to regain her health. After Burnaby's untimely death, Elizabeth threw off her widow's weeds and opened a new chapter of her life as a pioneering Alpine climber.

Lizzie, as she preferred to be called, moved to Switzerland, remarrying in 1900. Under her married name of Mrs Aubrey Le Blond, the indefatigable Lizzie quickly established herself as one of the world's foremost alpine explorers and mountaineers in a life of adventure that outshone her former husband's daredevil military exploits. Writing under the name of Mrs Le Blond, Lizzie wrote nine books including *The High Alps in Winter*, and *Adventures on the Roof of the World*.

She was also a prolific photographer and film-maker and, wearing breeches, she took part in over 100 ascents including Mont Blanc and twenty mountains never before climbed. Excluded from the men-only Alpine Club, Lizzie Le Blond formed the Ladies' Alpine Club in 1908, based at the Great Central Hotel, Marylebone.

Lizzie Le Blond met with a warm response from the Alpine Club who promptly recognised her club and affiliated it. Over 250 guests attended the Ladies' Alpine Club's first annual dinner, including many members of the Alpine Club. Queen Margherita of Italy was given the title of honorary president while Mrs Le Blond herself was president from 1908 until her death in 1934.

Pushing Boundaries

Given the physical limitations of establishing new clubs in St James's, it was inevitable the boundaries of Clubland would become blurred and extended. By the late nineteenth century, there were around 400 clubs in central London, representing a vast range of professional and sectional interest groups. Partly this was owing to the continued rapid growth of London's population. London's importance as a global city was now recognised, and established clubs were over-subscribed, leading inevitably to long waiting lists and pressure to meet demand by the creation of new clubs for a more tightly defined demographic.

The Turf Club, for example, appealed to the racing fraternity and at its height at least eight dukes were listed as members, more than any other club in London. Formed in 1861 as the Arlington Club and based at Bennett Street just off Piccadilly, the club changed its name to the Turf when it moved to Clarges Street on the corner of Piccadilly in 1875. At around the same time the Jockey Club, an even older institution founded in 1750, had grand premises in Pall Mall and fulfilled the joint functions of regulatory body for horse racing and an exclusive gentlemen's club. Meanwhile, Clubland was also extending its reach to include music and the arts, professions which had always been under-represented among the London clubs. This omission was rectified by the creation of four clubs, all highly individual in character.

The foremost club for actors, writers, and artists, the Garrick Club sprang to life at the committee room of the Theatre Royal, Drury Lane on 17 August 1831. Named in honour of the eighteenth-century actor manager David Garrick, the original members' list contained the cream of the English stage, such names as Charles Kemble, Charles Kean and William Macready who would have known Garrick in his later years. Soon the Garrick had recruited a new generation of actors such as the legendary Henry Irving and Herbert Beerbohm Tree. The literary world was represented by Charles Dickens, William Makepeace Thackeray and Anthony Trollope while eminent artist members included the Pre-Raphaelites, John Everett Millais and Dante Gabriel Rossetti. Initially, the Garrick Club set a limit of 300 members but this was soon expanded to 400 and raised the annual subscription to 6 guineas. The club was now attracting lawyers from the nearby Lincoln's Inn, although the membership continued to be heavily skewed in the favour of writers and artists.

By now a well-established club, it quickly became clear that the Garrick needed to fund a clubhouse. In 1864, the club moved to a purpose-built four storey classical mansion at 15 Garrick Street, built on the vacant site created by the redevelopment of slum dwellings on the edge of Covent Garden.

By now, Covent Garden was emerging as a distinct focus for creative talent. Founded in 1857 by the journalist and writer George Augustus Sala, the Savage Club held its first meeting at the Crown Tavern, Drury Lane. It appealed to a bohemian, slightly louche element of actors, musicians, writers, artists and individuals previously deemed unclubbable. These included the *Punch* editor Mark Lemon, the comic writers George and Weedon Grossmith, Mark Twain and Wilkie Collins. The Savage Club underwent frequent changes of address including Adelphi Terrace, the Strand, Fitzmaurice Place, Berkeley Square and latterly Carlton House Terrace. Oscar Wilde certainly knew the Savage Club, having been entertained there as a guest, and should have felt at home among convivial company. But having sampled the hospitality he is reported as commenting, 'I never enter the Savage Club. It tires me so. It used to be so gentlemanly Bohemian, but since the Prince of Wales became a member and sometimes dines there, it is nothing but savagely snobbish.'*

Oscar Wilde was not the only clubman to be making waves. Over at the Garrick Club its two most celebrated writers, Charles Dickens and William Makepeace Thackeray, had a very public falling out. In 1858 Dickens had recently separated from his wife but had already embarked on a secret long-standing affair with the Irish actress Ellen Ternan. Thackeray, who was probably repeating gossip from the Garrick, divulged the information. This could have been forgiven but for the involvement of Edmund Yates, a journalist protégé of Dickens and a Garrick Club member who published a scurrilous attack on Thackeray in the magazine *Household Words*. An incensed Thackeray accused Yates of basing his attack on private conversations held at the Garrick Club and he referred the matter to the club's committee for disciplinary action. Yates was duly expelled from the club and a bitter literary feud ensued. Dickens immediately resigned from the Garrick, blaming the club for siding with Thackeray. The two most famous authors of the nineteenth century were finally reconciled when they met on the steps of the Athenaeum, just a few months before Thackeray's death.

On quitting the Garrick, Dickens joined the Arts Club, an institution which had been founded in 1863 and was based in Hanover Square. This club promptly attracted a coterie of celebrated writers, musicians and artists, and besides Dickens the Arts Club was home to Wilkie Collins, musicians like Paolo Tosti and Franz Liszt, and the artists Frederic Leighton, Walter Sickert and John Everett Millais. The club subsequently moved to Dover Street in 1896, where it has remained to this day.

---

* Coulson Kernahan quoted by Barbara Black, *A Room of His Own A Literary-Cultural Study of Victorian Clubland*, Ohio University Press, 2012, p. 269

The Savile Club was launched in 1868. Initially called 'the New Club', the Savile attracted a louche set of *flâneurs*, or urban sophisticates. Located just off Trafalgar Square in Spring Gardens, the club moved in 1871 to Savile Row, taking its name from the street of tailoring. Despite the convivial fellowship, dining, snooker and poker playing, the club had no time for people it regarded as misfits. When in 1888 Oscar Wilde, a member of the New Travellers Club, was proposed for membership his election was postponed indefinitely.

By the late nineteenth century St James's was becoming a magnet for wealthy Americans seeking to integrate into London high society. The list includes Charles Yerkes, the Chicago entrepreneur who built some of London's first underground railways, store tycoon Harry Gordon Selfridge, the philanthropist Andrew Carnegie, society hostess Lady Maud Cunard, wife of the shipping magnate Sir Bache Cunard, and many others. The influx began to prise open the palaces of power, as money rather than family could now wield influence.

The American Multi-Millionaire

The most famous of the Anglophile Americans, politician, businessman and newspaper publisher William Waldorf Astor, was a member of the Garrick Club. Inheriting a fortune on the death of his father in 1890, Astor was for a short time the richest man in America. He built the luxurious Waldorf Hotel in New York as his cousin Jack built an adjoining hotel, the Astoria. Within the space of a year the businesses were merged to create the magnificent Waldorf-Astoria. A family feud led to a falling out and Astor and his family departed for London where he set to work building a publishing empire. In 1893, he bought the *Pall Mall Gazette*, adding to this a new quality periodical, the *Pall Mall Magazine*; in 1911 he also acquired *The Observer* which he built into Britain's premier Sunday newspaper. In 1899 Astor adopted British citizenship and was made Viscount Astor for his philanthropy under which he channelled a proportion of his vast wealth to support a wide range of medical and armed forces charities.

Astor's contemporaries at the Garrick Club included such literary luminaries as Arnold Bennett, Somerset Maugham, H.G. Wells, and T.S. Eliot. Along the way, Astor amassed an impressive property portfolio. His first purchase was the prestigious 18 Carlton House Terrace followed in 1895 by a gothic mansion on the Thames Embankment, Two Temple Place. To this he added Cliveden House in 1903, a stately home overlooking the Thames near Taplow, and Hever Castle in Kent, the historic home of Anne Boleyn. Following the outbreak of the First World War, Astor was so concerned at the mounting British casualties from the Great War that he loaned his Carlton Terrace home for the duration of the war to the British Red Cross for use as a hospital for the war wounded. By the time Astor died in 1919 his family had carved out a niche in British high society and in politics. That same year his daughter-in-law Nancy Astor, an American citizen, became the first woman Member of Parliament when she won a seat in Plymouth, Sutton for the Conservative Party. Nancy's husband, Waldorf Astor, had inherited his father's newspaper business, and his title. The Astors bought 4 St James's Square, now the home of the 'In and Out' Naval and Military Club. Nancy's political connections and her gift for entertaining the rich and powerful were an echo of the influential political salons from the days of Palmerston and Disraeli.

Clubland Around the World

The model of the St James's club inspired British expatriates to form social clubs wherever they put down roots. In India, for example, this led to the creation of such establishments as the Club of Western India in Poona, the Banglalore Club, the Calcutta Rowing Club and the Bombay Gymkhana Club. These clubs and many others too numerous to mention encouraged the St James's clubs to forge links with overseas clubs and reciprocal benefits were soon introduced. By extending honorary membership to visiting foreign dignitaries, St James's clubs acted as a catalyst for similar clubs to be created in the USA, Canada, Europe and Russia, as well as Britain's colonies and dominions.

By the turn of the nineteenth century the typical London members' club had become established as a model throughout the British Empire and the wider world. Overseas, some clubs extended reciprocal rights to members of certain London clubs with which they were affiliated. Reciprocal hospitality from partner institutions became an important benefit to club members. Clubs based around specific interests such as horse racing copied the St James's model and may even once have had formal links now lost in the mists of time. What is certain is that the British colonial administrators who set up the Singapore Turf Club, founded in 1842 to operate the Serangoon racecourse, would have been familiar with its St James's namesake. Likewise, in India there exists the Royal West India Turf Club which has much in common with its London namesake.

The Jockey-Club de Paris is a good example of an idea that has taken root in a foreign soil. Established in 1834 as a society for the encouragement and improvement of horse breeding, this highly prestigious club dates from a time when close ties between the upper classes of France and England developed during the reign of Napoleon III after he and his wife Empress Eugenie had spent several years living in exile in Great Britain. Other French clubs date from the same period such as the aristocratic Travellers Club Paris, established in 1903 on the Champs-Élysées, whose palatial interiors are decorated in the style of the Second Empire. Despite being independent institutions, members of the London and Paris Travellers Clubs enjoy reciprocal dining rights. During this period of instability that culminated in the Franco–Prussian War of 1870 and the Paris Commune, high status clubs disappeared and were reformed. Le Cercle de la Rue Royale was founded in 1852 but is now merged with the Jockey-Club.

A Transport Hub

Improved transport links were opening up the West End, making the entire area more accessible to ordinary Londoners, and Clubland could no longer remain a remote and introspective bastion of privilege. The more progressive clubs were starting to reflect a new and optimistic spirit of internationalism. Membership was becoming more diverse as clubs were open to new money, particularly from the United States. In the Victorian age central London was ringed by railway termini as companies had been forbidden from building their lines any closer than the outer fringes of the City and the West End. As a result, goods vans, omnibuses, hansom carriages and all forms of horse-drawn transport clogged the capital's streets. The busiest junction of all was the roundabout at Piccadilly where major routes converged. Early silent films show Piccadilly Circus as a mass of open-topped 'knife board' buses as pedestrians dart in and out of the slow-moving traffic. The arrival of the Underground was a game changer. Opened on 10 March 1906, Piccadilly Circus station was an interchange between two underground railways, the Baker Street and Waterloo Railway and the Great Northern, Piccadilly, and Brompton Railway. These would become the Bakerloo and the Piccadilly lines. In 1907, an annual 1.7 million passengers were using this station. The arrival of the Underground made the West End accessible to people in search of fun and entertainment. By the end of the Victorian era, public transport was opening up the area to East Enders and middle-class suburbanites.

Theatreland

By the late nineteenth century, Piccadilly's theatres, restaurants, shops and bustling nightlife had shifted Clubland's centre of gravity. Once home to Italian opera, the Haymarket during the late Victorian period was better known for popular theatre and eating houses. At the junction of five major roads – Regent Street, Piccadilly, Lower Regent Street, Coventry Street and Shaftesbury Avenue – Piccadilly Circus started to assume all the characteristics of a major shopping and entertainment district. In complete contrast to the nearby clubs of St James's and Pall Mall, Piccadilly's music halls, the London Pavilion, the Trocadero and the Criterion Theatre featured comedians, dance troupes and singers of comic songs and ballads. These working-class palaces drew crowds from the East End and the wider suburbs.

In the music hall's late Victorian and Edwardian heyday, jaunty songs drew inspiration far and wide from the costermonger who inherited a fortune and 'Knocked 'em in the Old Kent Road' to the flirtatious barmaid at 'the Old Bull and Bush in 'Ampstead'. The music hall allowed diversity to flourish like the effervescent male imperson-ators Hetty King, whose hits like 'Piccadilly' and 'Ship Ahoy!' struck a chummy note, and Vesta Tilley whose irreverent 'Burlington Bertie' mocked the genteel *flâneurs* and haughty denizens of Clubland.

Erected between 1892 and 1893 in memory of the energetic social reformer the Earl of Shaftesbury, and topped by a winged statue of Eros, Piccadilly's Shaftesbury Memorial Fountain came to symbolise the spirit of London's West End. The roundabout became known as the 'Hub of Empire' because its traffic never stopped and because of its gravitational attraction for Londoners and foreign visitors alike.

While improved transport links were opening up the West End, making the entire area more accessible to ordinary Londoners, Clubland could no longer remain a remote and introspective bastion of privilege. The more progressive clubs were starting to reflect a new and optimistic spirit of internationalism. Piccadilly and its surround-ing streets, the Haymarket, Piccadilly Circus, Shaftesbury Avenue and Cambridge Circus formed the nucleus of the West End's theatre-land. The Criterion at the corner of Jermyn Street and the London Pavilion at Piccadilly Circus which had been built on the site of the old White Horse coaching inn were synonymous with popular entertainment and musical shows. Standing opposite each other at the bottom of the Haymarket, the King's Theatre and Theatre Royal Haymarket established a reputation for quality. While in Duke Street St James's stood the St James's Theatre known in its time for putting on experimental productions. Oscar Wilde's plays *The Importance of Being Earnest* enjoyed a successful run at the theatre to be followed up by *Lady Windemere's Fan* which premiered here on 20 February 1892.

Tea at the Ritz

The Ritz Hotel on Piccadilly at the corner of St James's Street was opened in 1906 as the last word in luxury by Swiss hotelier Cèsar Ritz. The hotel was quickly established as an international venue. Cèsar Ritz died shortly after but the hotel changed hands and its name lived on. The Ritz saw some famous events. On 4 August 1914, Lady Diana Manner's future husband, Duff Cooper, then a Foreign Office official, hosted a dinner party at the Ritz and later that day announced that the First World War had broken out.

The hotel suffered during the war and lost nearly £50,000 in 1915 alone; the ballroom was usually empty and lights went out by 10 p.m., but rooms were still in demand and the hoteliers believed it to be worth keeping open.

The Duchess of Jermyn Street

Small family-run hotels were a feature of St James's during the Victorian and Edwardian period but none as celebrated as the Cavendish Hotel in Jermyn Street. Bought by society cook Rosa Lewis in 1902, the Cavendish, formerly Miller's Hotel, quickly became an institution. The original plan was that Rosa's husband Excelsior would manage the hotel while Rosa would continue her lucrative catering business in which she and a small army of assistants would produce extravagant cuisine for grand banquets or country house parties. Having cooked for the German Kaiser on his private yacht during Cowes Week and arranged state dinners for the Foreign Office, Rosa Lewis was at the peak of her fame.

From working-class origins in Leyton, East London, Rosa had come to the attention of the Prince of Wales in her role as cook to Lady Randolph Churchill in the early 1890s. Impressed as much by her discretion as her culinary skills, the future King Edward VII employed Rosa and her new husband Excelsior to manage a discrete establishment at Eaton Terrace where he enjoyed secret assignations with his lovers. The hotel in Jermyn Street was by way of a reward for services rendered, and in the early days of Edward's brief reign, Rosa kept a suite of rooms and a selection of his favourite clarets in readiness for a surprise visit.

In the event the king never stayed at the Cavendish. Even worse, Excelsior failed utterly at managing the hotel's finances, preferring the company of drunks and gamblers to more sober pursuits. The redoubtable Rosa confronted him, and after a blazing row threw him out. He vanished and is said to have emigrated to start a new life in the USA.

Rosa never remarried but she assembled a court of male admirers including Sir William Eden, father of the 1950s prime minister Sir Anthony Eden, and Lord Ribblesdale, a member of Brooks's — both semi-permanent residents at the hotel. The Cavendish was run as a club for which you needed society connections. Rosa Lewis's unique way of combining business with pleasure ensured a steady stream of guests, gamblers and after-hours drinkers. But her generosity meant the business was always precarious. Surviving the Great War, the Cavendish's heyday was in the 1920s and '30s when a new generation rediscovered the hotel's faded Edwardian elegance. Rosa was parodied by Evelyn Waugh in *Vile Bodies* as the foul-mouthed, indiscreet, dipsomaniac Lottie Crump, a depiction which caused grave offence and led to the author (and all other writers) being banned indefinitely. The original for the BBC series *The Duchess of Duke Street*, Rosa Lewis preserved the dress and the outdated mannerisms of the Edwardian era right up to her death in 1952 at the age of 85.

Votes for Women

If Lizzie Le Blond had raised eyebrows in England with her Ladies' Alpine Club, then she was behind her emancipated sisters in the USA. American women were far more active in forming clubs based on new professions that were opening up. The Women's Press Club of New York City was established in 1889 by Jane Cunningham Croly. Located at 126, East 23rd Street East Manhattan, the club was followed by a spate of women's press clubs across the US and Canada. In Britain two clubs were launched which had strong transatlantic and overseas links. The Ladies' Empire Club formed in 1902 and the Ladies' Imperial Club (1906) had a strong patriotic appeal.

In England, however, women were driven by another more serious priority, universal suffrage, or votes for women. By the turn of the twentieth century, the issue that would cause trouble for the clubs was votes for women. The women's suffrage party, the Women's Social and Political Union (WSPU) had begun life as a spin-off from the fledgling Labour movement. But support from the left-wing MPs George Lansbury and Keir Hardie was clearly not enough and in 1902, a group of ladies including Emmeline and Christabel Pankhurst broke away to kick-start a campaign of direct action. Emmeline Pethick-Lawrence had been introduced to the Pankhursts in 1906 and she and her husband joined the WSPU.

Frederick Pethick-Lawrence, Emmeline's husband, was a respected member of the Reform Club. The couple started the journal *Votes for Women* and offered their flat as the office for WSPU and as a place where women could rest and recover from their prison sentences. As Treasurer, Emmeline raised thousands of pounds as well as using her and her husband's money. This organisational support was significant in making the WSPU into a national movement.

After years of low-level protest during which the WSPU raised significant funding, established the Women's Press and formed a cohesive protest movement, members of the WSPU chained themselves to railings, disrupted political meetings, and protested at government offices. In 1910 the Liberal prime minister Herbert Asquith called a general election but lost his overall majority. To form a government, Asquith was forced into a coalition with Labour. Here was the opportunity the WSPU had been hoping for. The issue of universal suffrage (votes for men and women) was back on the agenda and the government duly tabled a Conciliation Bill, draft legislation which if enacted would have enfranchised 1 million women. As a gesture of goodwill, the WSPU suspended its political protest while the Bill moved through Parliament.

Then in November 1911, with politicians unable to reach a compromise agreement, the Bill was withdrawn. For the WSPU, the time for conciliation was past and its members, the Suffragettes, planned a campaign of direct action, vowing to break the law and face the consequences. At seven o'clock on the evening of 21 November, a steady stream of determined women poured out of the offices of the Women's Press at 156 Charing Cross Road carrying satchels full of rocks or armed with hammers. The Suffragettes set off in ones and twos, either on foot or by taxi bound for the West End, Whitehall, and London's Clubland. They had been instructed to wait until Big Ben chimed eight o'clock before starting their attack. Clubs with political affiliations were high on a list of targets which included government offices, the Post Office in the Strand, the Westminster Palace Hotel, Cunard's offices, and Swan and Edgar's department store.

By the end of an evening of mayhem, Bertha Brewster and her friend Edith Rigby had hurled rocks at the windows at the National Liberal Club in Whitehall Place. In Pall Mall, the window smashing raid caused extensive damage to the Carlton, the Junior Carlton and the Reform Club. One of the more controversial targets was the attack on the Guards Club, on the Mall, which had its windows broken by the actor Winifred Mayo. By the end of that month of action, 200 women would be behind bars at Holloway Prison. Most received a three-week jail sentence. Speaking later of the raid and specifically in relation to the Guards Club, Emmeline Pankhurst commented: 'The ordinary man is not much in politics; but he very often, because of his aristocratic and social connections, has considerable influence if he would use it.'*

The Reform Club's long-standing sympathy for women's suffrage appears to have been put under strain as the Pethick-Lawrences were

---

* Amy Milne-Smith, *London Clubland: a cultural history of gender and class in late Victorian Britain*, New York, Palgrave Macmillan, 2011, p. 198

arrested and charged with conspiracy. Prosecuted by the police in 1912, Frederick refused to pay a fine and court costs. He was declared bankrupt, a disgrace that led to his automatic expulsion from the Reform Club. Even when discharged, the club refused to have him back. Women were finally given a limited vote in 1918 following the end of the Great War.

Britain at War

Britain went to war with Germany in September 1914. Royal parks were commandeered for military training with Green Park transformed virtually overnight into a cavalry encampment with dozens of tents. Members' clubs lost the greater part of their male staff as men of military age volunteered or were conscripted. It was left to women to fill the gaps and they took a much more active and visible role above stairs, helping keep gentlemen's clubs open for members. The war changed the way clubs were run and it changed the employment prospects of women. Women volunteered to serve their country. Many joined the Voluntary Aid Detachment (VAD) as ambulance drivers, nursing assistants and other non-combat roles. Women also flocked to train as nurses, serving in field hospitals in France and Belgium or at the many military hospitals set up in Britain to take the war wounded.

While men had their officers' clubs or British Legion branches to fall back on, war service provided the impetus for women who had served their country to form clubs where they could share their experiences. With a clubhouse in Cavendish Square, and a royal patron, Queen Mary, the New Cavendish Club was set up in 1920 by Lady Ampthill for women who had served as VADs. A ladies-only club, the New Cavendish was run along the same lines as a members' club. In 1922, nurses who had trained at the Royal College of Nursing established the Cowdray Club, named after its founder Annie Pearson, Lady Cowdray. Not all members of the Cowdray were nurses. Beginning with 650 members the club quickly expanded beyond

3,000 members who included 55 per cent nurses, thirty-five other professions and the balance being women deemed sympathetic to the club's ethos.

During Clubland's heyday in the late nineteenth and early twentieth centuries, clubs were outward looking and expansive. Initially this was triggered by the enthusiasm and innovation of the new merchant classes. New clubs were formed to cater for emerging professions and an expanding middle class. Membership reflected new money and, in particular, the influx of wealthy Americans. As time passed, and particularly after the traumatic upheaval of the First World War, clubs became more democratic. Despite being ignored and overlooked for so long, women were now full members of society and on the verge of joining Clubland in their own right.

CHAPTER 8

THE JAZZ AGE: ST JAMES'S IN THE 1920S AND '30S

I've danced with a man, who's danced with a girl, who's danced with the Prince of Wales.
'It was simply grand,' he said 'Topping band' and she said 'Delightful, Sir,'
Glory, Glory, Alleluia! I'm the luckiest of females
For I've danced with a man, who's danced with a girl, who's danced with the Prince of Wales.

Lyrics by Herbert Farjeon 1927

Following the First World War, life started slowly returning to normal for the shops, cafes, restaurants and hotels of St James's and Piccadilly. In keeping with the spirit of the age, the area embraced popular culture. Women who had worked in factories and staffed the buses and public transport and who were soon to be given the vote were more visible on the streets. With long cigarette holder, beaded Charleston frock and bobbed hair, the 1920s 'flapper' shouted independence. The Great Depression which had spread to Britain after the Wall Street Crash of 1929 brought mass unemployment. In Britain 2 million workers had lost their jobs, mainly in the North, Wales and the Midlands. London did not escape its effects. What is sure is that the jazz age sparked a counterculture – a constellation of exciting new clubs and a night-time economy catering for a richer, more varied demographic than the traditional gentlemen's club.

Post-War Recovery

The First World War had cast a very long shadow over Clubland. During 1914–1918 almost an entire generation of young officers had been killed in action. Where once fathers would have arranged for their sons to be elected to their club, the generational link was severed. It would take many years to recover. Membership of some clubs fell sharply as new members were insufficient to replace older members after their death.

Some, however, view the interwar years as a golden age for members' clubs. Where once men in uniform were seen around the clubs, now clubs reintroduced Edwardian formality and members were expected to wear full evening dress for dinner. Likewise servants, in many cases men too old to have fought in the war, donned livery in club colours. The old order could not continue. Harold Macmillan, Tory prime minister from 1957–1963, was one of the first politicians to sever the tribal ties between politics and Clubland. In marrying Lady Dorothy Cavendish in 1920, Macmillan had joined one of the foremost families in the land. His father-in-law, the 9th Duke of Devonshire, was a leading member of the Liberal-leaning Brooks's and was the owner of the exclusive Pratt's Club. Despite being a Tory, family connections trumped political affiliation as the highly clubbable Macmillan joined the duke's inner circle. Although Macmillan subsequently became a member of the Tory Carlton Club, he was completely at home at Brooks's, the Beefsteak, and Pratt's Club.

For the new breed of clubman the accent was on fun and frivolity. In some senses, the behaviour is reminiscent of the post-Napoleonic scene and the rise of the dandies. Founded by Captain Herbert Buckmaster, an officer of the 'Blues' (Household Cavalry) in October 1918, Buck's was a young man's club. The club bought a small house in Clifford Street, Mayfair where it exists to this day. High spirited and high spending, members organised golf weekends in Le Touquet and attended race meetings at Goodwood and Ascot. Macmillan was a member. The comic author P.G. Wodehouse once said that Buck's was the nearest thing imaginable to Bertie Wooster's Drone's Club. But there are two other contenders for the title. The Bachelors' and the Bath Club, both based in and around Piccadilly, were home to the hell-raising rakes of the 1920s. These clubs abandoned deference and civility and instead encouraged the carefree antics of a *jeunesse dorée*, intent on partying. Ever receptive to the latest trends in Clubland, Wodehouse also wrote about the Junior Lipstick Club for the new breed of emancipated young women and the Senior Bloodstain for private detectives hired by husbands or wives to provide evidence for divorce proceedings. These fictitious clubs may sound far-fetched but in the early 1920s there was a Ladies' Carlton Club which some humourists referred to disparagingly as the 'Junior Lipstick'.

Some old established clubs were struggling and finally succumbed. The eighteenth-century Cocoa Tree Club in St James's Street, for example, shut its doors for the last time in 1932. Others decided to join forces. The East India United Service Club merged with the Sports Club in 1938. Further mergers took place in the 1970s and the club now goes under the name of the East India, Devonshire, Sports' and Public Schools' Club, taking care to preserve all of its many traditions.

The 'Bright Young Things'

An influential group of pleasure seekers was shaping the cultural life of the West End. The 'Bright Young Things' were precocious and talented young men and women whose creativity spun off in all directions from art and music, to photography, literature and poetry. The group included Evelyn Waugh, Cecil Beaton, Harold Acton, Robert Byron, Oliver Messel, Osbert, Edith and Sacheverell Sitwell, John Betjeman, Nancy Mitford, Beverley Nicholls and Anthony Powell. They were the first generation to come of age after the Great

War and they filled an intellectual vacuum created by the untimely death of so many talented artists and writers who had been killed in the battlefields of Flanders and northern France.

The term 'Bright Young Thing' was coined by a *Daily Mail* article that described the phenomenon. Being a 'Bright Young Thing' implied a dandified or eccentric dress code and an ambivalent sexuality. Evelyn Waugh satirised the phenomenon in his novel *Vile Bodies*. Written in 1930, the novel is based on the decadent lifestyle of the young and privileged upper classes whose empty lives revolved around clubs, society balls and entertainments in and around Mayfair and St James's. It is dedicated to Bryan Guinness and Diana Mitford who after marrying in 1929 became central players in London's heady social scene. The 18-year-old Diana had secretly become engaged to eligible bachelor Bryan, heir to the brewing dynasty and future Lord Moyne, shortly after coming out as a debutante. Rumours of their engagement fuelled society gossip for months. The debutante's frivolous lifestyle was parodied by Waugh whose larger than life heroine of *Vile Bodies*, the Hon. Agatha Runcible, is inspired by the real-life exploits of Diana Mitford.

From the late 1920s onwards the six Mitford sisters, Nancy, Pamela, Diana, Unity, Jessica and Deborah, the daughters of Lord and Lady Redesdale, joined other young ladies of their class in being presented to the king and queen at the Court of St James's at their coming of age. Idiosyncratic, self-assured and careless of public opinion, the Mitford girls almost single-handedly revived the flagging fortunes of the popular press. Banner headlines proclaiming 'Peer's daughter … ' became clichéd shorthand for juicy tittle tattle involving one or other of the Mitfords, as gossip columnists reported a succession of scandals including Jessica's elopement, Diana's divorce, Unity's personal invitation from the German Führer to attend the annual 'Parteitag' rally at Nuremburg, Diana's marriage to the leader of the British fascist party, Jessica's conversion to communism and Unity's failed suicide attempt.

In the opening pages of *Vile Bodies*, Waugh's heroine is mistaken for a jewel thief and is strip-searched by 'two fierce wardresses' after disembarking from a cross-channel ferry. Cue scandal, indignation and salacious press coverage. Real life headlines could be just as lurid as this example from the *Daily Express* of 1 March 1937 gives us: 'PEER'S DAUGHTER OF 17 ELOPES, SPAIN SEARCH', as a teenage Jessica ran away to marry her cousin Esmond Romilly.

The Mitfords moved in a rarified social stratum where nearly everyone was related either by marriage, friendship or through 'affairs'. In his novel, *A Buyer's Market*, part of his *Dance to the Music of Time* novel sequence, Anthony Powell describes a society ball given by Lord and Lady Huntercombe. The novel's narrator Nick Jenkins has been invited along with a restricted and diminishing pool of eligible bachelors to partner debutantes at a ball given by one of the girls' parents. When Nick Jenkins bumps into his fellow old Etonian and dipsomaniac Charles Stringham at an all-night coffee stall after leaving the ball, he strikes up a conversation. A hesitant navigator of social formalities, Jenkins is in awe of Stringham's connections and the ease with which opportunities just fall into his lap. 'How is it that everyone seems to know everyone else?' Stringham replies: 'That's just the way it is, Nick.'

One of *Dance to the Music of Time*'s engaging cast of 'Bright Young Things', Charles Stringham is in part a pen portrait of Alfred Duggan, Powell's contemporary at Eton, stepson of Lord Curzon, and half-brother to Lady Alexandra 'Baba' Curzon and her older sister Cynthia. Sir Oswald Mosley was briefly married to Cynthia Curzon and after she died prematurely of peritonitis, had a fling with her sister who, as Lady Alexandra Metcalfe, was already married to the Prince of Wales's equerry. Everyone did indeed know everyone else.

Being a 'Bright Young Thing' implied decadence, and a certain attitude of mind. St James's offered many pleasures for the discerning man or woman about town. The novelist and gossip columnist Beverley Nichols describes his typical 1920s evening attire:

... waistcoat by Hawes and Curtis of the Piccadilly Arcade, silk hat by Lock in St James's Street, monk shoes by Fortnum and Mason of Piccadilly, crystal and diamond links by Boucheron ... gold cigarette case by Asprey of Bond Street, a drop of Rose Geranium on my handkerchief from the ancient shop of Floris in Jermyn Street.[*]

A Cultural Melting Pot

St James's in the interwar years was a magnet for bohemians, including writers, poets, artists, photographers, composers, jazz musicians and playwrights. Its rich mix of cafes, theatres and clubs contributed to a colourful nightlife. Jazz and dance music was more than mere entertainment. With roots in black music it was an engine for social change. The Original Dixieland Jazz Band started the ball rolling in 1919 with their London tour. They appeared in the revue 'Joy Bells' at the London Hippodrome on 7 April. This was followed by a royal command performance for King George V at Buckingham Palace. The band members were less than impressed by the assembled aristocracy who peered at them 'as though there were bugs on us'. The final act was the pursuit of the band to Southampton docks by Lord Harrington, enraged that his daughter was infatuated by the lead singer. The jazz musicians who played nightly in the St James's clubs, restaurants and hotels brought a rich cultural heritage and sexual magnetism. Black trumpet soloist Louis Armstrong played residences in London followed by band leaders Duke Ellington and Coleman Hawkins. The Jamaican trumpet player Leslie Thompson joined the Emperors of Jazz, a band fronted by West Indian dancer turned bandleader Ken 'Snakehips' Johnson. Johnson went on to form one of the top swing bands in the country, known as the West Indian Orchestra, which became the resident band at the highly fashionable Café de Paris.

---

[*] Beverley Nichols, *Twenty-five: An Autobiography*, Pomona Books

The West End attracted significant numbers of gay men and lesbians. In an age when homosexual behaviour was against the law, prominent gay men like the actor and playwright Noel Coward, John Gielgud and Ivor Novello had to rely upon a close knit and sympathetic community to help them keep their private lives a closely guarded secret. They were also forced to present themselves to the ever-inquisitive press as unattached bachelors, a fiction that necessitated constant rumours of amorous intrigue with mystery women. Coward's name was often linked with his leading lady Gertrude Lawrence, his co-star in *Brief Lives,* while Ivor Novello was forced to invent fictitious women friends to cover up his lifelong love affair with the actor 'Bobbie' Andrews.

A missing generation of young men killed in the Great War led to a significant increase of activity, both in employment and leisure, of young single women. Filling jobs previously done by men were now done by women, who enjoyed greater freedom than previous generations. The urban zeitgeist was captured by the lesbian author Radclyffe Hall whose novel, *The Well of Freedom*, provided an alternative model for same sex relationships.

It is hardly surprising therefore that St James's and Piccadilly had an active gay scene with recognised cafes or pubs where same sex encounters could take place, as well as gay nightclubs – mostly in neighbouring Soho where members could meet without fear of being arrested for indecency. Noel Coward was a member of the Fifty-Fifty Club run by Ivor Novello and Constance Collier, and catering exclusively to the theatrical elite. A heady mix of high society, artists and bohemians patronised the Gargoyle Club which occupied the first floor of a pair of adjoining Georgian houses, 69 and 70 Dean Street, Soho. Opened in 1925 and owned by the Hon. David Tennant, son of Lord Glenconner, this club encouraged sexual experimentation. The décor featured original works and murals by Matisse and Augustus John. Matisse was made an honorary member and he might have rubbed shoulders with the likes of Somerset Maugham, George Grossmith, Nancy Cunard, Adele Astaire and Noel Coward. Tucked away in a basement in

Endell Street, the Caravan Club was advertised as 'London's Greatest Bohemian Rendezvous'. Virtually invisible to all but those 'in the know', this exclusively gay club operated below the radar as indeed it had to: homosexuality was at the time illegal.

With its vibrant night-time economy, Piccadilly Circus was a magnet for repressed homosexuals from the suburbs, flamboyant actors, as well as queer servicemen and sailors. The Criterion theatre and restaurant on Piccadilly Circus and the Long Bar at the Trocadero were well-known pick-up points for gay men. Referred to by those in the know as the 'Lillypond', Lyons Corner House in Coventry Street was a gay meeting place. Male prostitutes who cruised openly for men were known as 'Dilly Boys'.

London Lets its Hair Down

The arrival in Britain of the Original Dixieland Jazz Band from the USA in 1919 started a trend. Dance crazes like ragtime, the Charleston, the black bottom, the tango and the foxtrot made their way across the Atlantic in swift succession as post-war Britain began to relax after the war. Jazz reigned supreme as cafes, restaurants and hotels in and around the West End vied to attract the best dance bands. Hosting some of the most popular jazz bands of the 1920s and '30s were the Café de Paris in Coventry Street, the Café Anglais in Leicester Square, the Kit Kat restaurant and club in Haymarket where Al Starita's Kit Kat Band held sway, the Criterion, and the Trocadero in Piccadilly. The dance craze led to restaurants being fitted out with tables grouped around a stage and a dance floor where couples danced to the music of a resident orchestra late in the evening after finishing their meal. The more exclusive clubs and restaurants such as Ciro's, Quaglino's and the Embassy Club attracted international high society. Situated off the Haymarket in Orange Street, one of the first exclusive dance clubs, Ciro's was famed for its exhibition dancers and haute cuisine. Part of an exclusive international restaurant chain, there were branches of Ciro's in Paris, Biarritz and Monte Carlo.

C.B. Cochran

If one man came to dominate the world of West End entertainment it was the theatre manager and impresario Charles Blake Cochran, invariably referred to as C.B. Cochran. Cochran was born in Sussex and at the age of 18 travelled to New York in 1890 to make a career on the stage. His acting may have been average but the young Cochran discovered his talent as a producer and publicist. He lived on his wits, taking a succession of jobs from promoting rodeos and boxing tournaments to promoting Vaudeville acts. He returned to London in 1902 where he tried his hand as a theatrical producer and a promoter of wrestling matches.

C.B. Cochran's entrepreneurial spirit and the bulging address book full of contacts he had made in New York stood him in good stead in London of the Edwardian era when American popular songs and musical shows were enjoying a surge in popularity. In a career which spanned the Edwardian era to the 1950s, Cochran brought a musical revue starring an all-black cast to the London stage in 1903. *In Dahomey* was an immediate sensation giving rise to the dance craze 'the cakewalk'.

C.B. Cochran's career as an impresario took off in the immediate post-war years when he established the London Pavilion at Piccadilly as the home of the musical revue. In 1923 his revue *Dover Street to Dixie* at the Palace Theatre had an all-white cast in the first half of the programme, followed by an all-black cast who took the stage for the second half. Star of the show Florence Mills received a standing ovation for her song 'Bye-bye Blackbird'. Florence and an African American cast headlined in Cochran's revue *Blackbirds*, which opened at the London Pavilion in 1926. With an eye for talent, Cochran promoted rising stars like Noel Coward, Gertrude Lawrence, Jessie Matthews and Jack Buchanan. Known as 'Cocky' to close friends like Noel Coward, Cochran was a very private individual. His long-standing collaboration with Coward, whom he had first spotted as a rising young talent, resulted in *On With the Dance* in 1925, followed up by two hugely popular Noel Coward musicals, *Bitter Sweet* and *Cavalcade*.

In 1934 and with box office sales flat, the revues ended and the London Pavilion was converted to a cinema, acknowledging the popularity of the new talking pictures. Once cinema embraced sound it became a more versatile medium that was quick to ride the wave of popular culture. Cinema-going rose in popularity after the Capitol Cinema opened in 1925 in the Haymarket in premises that had once been the Kit Kat Club. In 1929 it had premiered the first British 'talkie', Alfred Hitchcock's *Blackmail*. In 1935 the cinema, which still exists, was taken over by Gaumont and the building was completely gutted and the interiors remodelled in the popular art deco style of the period. The cinema re-opened on 4 February 1937 with a royal performance of *The Great Barrier* starring Richard Arlen and attended by HM Queen Mary. C.B. Cochran suffered chronic ill health in his later years although his appetite for theatrical productions appeared undimmed. From around 1936 he managed the Royal Albert Hall, a position he held for twelve years. He was knighted in 1948 but died tragically a few years later after becoming trapped in a bath of scalding water.

Catering for the Masses

If there is one institution that helped light up the West End and make it more accessible to ordinary Londoners it was Lyons' Corner Houses. Providing tea and entertainment, Lyons' tea rooms and Lyons' Corner Houses chimed with the spirit of the jazz age. Lyons, an offshoot of the highly successful tobacconists chain Salmon and Gluckstein, opened the Popular Café at Piccadilly Circus in 1898. It was following a trend set by the opulent and unmistakeably Victorian institution, the Monico, which served afternoon tea with cake at 1s 6d and boasted a billiards room.

From the start, Lyons' Corner Houses were places where single women felt comfortable and were welcome. From the 1920s to the 1970s, Lyons dominated the fast food market in London's West End. Lyons' Corner Houses attracted office workers in their lunch break, while by night they provided affordable dining for couples out for an evening as well as single women and gay men.

Based at Cadby Hall, the Lyons group of companies was at one time Britain's biggest caterer and its food company was rightly famed for its 'individual fruit pies', tea, coffee, and chicory essence. For the first time, ordinary people from the suburbs could visit London's West End and enjoy a meal and a show in comfortable surroundings without breaking the bank. This had the effect of revitalising tourist attractions, store shopping, music halls, cinemas and art galleries. In 1923, the Lyons' Corner House on Coventry Street was extended to create four floors containing a food hall, restaurants and a tea room – all with their own musicians. This flagship store could seat a total of 2,000 diners. The Lyons' at Trocadero on Piccadilly was a similar size. Other Corner Houses were located at Tottenham Court Road, the Strand, and Marble Arch.

Some Lyons' Corner Houses even had dance floors such as Lyons' in Oxford Street, which hosted dance music from 1923. Lyons' Popular Café in Piccadilly opened the summer season of 1931 with Harry Singer and His Band. In 1924 Lyons launched what was to become an institution – a new uniform and a name for its wait-resses. Called 'Nippies', the Lyons' waitresses wore starched caps with an embroidered black alpaca dress with detachable white collar and cuffs.

Strong competition also came from the ABC Tearooms – short for the Aerated Bread Company – whose distinctive canary yellow glass fascia and red art deco lettering remained a feature on London streets until 1982 when the company ceased trading.

During the 1920s and '30s it has been estimated that in the West End you could find at least one tea shop every 100 yards.

The jazz craze cut right across the social scale and there were many modestly priced restaurants and dance halls which attracted ordinary Londoners. The near universal popularity of dance bands was fed by the recording industry which churned out thousands of hits on 78 rpm records at affordable prices. Competition from popular record labels such as Regal, Zonophone, Columbia, Decca, Rex, Imperial and His Master's Voice lowered the price of gramophone records to a few shillings, while portable 'wind-up' record players were mass produced for a buoyant market. The advent of radio in 1922 brought jazz into people's living rooms with BBC recordings live from the Savoy. Radio brought dance bands to the forefront of popular entertainment. The band became a 'band show' with a variety of musical entertainments, singing and dancing. Bands even made the leap into the television age post-war. With its band leader's raucous cry of 'Wakey, Wakey!', the Billy Cotton Band Show became a permanent fixture of BBC's Saturday night output from the 1950s through to the end of the '60s.

Sweetheart

At the close of the 1920s, the Savoy Hotel's resident band Fred Elizalde's Orchestra played syncopated jazz to a young and enthusiastic audience. Judged too 'fast' by an older clientele who yearned for a slow waltz, the Savoy's management failed to renew Elizalde's contract, leaving the band's singer Al Bowlly temporarily at a loose end. Bowlly had arrived in London in 1928. The son of a Greek father and a Lebanese mother and born in the Portuguese colony of Laurenço Marques, now Mozambique, Bowlly spent his early years in Johannesburg, South Africa where his family eventually settled. Apprenticed to his father's barber's shop, Bowlly discovered his true talent for singing and playing the guitar. Before long he was making a name for himself among local bands before striking lucky and joining Edgar Adeler's touring orchestra.

The 1930s was to become the era of the big band sound, and Bowlly's singing talent was quickly recognised. He recorded a series of hits with Lew Stone and subsequently Ray Noble's Orchestra on HMV. Hits like 'Night and Day', 'Love is the Sweetest Thing', and 'The Very Thought of You' conjure up the mood music of the interwar years. No dance was complete until the last waltz, another Bowlly/Noble collaboration, 'Goodnight Sweetheart' was played. Prior to Bowlly, jazz singers or 'crooners' as they were often called, were rarely acknowledged or given star billing; all the credit was given to the band leader. Before the invention of the microphone they had to sing into a megaphone while the recordings they made unhelpfully described dance music as 'with vocal refrain'. The first jazz vocalist to use a microphone, Al Bowlly's 'melt in the mouth' singing voice created a sensation. Emerging as the pre-eminent British singer of the 1930s and credited on records as a solo artist, for a time Al Bowlly's reputation and his fan following eclipsed that of the rising US vocalist Bing Crosby.

High Society

On 27 May 1931, Jack Upson, a businessman who had made his fortune from the high street chain the Dolcis Shoe Company, opened a new dance venue, the Monseigneur Restaurant at Piccadilly House, Jermyn Street. Upson had invested his entire fortune in a bid to create the best and most prestigious dance club in London. He hired an American band leader Roy Fox from Hollywood to put together an orchestra. Vocalist Al Bowlly, trumpet-player Nat Gonella and pianist Lew Stone were among the talented line-up on the opening night. Billed as 'Roy Fox, the Whispering Cornettist', Fox was a perfectionist in every sense. As well as being carefully rehearsed, the entire orchestra was kitted out in white tie and tails – mirroring the dress code of the high society couples on the dance floor. To preserve exclusivity, Upson introduced a membership fee but made an exception for the Prince of Wales and his circle whose occasional patronage would set the seal on the Monseigneur's reputation with the in-crowd. Bear in mind that in 1931, Britain was suffering large scale depression and with around 2 million workers on the dole, the Monseigneur Restaurant represented unimaginable luxury that London's poor could only dream about. For those who could afford it, a dinner and dance at the Monseigneur was a glorious escape from the depressing reality of newsreels showing lengthening dole queues or foreign dictators whipping up frenzied support for their aggressive militarism.

Joyce Stone, Lew Stone's wife, recalls the Monseigneur in its heyday as a most beautiful restaurant with a lot of gilt decorations and an elaborate staircase. She was particularly impressed with the cloak-room whose attendant was dressed as a Monseigneur!

> He had a white wig and a blue velvet coat with lace ruffles. The head waiter who showed you to your table was also dressed in the same kind of uniform. The bar served a Monseigneur cocktail which was light blue. I imagine its base was gin. I had two sips and saw everything in triplicate so I gave up drinking it!*

Favoured by jazz–loving Edward, Prince of Wales, the Monseigneur was soon attracting royalty, high society and showbiz celebrities. Lady Diana Cooper, Hoagy Carmichael, Noel Coward, Jack Buchanan, the Maharanee of Sarawak were among the regulars. Always a vanity project, lavish overheads together with a long-running contractual dispute with Roy Fox drained its owner's considerable fortune. Struggling to balance the books, Jack Upson decided to quit and in September 1934 the Monseigneur closed for good and was converted to a cinema.

Relaxed Morals

The dance craze may have breathed new life into London's West End but there were other influences at work that would transform society. Dance restaurants and nightclubs provided an opportunity for sexual adventure. Independent, working, and with money to spend, young women enjoyed a new-found freedom in the 1920s. The relaxed attitudes were more common among the upper classes and among the West End's international smart set who partied without restraint. One of the Maharanee of Sarawak's jazz–obsessed daughters married the bandleader Harry Roy, a match that must have disappointed her parents who showed rare fortitude when

---

* Sid Colin and Tony Staveacre, *Al Bowlly,* Elm Tree Books, London, 1979, p. 40

confronted with the inevitable. With his shock of wavy black hair side-parted, Latin looks and his seductive singing voice, Bowlly was irresistible to the ladies. Band leader Ray Noble has this to say: 'During the time I knew him, he fell victim to every pretty redhead, brunette or blonde. Although neither young, nor handsome, he exerted a fascination on the fair sex which I found almost frightening.'**

Sexual liaisons among society women provided ammunition for newspaper gossip columnists as well as sparking lawsuits from jealous husbands. Notoriety surrounded the handsome and virile Grenadian cabaret singer Leslie Hutchinson, better known by his nickname, 'Hutch'. Starring at the Café Anglais and the Café de Paris, Hutch was one of the highest paid entertainers of the pre-war era. He bought a Rolls-Royce, a house in Hampstead, was dressed by Savile Row tailors, spoke six languages and was on friendly terms with the Prince of Wales. Despite Hutch's numerous accomplishments, he suffered serious racial discrimination typical of the period. When hired to perform at lavish society parties, the black singer was often obliged to go in by the servants' entrance. The first scandal came in 1930, when Hutch was accused of making the debutante Elizabeth Corbett pregnant. Her father pursued Hutch through the courts but Elizabeth managed to get a Guards officer to marry her. The couple had a society wedding in Sloane Square by which time she was already three months pregnant. Subsequently Hutch's name was linked to a number of society ladies including Edwina Mountbatten. A scandal ensued but nothing was ever proven.

Queen of Clubs

Typically, a West End dance venue such as the Monseigneur would close at 2 a.m. Unwilling to call it a night, members of the band bent

_____

** Ray Pallett, *Goodnight Sweetheart: Life and Times of Al Bowlly*, Spellmount Ltd Tunbridge Wells, 1986, p. 82

on partying would head off to an all-night drinking den joined by upper-class night owls in search of clubs where they could drink till 5 a.m. or, on occasion, well into the next day. Then it would be off to the Lyons' Corner House in Coventry Street for an early morning breakfast.

Undisputed queen of London nightclubs, the indomitable Kate Meyrick, known to one and all as 'Ma', was an astute operator. At one time the dowdily dressed and gimlet-eyed Ma Meyrick owned and managed half a dozen clubs around Piccadilly including the Bag O'Nails in Kingly Street, the Slip-In, the Manhattan, and the Silver Slipper in Regent Street which boasted a glass dance floor. Ma drew on her considerable reserves of animal cunning to earn a crust. Deserted by her husband and left to support three boys at Harrow and three girls at Roedean, Ma Meyrick needed a reliable income stream and nightclubs were a money spinner.

The most notorious of Ma's louche enterprises was without a doubt the 43 Club at 43 Gerrard Street which opened in 1923. A magnet for bohemians, film stars, gangsters, good time girls, jazz musicians and aristocrats, the club circumvented late night licensing laws by claiming they were invited to a 'bottle party'. Guests simply had to claim they had pre-ordered a bottle of wine or spirits and a runner was sent to fetch the alcohol from an all-night off-licence. Ma made a healthy profit from selling champagne after licensing hours at £2 a bottle. The Lancashire millionaire Jimmie White once brought six Daimlers full of showgirls to a champagne party at the 43 Club costing £400. Besides welcoming free-spending toffs, clubs like the 43 and the Bag O' Nails employed dance hostesses whose job it was to sit with unaccompanied male guests in time-honoured fashion, and coax them into buying the most expensive champagne in the house as well as one or two of the establishment's exorbitantly priced cuddly toys. Based on the assumption of sexual favours to come, these seedy transactions ended predictably once a man had been relieved of all of his cash or had been rendered unconscious by drink, by which time the hostess had vanished. This discreet operation went side by side with convivial drinking and dancing: 'At the 43 Club the underworld and aristocracy met on equal terms, free spending burglars like Ruby Sparks mingling with the owners of the jewels and furs from whom they stole.'*

At a time when nightclubs which sold drink after hours and had no dancing licence were routinely raided, Meyrick's clip joints appeared to flout the law with impunity. Her clubs were seldom targeted, or if they were then advanced warning was given to enable the guests to disperse quietly. It was said that members of her clubs included some prominent establishment figures for whom the publicity of being caught in flagrante would have caused a sensation. Meyrick also offered regular bribes to the local police. However, the law had to be upheld and Meyrick was fined on several occasions. In 1924 she was sent to Holloway prison and in 1929 she was sentenced to eighteen months for corrupting the police. Two more spells in prison culminated in 1932 with a solemn undertaking to have nothing more to do with nightclubs. A year later Ma Meyrick was dead but not before marrying her three daughters into the aristocracy.

The 'Playboy Prince'

Just as in the Georgian era, Almack's assembly rooms provided the setting where debutantes might find a suitable husband, so the twentieth century evolved its own version of this aristocratic marriage mart, the dance restaurants and exclusive nightclubs of St James's. Britain's most eligible bachelor, the pleasure-loving Edward, Prince of Wales, was an avid jazz fan. The arrival of the prince and his party would grant the seal of royal approval to any nightclub.

The prince, known to his inner circle as David, was well known for his musical talents and his love of showing off. He would often be invited on stage by the band to play the drums as a 'party piece'. Having enlisted as an ensign in the Grenadier Guards during the First World War, Edward served in France and toured the various

---

* Robert Murphy, *Smash and Grab,* Faber and Faber, London, 1993

theatres of war as a junior staff officer. It was in the army and on leave in Paris that Edward had acquired a love of fast living and the demi-monde. The Prince of Wales occupied York House, part of the St James's Palace complex. And when in residence, he frequented all the fashionable nightclubs including Ciro's, the Café de Paris and his favourite haunt, the Embassy Club in Old Bond Street, where he pointedly ignored debutantes in favour of actresses and fashionable demi-reps.

One of the hits of the period was a song written in 1927 by Herbert Farjeon and sung by many female singers reflecting what must have been many a society woman's ambition: 'I Danced with a Man who's Danced with a Girl who's Danced with the Prince of Wales'. The 'girl' who inspired the song was ballroom dancing champion Edna Deane. When his first love Lady Rosemary Leveson-Gower, daughter of the Duke of Sutherland, married another man, the prince recovered quickly. On the rebound, the prince seems to have developed a penchant for American divorcees, forming a relationship first with Freda Dudley-Ward, before falling madly in love with Gloria Vanderbilt's twin sister, the attractive and vivacious Thelma who by her late 20s was already on to her second husband, shipping magnate Lord Furness. Mindful of his son's wayward conduct, King George V arranged for the prince to tour the Empire. A tour of India and the Far East in 1922 was followed up with a visit to the United States in 1924 and South Africa, the Gold Coast and Nigeria a year later. The prince developed a passion for big game hunting and on one of his subsequent visits to East Africa in April 1930, he invited his mistress Thelma Furness, to join him on safari.

Married to shipping magnate Lord Furness, Thelma's behaviour scandalised polite society, leading eventually to her divorce in 1933. The prince and Thelma continued their liaison at the prince's newly acquired country retreat Fort Belvedere, meeting regularly until the affair was broken off in 1934 when Thelma departed for America. While his public life was packed with speaking engagements and goodwill tours – the prince was by far the most photographed member of the royal family – Edward's private life revolved around going out and having a good time. Here he had a co-conspirator in his equerry, the tall and cheerful Irishman, Major Edward Dudley Metcalfe, 'Fruity' to his friends. Edward had met Fruity on the royal tour of India when, as a junior officer in the Indian army, he had been given the task of managing the prince's polo ponies.

'Fruity' Metcalfe was promoted to major and followed the prince back to England as his equerry, a key member of the royal household. Surrounded as he was by respectful courtiers and hemmed in by formality, the prince enjoyed Fruity's bluff banter. Referring to his boss as 'the little man', Fruity Metcalfe always gave him an honest opinion although he never overstepped the mark. Behaving more like pals together, the prince and 'Fruity' frequently spent their nights on the town.

Writing as the Duke of Windsor many years later, Edward recalls these carefree times in his memoir *A Family Album*. A typical evening would begin with a cocktail in York House. Suitably fortified, the prince and Fruity would gather a small group of friends to go out to a restaurant or take in a show. Then it would be off to a nightclub to dance into the small hours of the morning to the lively jazz bands of the Roaring Twenties.

These riotous outings led by the prince included all three of his younger brothers and Lady Alexandra 'Baba' Curzon, daughter of the foreign secretary and soon to be Viceroy of India, Lord Curzon. Together with the indefatigable Fruity Metcalfe, the young royals would return to York House to continue partying, often with a posse of celebrity guests in tow. The Duke of Windsor's memoirs relate a particularly memorable night when Fred Astaire and his sister Adele were invited back to York House to dance. On another occasion the prince decided that he and his party were not going to be prevented from dancing simply because the nightclub was closing and the orchestra were packing away their instruments. He therefore invited the whole of Paul Whiteman's Orchestra back to York House where he would attempt to smuggle them in through a back entrance. When it was pointed out to him that this might be a breach of royal security, Lady Baba offered to host the party at her place. Her father, Lord Curzon, the foreign secretary was abroad, and the family house in Carlton House Terrace would be empty. Stopping only to collect an ample supply of champagne from York House, the royal party duly arrived at Lord Curzon's mansion, stripped the dust sheets off the furniture and danced through until 6 a.m., drinking champagne. Lord Curzon might never have known of this wild party but for the fact that the prince's brother Harry, Duke of Gloucester, sat down on his Lordship's antique Georgian mahogany dining table and broke it in two. The incident was eventually papered over by some skilful diplomacy on the part of Lady Curzon. Baba and Fruity subsequently married, with his youthful bride known by her formal title, Lady Alexandra Metcalfe.

Despite occasional forays into the West End, the Prince of Wales was seen less and less. In 1934 Edward swapped York House, St James's for Fort Belvedere, a large secluded house in the grounds of Windsor Great Park. By a strange coincidence, later that year the prince met the woman who was to share his life and lead to his abdication, Wallis Simpson. Wallis, then married to husband Ernest, had been urged by her friend Thelma Vanderbilt (Lady Furness) to look after the prince and to see he didn't get lonely while she was away on an extended vacation. It was a commission she executed to perfection.

King George V died at Sandringham on 20 January 1936 after a short illness, surrounded by his closest family, including the Prince of Wales. At 40 years old the prince had prepared himself for the moment he would inherit his father's throne and be crowned Edward VIII. He was adamant that he was going to marry Wallis Simpson who would then become Queen Consort of a modernised monarchy. He had also decided he and his bride would live in York House, St James's in comfortable, less ostentatious style than the grandeur and formality of Buckingham Palace. But it was not to be. Throughout 1936 frantic negotiations were taking place behind the scenes which might yet broker a solution to a constitutional crisis. As upholder of the Church of England, the king could not marry a divorcee. In his last act as king,

Edward signed the instrument of abdication on 10 December, paving the way for his younger brother to be crowned King George VI. The former king was given the title the Duke of Windsor. The duke joined a recently divorced Wallis Simpson in France where they would soon tie the knot with Fruity performing the duties as best man. Edward was rarely to set foot in Britain ever again. In a little over two years the country would be at war.

Dressed to Impress

The jazz age is synonymous with the London Look. Jermyn Street, St James's and Savile Row became the epicentre of male fashion. The iconic Simpson's of Piccadilly opened in 1936 to a fanfare of popular acclaim. The store's founder Alec Simpson had a mission to offer smart ready-to-wear tailoring at affordable prices. He even set up one floor of his art deco emporium as a tailoring and cutting room offering a bespoke 'Savile Row' service for customers prepared to pay a little extra.

One of Simpson's best-selling lines was its new patent trousers with 'adjustable waist fastenings'. Manufactured under the trade name of DAKS at Simpson's own London factory, these trendy high-waisted trousers could be worn without braces and retailed for 30s. At Simpson's grand opening on 29 April, the store's designers created dramatic displays of clothing around three aeroplanes which had been partially dismantled and re-assembled on the fifth floor as a talking point. Celebrities flocked to the event and the newly opened store included a pet shop, a cigar store, a florist, and a hairdressing salon.

Simpson's stocked a full range of suits, trousers, raincoats, overcoats, hats and accessories which today's shopper would be hard-pressed to find under one roof. Less than a year after it opened, Simpson's branched out into ladies' wear with a women's department on the fourth floor stocked with country tweeds, two-piece suits, blouson jackets and golfing slacks. The store established a fashionable brand image. Just as Beau Brummel had created the style we associate with dandyism, so 100 years later, a new Prince of Wales became closely associated with men's fashion. His was a more exclusive brand. Slim and with film star good looks, Edward, Prince of Wales, was the most photographed member of the royal family. Whether attired in formal morning suit, dressed in one of his trademark check suits, or relaxing in plus fours and Fair Isle pullover, the prince was a walking advertisement for British tailoring.

From 1919 to 1959 when he closed his business and retired, Scholte of Savile Row was the prince's preferred tailor. Having served a ten-year apprenticeship as a cutter, Scholte came from a long tradition of master tailors who frowned on fashion's wilder excesses. The Duke of Windsor recalled an incident when the tailor refused to cut a suit for Fruity Metcalfe – much to that gallant officer's mortification:

> As befitting an artist and a craftsman, Scholte had rigid standards concerning the perfect balance of proportions between shoulders and waist in the cut of a coat to clothe the masculine torso. Fruity who, for all his discretion of costume was always ready to experiment, had sinned by demanding wider shoulders and a narrower waist.[*]

The prince championed a more casual look, substituting formal white tie and tails for the more comfortable dinner jacket and adopting soft turn-down collars of his Hawes and Curtis shirts in place of the conventional detachable boiled and starched collars of the period. He was aware of his role as an ambassador for British tailoring:

> I myself played a fairly prominent and for the most part equally unconscious role in this process. After all, it was part of my job as the Prince of Wales to support and stimulate British trade in general, and this inevitably included men's clothes.[**]

---

[*] The Duke of Windsor, *A Family Album*, Cassell, London, 1960, p. 99
[**] Ibid., p. 114

While Parisian haute couture was widely adopted by upper class women and film stars, the impeccably cut Savile Row suit was its male equivalent. Hollywood's leading men – and some of its leading ladies – were dressed by Savile Row. Huntsman, Norton and Sons, Kilgour and French, and Anderson and Sheppard established a name for themselves by dressing Hollywood 'royalty' including Douglas Fairbanks Junior, Rudolph Valentino, Clark Gable, Stewart Grainger and Gregory Peck. Prepared to risk a little flamboyance, Anderson and Sheppard was chosen by Marlene Dietrich to tailor her trousers and blazers. Fred Astaire was a particularly avid fan of tailoring, having been personally introduced to the Row by the Prince of Wales. Savile Row tailoring was and remains an important British export.

Redevelopment

Depressed property prices in the economic crash of the early 1930s acted as a spur to property developers who saw reduced land prices and cheap labour as an opportunity. Large swathes of the West End were redeveloped including John Nash's Regent Street which was demolished and rebuilt from 1921 to 1927. Owned by Crown estates, the early nineteenth-century shops lining Regent Street between Piccadilly and Oxford Street were demolished and replaced with the modern stores.

Nor did St James's Square escape the wrecking ball. Irreplaceable heritage was casually tossed aside as one after another the square's stately seventeenth-century mansions were sold for redevelopment. In 1934, for example, Winchester House was pulled down to make way for an undistinguished office building while in 1938 the historic Norfolk House on the south-east corner of the square, London home of the Dukes of Norfolk, was demolished. A year later, the Sports Club which had stood on the corner of the square was torn down to make way for an architecturally unimpressive modern office block.

The only evidence of these missing architectural gems is the ball-room of Norfolk House which was carefully dismantled and sold to the Victoria and Albert Museum where it was painstakingly re-assembled. Today, the Norfolk House Ballroom occupies pride of place in the museum's early furniture gallery. But it was not all bad news. Famous for its art deco style, the jazz age left a subtle legacy in the form of building refurbishments and improvements to transport links. Reflecting the importance of this underground railway interchange, Piccadilly's circular domed subterranean ticket hall clad in expensive travertine marble makes an elegant statement. The station's art deco bronze signage with white enamelled lettering still exists although in a somewhat tarnished state. Designed by Joseph Emberton, the clothing store Simpson's of Piccadilly was built on the site of the former Geological Museum which had been demolished in 1935. With art deco interiors by former Bauhaus architect Lazlo Moholy-Nagy, a refugee from Nazi Germany, Simpson's flagship store occupied a site reaching from Piccadilly to its rear entrance in Jermyn Street.

Simpson's store was a sophisticated building whose non-reflecting, concave curved glass windows on the ground floor level give amazing depth and clarity to shop window displays. Illuminated in coloured lighting, the store's upper floor terrace and loggia just below the roof-line represented all that was best of the 1930s modernist movement. Today the Grade 1 listed building is a Waterstone's bookstore. That other art deco landmark, 55 Broadway, the former headquarters of London Underground above St James's Park Station, deserves honourable mention. Built in 1929 and once the tallest office building in London, 55 Broadway is famous for its statues – one of which, a male nude, had to be modified after its explicit nature provoked a storm of public protest.

Just as important as the grand architecture, people continued to live in St James's – within the maze of historic buildings. Unlike many other parts of the capital the area retained much of its pre-war character and *cachet*. The sixty-nine bachelor flats created in 1804 within the stately three-storey mansion Melbourne House next door to the Royal Academy and known as the Albany, appealed to the artistic and intellectual elite. During the 1920s and '30s Bryan Guinness, Aldous Huxley, Sir Thomas Beecham, J.B. Priestley and many others lived in this exclusive gated apartment building. The grand houses not yet converted into flats, clubs or office buildings could make a desirable London pied-à-terre for the super-rich. Nancy Astor, Britain's first woman MP, wife of Waldorf Astor and chatelaine of Cliveden, purchased number 4 St James's Square. She had bought the house in the early 1920s after being elected MP for Plymouth, Sutton in 1919 to be near Parliament and to entertain on a lavish scale. It is clear that St James's reputation as an elite village was as strong in the twentieth century as it was in the reign of Queen Anne.

CHAPTER 9

CLUBLAND AT WAR

We picked our way up St James's Street,
and when we came level with King Street,
we had the impression of looking into Dante's Inferno.
From St James's Theatre to St James's Square
all seemed wreckage and fire.

Mrs Robert Henrey, *The Siege of London*

Madeleine Henrey's first-hand accounts of the Blitz in *A Village in Piccadilly* and *The Siege of London* offer a clear insight into the impact of war on St James's and Piccadilly. Born Madeleine Gal in the Paris suburb of Clichy in 1906, she was taken to London as a teenager by her mother, a seamstress. Mother and daughter settled in Soho and after finishing her education at a convent school, Madeleine landed a job as a manicurist at the Savoy Hotel. Here she met her future husband, the journalist and gossip columnist, Robert Henrey. The couple married in 1928 and moved to Normandy where they lived on a farm. By now fluent in English, Madeleine tried her hand at writing novels while raising her young son, Bobby. Her first book, *A Century Between*, was published in 1937.

Writing under her husband's name, Madeleine's novels might have sunk into obscurity. But Hitler's invasion forced the Henreys to flee to England in 1940 where they rented an apartment off

Piccadilly. Madeleine's account of wartime life in the West End is social reportage at its very best. Buoyed by critical acclaim, Mrs Henrey went on to publish more than thirty books over the next four decades.

Impressions of War

Walking the busy arteries and peaceful backwaters of St James's, it is hard to comprehend the sheer destructive force on buildings and lives unleashed by the Second World War. After a particularly devastating raid on the night of 23 February 1944 when St James's was attacked by the Luftwaffe, Madeleine Henrey and a friend took a night-time walk through the fires and rubble. Miraculously escaping a direct hit, the ancient glass windows of the Chapel Royal, St James's Palace had been blown out while a 'Dante's Inferno' of fires had taken hold in the wreckage of St James's Street and King Street: 'Heavy gilt picture frames from the shattered establishment of a famous art dealer lay in the middle of the street. Spink's was on fire. The already charred skeleton of Christie's stood out like a fantastic light in a Roman temple.'

Dante's *Inferno* is also evoked by Charles Gillen, an American GI (general infantryman) from South Orange, New Jersey who recorded his impressions in a diary. On leave in London in 1944, Gillen visited a West End show. With only a tiny electric torch to light his way around a blacked-out Piccadilly Circus, he was confronted by a degrading sight which he describes as Dante's 'Third Circle of Hell'. Women were lined up, visible only by the light of a multitude of feeble torches. Gillen observed:

Packed along the sidewalks of the Circus in what seemed to be thousands, were prostitutes of every age, shape and size, although one couldn't be sure of individual looks because the pitiful torches revealed very little even when swept upwards closely from toes to head … One was solicited every few steps, sometimes in the baldest words, sometimes in more genteel phrases like: 'Want to come home with me, love?' *

Even though the Allies were on the brink of winning the war in Europe, years of bombing and privation were sapping civilian morale. In their different ways the American soldier and the young Frenchwoman had captured a moment of living hell.

Preparations for War

After the evacuation of the British Expeditionary Force from the beaches of Dunkirk in June 1940, Hitler's forces looked poised to invade Britain. Urgent preparations were made for the defence of London. The lake in St James's Park was drained to avoid the reflection of the water being used as a landmark by Luftwaffe pilots, and searchlight batteries and barrage balloons were tethered in St James's and Green Park. At the outbreak of war, the illuminated billboards in Piccadilly Circus were switched off for the duration as part of the general blackout of lights from buildings. They would not be switched on again until 1949. Cars, buses and motorcycles drove with hooded lights. Meanwhile, the statue of Eros was removed to Egham Park in Surrey for safekeeping and its base boarded up. Posters advertising war bonds were pasted around the hoardings.

Yet many aspects of daily life in London's Clubland remained unchanged. At Piccadilly Circus, crowds of people still took their eighteen-penny afternoon tea at the Monico, or gazed at the windows of the jewellers Saqui and Lawrence. The clothing emporium Simpson's of Piccadilly switched from civilian dress to military uniforms. On the first floor, young officers were kitted out under the watchful eye of the immaculately pinstriped Major Huskisson MC, a veteran of the First World War. The store had a near monopoly of

---

* Leonard Mosley, *Backs to the Wall, London Under Fire 1939–45,* Book Club Associates, London, p. 331

Royal Navy tailoring and was a major supplier of well-cut khaki officers' uniforms. For those unable to call in person, Simpson's ran an efficient mail order business. Apart from the obvious items, officers were advised to purchase 'wool pyjamas, a waterproof trenchcoat, and heavy 'acquatite' shoes.' An advertisement reminded the reader that, 'a commanding officer forms his first impression from your uniform.'**

Savile Row, the home of London tailoring, switched from civilian suits to military uniforms and offered a bespoke service to officers of elite regiments like the Cavalry and Guards. Soon shortages began to hinder war production. Clothing was subject to purchase tax in 1940 and from June the following year, clothing was rationed and 'utility' garments – economically cut according to Ministry of Supply guidelines – were identified with a label bearing the utility mark. Rationing started to affect members' clubs from the outset and chefs found their menu choices constrained as milk, cheese and butter were put on ration in January 1940.

The real issue, however, was not basic cooking ingredients but the indispensable luxuries like vintage clarets, brandies and port stored in club cellars. As soon as France was overrun it became obvious that stocks would have to be conserved as no one knew when they might be able to resume purchasing vintages from the continent. The war saw a flourishing black market in all forms of wine and spirits, most of which were available at highly inflated prices. But club bars continued to serve members from their well-stocked cellars and it was only gradually that prices began to rise. Prudent clubs introduced rationing early on. At the Army and Navy Club, for example, vintage port could only be served at luncheon and then only on two days of the week. Members were limited to 2 quarts of champagne and 2 quarts of French or German wines in each calendar month. Price was used as a form of rationing and a 25 per cent surcharge was levied on the sale of whisky and gin.

** David Wainwright, *The British Tradition: Simpson's – a World of Style*, Quiller Press, London, p. 30

Things got decidedly tough at the Army and Navy Club. In June 1940 seventy members of staff were called up for military service. With conscription in full swing, clubs had to make do with fewer, mainly elderly, male servants, and recruit young women to fill the gaps. With many members volunteering to join the armed forces, clubs were forced to introduce cuts. No longer could there be any pretence that things could carry on as normal and many formalities were cast aside. At Boodle's, for example, members were generally permitted to dine 'undressed', a practical relaxation of rules allowing officers to wear uniform or mufti rather than taking the trouble to change into the time-honoured dinner jacket and black tie.

The entry of Italy into the war in June 1940 prompted the immediate rounding up of all Italians living in Britain. The Army and Navy Club reacted promptly by cancelling the honorary membership of the Italian head of state, King Victor Emmanuel. The internment of Italians, most of whom were sent to a prison camp on the Isle of Man, played well to British public opinion but it was a minor disaster for St James's and Piccadilly whose sizable Anglophile Italian community ran most of the area's fine dining and hospitality businesses. Chefs and proprietors of some of the most prestigious hotels and restaurants like Giovanni Sovrano, formerly maître d' of the Savoy, and the Quaglino brothers, Giovanni and Ernesto, whose restaurant re-opened under new management as the Meurice, were banished. In a matter of days, Italian proprietors placed their premises in the hands of caretaker partners who undertook to look after their business interests. Luigi Stocco, owner of the Embassy Club and the Café de Paris, handed over to his Danish partner Martin Poulsen who became for a time the undisputed king of West End nightlife.

The Ritz remained a quintessential fixture of London's high society. It came to symbolise romance. In the words of the song 'A Nightingale Sang in Berkeley Square' (written in 1940 and performed by Vera Lynn), 'There were Angels dining at the Ritz.' The hotel became synonymous with an idealised way of life far removed from the harsh realities of war.

Governments in Exile

With the entire country on a war footing, the stiff social etiquette of St James's came under attack. A new informality ruled and military matters took precedence over ceremony. Foreign governments in exile set up headquarters for the duration of the war in buildings loaned by the government. General Charles de Gaulle led the Free French from temporary headquarters in a spacious modern office block in Carlton Gardens where a giant tricolour flag few above the entrance. Meanwhile, the free Polish army under General Sikorski co-ordinated their efforts from the Hotel Rubens in Palace Place. Having escaped capture by Hitler or internment by the Soviets, the rump of the Polish armed forces numbering 17,000 men was stationed in Scotland. In addition to the French and Polish, the West End played host to Dutch, Belgian and Scandinavian free forces. The St James's clubs, particularly those with a strong connection to the military, regarded it as their patriotic duty to open their doors to comrades in arms. Officers of allied armies, for example, were automatically given free membership of the Naval and Military Club in Piccadilly. Daily life underwent a transformation as St James's began to see a steady stream of troops of every nationality pledged to the allied cause. Madeleine Henrey recorded these changes:

> The cocktail bars in Piccadilly were crowded with soldiers, sailors, and airmen, not only of the home country but of the Dominions, the free allied nations. Norwegians and Dutch, French and Poles in their respective uniforms crowded the hotel foyers. Some airmen and a few technicians back from Murmansk and Leningrad, told stories of the Russian campaign fought in temperatures of twenty to thirty degrees below zero. A young officer wearing a picturesque headgear with a wide brim turned up on one side and decorated with a bunch of bright green feathers was just back from Gambia ...*

---

* Robert Henrey, *A Village in Piccadilly,* J.M. Dent, London, 1942, p. 65

The clientele of clubs and restaurants changed almost overnight to reflect the influx of foreign allies and governments in exile. Clubs, restaurants and hotels found they were far busier than in peacetime. The Albanian royal family took a permanent suite of rooms at the Ritz. So too did royals from Denmark, Luxembourg and Norway. Rumour had it the Albanians paid their bills with their country's gold reserves and had their own private air raid shelter installed. Fashionable restaurants were patronised by leaders of various foreign governments or armies in exile. The problem was that these individuals represented widely diverging political interests. Apart from desiring the overthrow of Hitler, there was little common ground.

British Army liaison officers, particularly those able to speak foreign languages, played an important role in communicating Allied strategy to these groups and weaving them into the overall war effort. They also performed a valuable role in intelligence gathering. The historian Leonard Mosley paints a vivid picture of the air of intrigue pervading St James's:

> At Claridges or the Ritz it was not unusual to see lunching simultaneously Moshe Shertok, head of the Jewish Agency, General Sikorsky, leader of the Poles, Admiral Muselier of the Free French Navy, King Haakon of Norway, Colonel Passy of Free French Intelligence and Colonel Maurice Buckmaster of SOE. They almost always occupied separate tables, eyeing each other with cold suspicion.*

There were plenty of unofficial watering holes around St James's where plots could be hatched. Just around the corner from the Free French HQ in Carlton Gardens, tucked away in a mews behind St James's Street was *Le Petit Club de France*. This open-all-hours club was operated by an enterprising Welshwoman, Olwen Vaughn. Inhaling the unmistakable aroma of Caporal cigarettes and listening

---

* Leonard Mosley, *Backs to the Wall, London Under Fire 1939–45,* Book Club Associates, London, 1974, p. 208

to the clink of *pastis* glasses, French staff officers rubbed shoulders with Resistance fighters back from missions behind enemy lines. The place was a den of intrigue with rival factions of the Free French Army and Free French Navy perpetually jockeying for power and influence. One result was a clumsy attempt to frame Admiral Muselier with forged correspondence supposedly implicating him in a Vichy plot to overthrow de Gaulle and for which the innocent Muselier was imprisoned briefly by the British authorities as a spy.

Blitzkrieg

The first air raid on London on the afternoon of Saturday 7 September 1940 heralded the start of the Blitz, which was to last almost without break until 11 May 1941, after which raids became less frequent but no less damaging. Although the civilian population had been drilled by the government in how to respond by donning gas masks and heading for the nearest air raid shelter, the aerial attacks caught many people off guard. Germany's original aim was to knock out RAF airfields, Britain's first line of defence, in preparation for a seaborne invasion. But when this strategy failed to yield results, Hitler switched tactics and ordered mass bombing raids on the City and the East End to destroy London's commercial heart.

On 13 September a German bomber that had strayed off course dropped a bomb near Buckingham Palace. Four days later Marble Arch Underground station was hit, killing over twenty civilians and injuring many more. Nowhere in London was now safe from attack. By mid-October air raids had switched from the docks and had begun to target the West End. On the night of 14 October 1940, St James's Church, Piccadilly was badly damaged by incendiary and conventional bombs which left the roof of the nave a charred shell. But firefighters had saved most of the building and by Christmas, services were once more being held in the south aisle which had escaped damage. Walled off from the ruins of the church and under a temporary corrugated iron roof, worshippers braved the cold and followed the service from fire-singed and water-stained prayer books. An upright piano replaced the magnificent seventeenth-century organ with its gilded angels carved by Grinling Gibbons which had escaped destruction. The church crypt was used as an air raid shelter throughout the Blitz and the church remained a battered shell until restoration was completed in 1954.

The first and greatest loss of the wartime raids on St James's was the Carlton Club which had stood on the corner of Carlton Gardens and Pall Mall next to the Reform. The grand clubhouse sustained a direct hit on 14 October 1940: luckily there were no casualties, although Harold Macmillan, then Parliamentary Secretary to the Ministry of Supply, was in the building at the time. The club moved to the newly vacated Arthur's Club at 69 St James's Street where it remains to this day.

The Blitz saw an unprecedented spirit of unity as clubs collaborated to offer each other support. Several clubs were bombed out and as their buildings were evacuated other institutions came to the rescue, offering hospitality and temporary membership to displaced members. The following month it was the turn of the Naval and Military Club, the 'In and Out' on Piccadilly, which sustained heavy damage to its top two floors when a stick of three high explosive bombs hit the club's west wing and nearby buildings on Half Moon Street on the night of 4 November. Two club members were seriously injured and later died in hospital.

Over the following weeks, the club was patched up, re-roofed, cleared of debris and reopened for 'business as usual'. An impromptu cocktail bar was set up in a grand reception room full of leather armchairs while servants kept a large open coal fire burning in the grate. The Caledonian Club took a direct hit later that same month, its members transferring to the East India and Sports Club where they stayed until 1943. Waiters ferried undamaged bottles of rare wines and port to their temporary haven on the corner of St James's Square and Charles the Second Street.

Christmas 1940

Mercifully, there was an unofficial suspension of bombing by both the Luftwaffe and the RAF which by this stage in the war was mounting retaliatory raids on Berlin. Lasting from Christmas Eve until 27 December 1940, the second Christmas of the war would bring a welcome respite. Madeleine Henrey recalls the temporary truce fuelled a rush to enjoy Christmas as jostling crowds returned once more to the West End:

> The desire to spend money was staggering ... Oxford Street, Regent Street and Piccadilly were crowded until the official closing time for shops at 4 p.m. ... Now thousands of children had come back from the reception areas and even the most cautious of grown-ups felt they could risk a few nights in town.[*]

Food rationing and shortages of imported luxuries were beginning to bite and long queues formed outside butchers' shops, market stalls and department stores. The lucky few came home with a small chicken, some sausages, and perhaps a bottle of ginger wine or sherry. West End shows were well attended and the pantomime put on at the Stoll Theatre, Kingsway, *Babes in the Wood*, took £5,000 in advance bookings.

But that Christmas was short-lived. The truce was broken suddenly on Sunday 29 December by the biggest raid ever mounted by the Luftwaffe in which the target was St Paul's Cathedral. The bombing was so intense it caused what became known as the Second Great Fire of London. The City of London from Aldersgate to Aldgate East became a raging inferno in which virtually no building survived. In a single night, a quarter of the 'Square Mile' was razed to the ground as firefighters looked on in despair. For on that night the fire hydrants failed and the Thames was at its lowest ebb, its water well beyond the

---

[*] Robert Henrey, *A Village in Piccadilly*, J.M. Dent, London, 1942, p. 65

reach of the pumps. The fact that St Paul's Cathedral escaped was down to luck and an army of firewatchers who stood by ready to extinguish any incendiary bombs that landed on the roof. Despite their vigilance, one bomb smashed its way through the dome but miraculously failed to detonate.

Club Hospitality

Throughout the German bombing raids, there was unprecedented pressure to find accommodation for military personnel based in London, overseas delegations, and Whitehall staff leading the war effort. Beds were often booked months in advance and efforts were made to press every available bed into service. Cabinet ministers, most of whom were club members, made full use of their club dining facilities which were conveniently near Whitehall. Clement Attlee, deputy PM in Churchill's wartime Cabinet, was to be discovered most nights at the Oxford and Cambridge Club tucking into a modest meal. The clubbable Harold Macmillan was frequently to be found at the Beefsteak, Pratt's Club, Buck's, and the Carlton Club. Foreign secretary Anthony Eden and Churchill rarely visited clubs.

Hotels continued to attract visitors but bomb damage forced closures. The author Anthony Powell, now a liaison officer to the Free Polish forces, recalls the Cavendish Hotel in Jermyn Street run by the elderly and eccentric Rosa Lewis:

> People went to the Cavendish fairly late, after 11 o'clock, probably after midnight, when drinks in general ceased to be procurable in public places … A couple of pink-faced guards ensigns would not be unexpected, nor an American … Augustus John, sitting alone in the corner was always a possibility.*

---

* Anthony Powell, *Messengers of Day,* Vol. 2 of *To Keep the Ball Rolling,* Heinemann, London, 1978, p. 51

The American artist J.O. Mahoney stayed at the Cavendish possibly out of curiosity or a sense of danger. Powell provides an account:

> In consequence of the Blitz, the glass had long vanished from Mahoney's bedroom windows at the Cavendish where he looked on to Jermyn Street, though some protection was afforded by thick 19th century embroidered Japanese curtains. For a long time no water had run from the taps of his bath which was also filled with plaster from the ceiling ... Rosa Lewis would sit in the capaciously hooded porter's chair in the hall, greeting returning guests with the words, 'Jerry has been very naughty tonight, very naughty indeed.'**

Virtually all of the St James's clubs that remained undamaged offered overnight accommodation to members. A comfortable bed for the night could be often had for as little as 5*s*, a considerable saving on the cost of a hotel. Some even had beds for women. The Naval and Military Club, for example, which had admitted women as associate members since 1934, provided them with their own sleeping quarters. An essential part of providing overnight sleeping was the air raid shelters. Civil defence air raid precautions encouraged clubs to designate cellars or basements as shelters for use during an air raid. These places were made as bomb proof as possible by shoring up ceilings and reinforcing them with steel beams. Blackout shutters were fixed up and panes of glass in windows were taped up to avoid flying splinters of glass from bomb blast.

At the Army and Navy Club, half the basement at 46–47 Pall Mall was converted into a shelter with two-tier bunks for twenty-four members and three-tier bunks for thirty-six male servants. The charge for the use of bunks by members was 2*s* for one night, 10*s* for a week and 30*s* for a month.

Some clubs installed diesel generators as a back-up in case the power supply failed, while at the Army and Navy, primus stoves were

---

** Anthony Powell, *Messengers of Day* ibid p 137ssn

supplied to the kitchen as a standby for cooking breakfast. Besides the clubs, hospitality could be found in some unexpected quarters. In June 1940, Simpson's of Piccadilly opened its fifth floor rest room to soldiers returning from Dunkirk. Staff would telephone messages to family members and even offer them a room, a change of clothes and a meal. Later that year the store decided to launch its own club. Called the Simpson Services Club, free membership was granted to officers of both sexes, the sole proviso being that an individual had to be proposed and seconded. Throughout the duration of the war around 12,000 officers took advantage of this arrangement to relax and recharge their batteries. A few doors down from Simpson's on Piccadilly, the BBC's recording studio opened its 'Stage Door Canteen' to the armed forces. Over the course of the war, thousands of servicemen and women who were passing through the West End dropped in for a hot meal and a cup of tea.

Party Like There's No Tomorrow

At the outbreak of war all West End theatres, clubs and dance halls had been forced to close by order of the government, but this ruling had been relaxed after twelve days when it was realised that they were in fact an important morale boost. During the dark days of the Blitz a sort of frenzy overtook West End nightlife. People started going to the theatre and to cinemas. Dance bands attracted revellers to nightclubs and restaurants where couples, many in uniform, swayed drunkenly to the music in an effort to keep their spirits up. Nightclubs circumvented strict licensing laws and served alcohol after hours by allowing people to pre-order drinks if they were part of a private party. 'Bottle parties', as they were known, were billed as invitation-only gatherings but in reality, anyone could join in and order alcoholic drinks at any time of day or night. Madeleine Henrey recalls how an endless supply of alcohol fuelled riotous all-night dancing. In wartime, the Embassy Club had 'nothing in common with the elegance of its regal days when every woman's dress was a masterpiece and Jackson, the sleek black cat, used to jump on the royal table to be stroked by two sons of a king'.*

The possibility of sudden death acted as an aphrodisiac. Revues at the Windmill Theatre in Great Windmill Street off Shaftesbury Avenue were hugely popular during and immediately after the war. Timed at around an hour and a half, non-stop performances staged from noon until 10.35 p.m. featured a dancing troupe, comedians, and a *tableau vivant* where a young lady would strike a dramatic pose wearing nothing but a wisp of gauze or a strategically placed feather to cover her modesty. The front six rows of the tiny intimate theatre were the most popular as members of the audience near the footlights could almost reach out and touch the performers. Under the management of the prim Mrs Laura Henderson and impresario Vivian Van Damm, showgirls were instructed to remain completely motionless. Failure to observe this rule meant the theatre's performance licence would be revoked by the Lord Chamberlain. Things did not always run smoothly. Journalist Vivien Goldsmith whose mother, a Windmill Girl, appeared under the stage name Joan Jay, recalls an amusing story of the theatre in its heyday:

> The only time a nude moved was when a bomb dropped on the Regent Palace Hotel. The theatre shook and the 'statue' ran for her life as a dead rat fell out of the rafters. The nudes were never allowed to sing, because that would involve too much deep breathing and heaving of their fulsome chests.**

Many post-war comedians including Bruce Forsyth and Peter Sellers cut their teeth as warm-up acts to the showgirls who formed the Windmill's star attraction. Van Damm's flair for public relations created the legend of the Windmill as 'the theatre that never closed'. In 1944 Mrs Henderson left the theatre to her partner Van Damm and he ran it until his death in December 1960. But the Windmill

---

* Robert Henrey, ibid., p. 16

** Vivien Goldsmith, *The Daily Telegraph,* 24 November, 2005

was tame in comparison with some other nightclubs, some of which managed to circumvent the rules governing public entertainment. One club popular with young RAF officers boasted an artificial pool full of topless mermaids.*

Considered one of the safest places in an air raid, the dance floor in the basement of the Café de Paris on Coventry St was 20ft below ground level. But on the night of 8 March 1941 the packed nightclub took a direct hit when, by a freak chance, two German bombs came crashing down the ventilation shaft. The bombs exploded in front of the stage where the West Indian band leader Ken 'Snakehips' Johnson was in full swing with an Andrews' Sisters' hit 'Oh Johnny Oh'. The blast severed Johnson's head which landed among the terror-stricken couples on the dance floor. He and thirty-three others including band members, waiters and couples on the dance floor died in the blast which severed limbs and left a further eighty people seriously injured. Martin Poulsen the Café de Paris's proprietor and his Swiss manager were killed on the balcony overlooking the dance floor. Ambulances were quickly on the scene as doctors and paramedics offered first aid and survivors were guided to safety. Some of the victims were horribly mutilated, others were apparently unharmed, sitting at tables in full evening dress. Looking like shop window dummies, people had died of asphyxiation, having had all the air instantly sucked out of their lungs by the blast. But there were also stories of miraculous survival. A troupe of dancers waiting in the wings were unharmed; one man carried out on a stretcher told the anxious crowds outside, 'At least I didn't have to pay for dinner!' That same evening, Buckingham Palace was hit with bombs narrowly avoiding killing the king and queen who had stayed in London to share the capital's fate.

Tragically, just two weeks after the bombing of the Café de Paris, jazz singer Al Bowlly was killed in an air raid that took place on 17 April 1941. For almost a decade, Bowlly had been one of the best-loved jazz singers in the world. Just before the war his popularity nose-dived as a new generation of singers like Bing Crosby and

---

* Interview: Marjorie Chipperfield, secretary at the Air Ministry, 1940–46

Frank Sinatra took his place. He stayed around and he was beginning his comeback as part of a double act with guitarist Jimmy Messene, called Radio Stars with their Guitars. Bowlly was killed by a parachute mine that landed at the Haymarket end of Jermyn Street. Parachute mines were a deadly new weapon packed with high explosives. Timed to detonate before hitting the ground, they had the explosive force of ten conventional bombs and could destroy everything within a radius of 500m. The raid was one of the biggest to hit the West End. Hundreds of casualties were buried in a mass grave at Hanwell cemetery, among them Al Bowlly, one of Britain's greatest jazz singers.

Business as Usual

The Army and Navy Club at 46–47 Pall Mall suffered extensive damage on the night of 23 February 1943 from four high explosive bombs which fell nearby. The roof was damaged and ceilings, partitions, windows and interiors were wrecked, and the north wall had to be shored up. But the club never closed. Although many club members received minor injuries, most were treated at the scene and went on to make a full recovery. Fortunately, the club's wine cellar and its store of valuable paintings crated up for the duration were undamaged, which greatly assisted the club in getting back on its feet. A member wrote expressing praise for the club secretary Miss Vennard and her staff:

> I feel I should express to you as our Chairman my sincere admiration at the coolness and energy displayed by Miss Vennard. She, though wounded in the head, quickly organised a first aid post and by her complete calm set an example to the rest of the staff who backed her up magnificently.[**]

[**] Anthony Dixon, *The Army and Navy Club 1837–2008* (published by the Army and Navy Club 2009), p. 92

But worse was to come on 23 February 1944 when a 500lb bomb sliced through the London Library in St James's Square, one of the capital's most important cultural assets, totally wrecking the newly built back stacks. Madeleine Henrey recalls: 'The building's façade was intact but inside was a terrible mess of broken glass and torn volumes.'[*]

Over 1,600 books and periodicals in this private members' library had been destroyed. The following morning, Henrey joined volunteers including the writers James Lees-Milne and John Pope Hennessy and the library staff in trying to save as many books as they could from the smouldering wreckage before water from the firemen's hoses could wreak further damage. The real damage was in the art room where the bust of Thomas Carlyle had been hurled from its niche and decapitated, while among the biographies on the third and fourth floors the books had been thrown from the shelves and covered in a white dust. Henrey writes:

A number of twisted girders were holding back a load of rubble and pulverised literature ... When I returned later in the day I found nearly twenty of the girls already at work. Eleanor Rendall, her hair clogged with brick dust and her arms black with dirt, was climbing over the debris with no thought for her safety. 'For thirteen years I have put the biographies away,' she said. 'I must save what I can.'[**]

UK and US servicemen helped in the clean-up, moving books by wheelbarrow to be housed in the cellar of the National Gallery until the building could be repaired and the library re-opened. The marble bust of Carlyle was subsequently restored but evidence of the bombing is still turning up in the form of tiny pieces of shrapnel found buried in the pages of some of the library's more obscure and little-read theology books.[***]

---

[*] Robert Henrey, *The Siege of London*, J.M. Dent, London, 1946, p. 23
[**] Ibid., p. 24
[***] Interview: Helen O'Neill, Senior librarian, The London Library

Allied Nerve-Centre

Even as war was declared, a warren of deep tunnels and underground bunkers was being constructed under Whitehall as a precaution in the event of enemy attack. Each of the main ministries would have its own bombproof 'citadel', and all were linked by deep underground tunnels. Today evidence of the fortifications can be seen above ground, some of the most visible being the Admiralty Citadel next to Horse Guards, an enormous concrete blockhouse now mellowed and clad in ivy, and the circular Home Office citadels in Great Peter Street, built on the site of two long demolished gasholders. No one knows the full extent of the tunnels beneath Whitehall and St James's: a deep shelter is known to exist beneath a former government building on Piccadilly, while another tunnel runs deep below Trafalgar Square.

With its entrance at Clive Steps just opposite St James's Park, the Cabinet War Rooms beneath the Treasury is the only citadel open to the public. Here, Churchill and the Chief of Imperial General Staff (CIGS) General Brooke, subsequently Field Marshall Lord Alanbrooke, directed Britain's war against Germany. What the public sees is only a fraction of tunnels and the maze of shelters that once connected the Cabinet War Rooms to the Air Ministry in Whitehall and the Admiralty Citadel.**** On 22 July 1942 another Allied command centre was added to this network. It is a large art deco office building at 31 St James's Square. Formerly the site of an aristocratic mansion, demolished just before the outbreak of war, Norfolk House was requisitioned to house the Allied Forces' Headquarters (AFHQ). Staffed jointly by senior British and American service heads under the command of General Dwight D. Eisenhower, Norfolk House was where the preliminary plans were made for the invasion of North Africa and Italy and the D-Day Normandy Landings. It is unlikely that Norfolk House had any underground infrastructure but it is likely that the building was chosen for its deep basement which

---

**** Interview: Marjorie Chipperfield, secretary at the Air Ministry, 1940–1946

would have been made bombproof. But even this precaution was hardly necessary as Eisenhower was always on the move. He made periodic flights to Washington to report to President Roosevelt, while he and his immediate staff including Brigadier General Walter Bedell-Smith and General Mark Clark made tours of inspection to the different theatres of war.

The air raid of February 1944 which hit the London Library in St James's Square could quite easily have killed the supreme allied commander and set back planning for D-Day. It was an incredible near miss. The bombs which hit the London Library were less than 200 yards from Eisenhower's headquarters. Taking no chances, Eisenhower ordered the immediate evacuation of Norfolk House and the entire staff had decamped within a matter of days, swapping the comforts of St James for a tented and camouflaged compound in Bushey Park. The immediate run-up to D-Day itself found the supreme allied commander based at Southwick House near Portsmouth, a country estate with sweeping vistas of the coast.

The Guards' Chapel

The sung Eucharist held at the Guards' Chapel, Wellington Barracks on the morning of Sunday 18 June 1944 was no ordinary religious service: it was a celebration. Not only was this the anniversary of the battle of Waterloo, but also the assembled congregation of over 200 soldiers and civilians were giving thanks for the success of the Normandy landings twelve days earlier. Then, as every Sunday, the service began at 11 a.m. The band of HM Coldstream Guards provided rousing music to accompany the choir. Even as people were filing into church far away in the Pas de Calais, a vengeance weapon, one of Hitler's new V1 flying bombs, was fired from a ramp pointed in the direction of London. At 11.20 a.m., just as a lesson was being read, in the skies above London the V1's sputtering pulse jet engine cut out and the missile glided groundward. It could have landed anywhere within a radius of several miles as the 'Doodlebug's' crude gyro compass made this a random if terrifying weapon. The flying bomb hit the chapel roof, exploding inside the building, virtually obliterating it. The death toll was 121 killed and a further 141 injured, trapped by the falling masonry. Only the apse remained undamaged. Within minutes, fire crews and air raid wardens rushed to the scene and began the task of rescue. Heavy lifting equipment was called as more people were dug alive from the wreckage. At the time the threat of V1s was not widely known as these sporadic attacks had begun only five days earlier. But the Guards' Chapel was to be the worst atrocity of this new campaign of terror launched on London and the most high profile.

As Allied armies began to overrun the V1 launch sites and the RAF achieved small success in bringing down these weapons in flight, Germany switched to an even more deadly rocket, the V2, which could exit the earth's atmosphere and drop without warning at supersonic speed. By this time a news blackout and a campaign of disinformation persuaded the Nazis that their V weapons were overshooting their target causing them to re-calibrate their weapons. The majority fell on South London. On 27 March 1945 the last V2 fell on a block of council flats at Vallance Road, Stepney. The German rocket engineer Werner Von Braun was captured by the Americans in the final days of the war and the scientist and his highly skilled team were offered an immediate pardon on condition that they employed their knowledge to help America lay the foundations of NASA's ambitious space programme. The V2 was the forerunner of the US Saturn rockets and the Apollo mission that put men on the moon.

The war had left Clubland battered, bloody, but unbowed. The clubmen and women were ready to rally the spirits of Britain's wartime government and foreign governments in exile throughout the war. The spirit of co-operation across Clubland resulted in servicemen and officers being given club membership at vastly reduced rates, so that they could enjoy some respite from the war even in the heart of London. Rebuilding would take time and had to extend to areas of club management, not just the fabric of the buildings and their stocks of wine, brandy and port. Prudent club officials took down the valuable portraits and stored them safely below ground. An early raid on the National Liberal club demolished its wonderful circular stone staircase, and the same bomb ripped apart a full-length portrait of Winston Churchill as First Lord of the Admiralty. The portrait was salvaged from the ruins, carefully restored and now hangs below the rebuilt staircase: an example of the careful conservation of our national heritage that we owe to Clubland.

CHAPTER 10

CLUBLAND REBORN

Life in a club includes an element of fantasy,
no man it has truly been said behaves quite naturally in his
own club.

George Webb, former chairman of the Travellers Club

From a peak of 400 gentlemen's clubs in the late nineteenth century, Clubland now comprises fewer than fifty clubs. The best-known and most historic have survived, because of their unique character. The 'element of fantasy' which George Webb of the Travellers Club describes is increasingly bolstered by the reality of sound financial management. Clubs continue to be associated with the 'establishment', a nebulous and erratic concept – often used as shorthand for the upper reaches of government, Parliament, the Civil Service, the legislature, academia, business, finance, the media and the arts. But these institutions are no longer all-pervasive as in their Victorian heyday when their proliferation was driven by international trading links to the Empire and the wider world. After spending the greater part of the twentieth century stagnating, West End clubs are enjoying a renaissance. This includes not just those characterful survivors but an entirely new breed of clubs. Clubland has come full circle. The risqué, rebellious mid-nineteenth century clubs founded by writers, artists and actors like the Garrick Club, the Savage, or the Arts Club in Dover Street, are still going strong. Meanwhile, a new generation of entrepreneurs, media executives, rock stars and an international jet set embrace modern clubs like the Groucho Club, Quo Vadis, Soho House, Black's Club, Chelsea Arts Club and Home House.

Sought out for their international focus, professional networks, and business-friendly facilities, these clubs enjoy relaxed rules around drinking and entertaining. At the same time, powerful women in those industries, a constituency that barely existed in the nineteenth century, might join the all-female clubs such as Grace in Belgravia, a women-only fitness, wellbeing and lifestyle club, or the Trouble Club in Kingly Street, Soho, billed as a 'spot for all the talented, witty and cheeky women of today'. Changes in fashion could mean that, in time, these institutions will be superseded, and may even come to appear conservative or quaint to future generations. Which ones will stand the test of time is anyone's guess. Clubs are social constructs, influenced by contemporary socio-economics and the business world around them.

St James's and Piccadilly are a destination for luxury shopping, fine dining, and high-class hotels. Stores like Dunhill, Fortnum and Mason, and speciality shops like the wine and spirits merchant Berry Bros & Rudd, the perfumer Floris, the cheesemonger Whitfield and Paxton, hatters Lock and Co, and Lobbs, the bespoke shoemakers, attract a wealthy, international clientele. Luxury shops and luxury brands, theatres and Michelin starred restaurants are not only synonymous with London's Clubland, they are also the hallmark of a global city.

Post-War Revival

After the Second World War, it was believed by many that the glory days of Clubland would never return: a gradual decline was predicted. Post-war austerity together with changing habits in leisure and male sociability meant that fewer people had the appetite (or the money) for fine dining, card playing, or billiards that characterised the Victorian age. Members' clubs appeared to be facing slow extinction.

The rebirth of London's Clubland was no overnight success story. Throughout the 1950s and early '60s, the average age of club members had been rising steadily, the result of a missing generation of young men killed in the Great War. The stereotypical image of old men snoozing in leather armchairs, faces covered by a broadsheet newspaper is no exaggeration. It is small wonder so many clubs closed down. This ageing demographic precipitated a crisis in the 1960s and 1970s when a combination of soaring central London land values and a declining membership base persuaded some management committees to recommend demutualisation. Members who were shareholders stood to make large sums if the club was wound up, a further incentive to club closure.

Founded in the eighteenth century, the St James's Club typified the accelerating decline of Clubland. In 1975, with the lease on its premises at 106 Piccadilly due to expire, the St James's Club felt it had no option but to dissolve. Unable to raise the money to buy a lease extension, the club was wound up and merged with Brooks's. Shareholders were given a choice of either receiving £500 cash to resign their membership or join Brooks's. Many chose the latter.

But Clubland has never been static. In 1963, with the lease on its building falling due, the Junior Carlton obtained planning permission to demolish its clubhouse on Pall Mall and replace it with a modern office block, the top two floors of which could be rented out to raise income. The building re-opened in 1969 but its modern design and cramped accommodation proved so unpopular with members that the club was wound up and merged with the Carlton. In the case of the Carlton and Junior Carlton, and the Guards and Cavalry clubs, mergers were the obvious route to salvation as members shared a common interest. Some mergers have been more opportunistic. The East India Club in St James's Square, for example, absorbed the Public

Schools' Club in 1972, and three years later joined forces with the Devonshire Club, injecting new blood and significant finances to secure its future. To give it its full title, the East India, Devonshire, Sports and Public Schools' Club, embraces a wide and highly club-bable demographic.

An even bigger series of mergers and hosting arrangements under-pins the Naval and Military Club which for many years occupied Lord Palmerston's former home, Cambridge House, on Piccadilly. The club is still known affectionately as the 'In and Out' from the two massive pillars on which were painted in large letters 'In' and 'Out' to enforce a one-way traffic rule on the tiny forecourt on Piccadilly. The Naval and Military Club has continued to thrive by offering accommodation to smaller and less successful clubs unable to afford premises of their own. This trend began as early as the 1960s when the Naval and Military absorbed the Ladies' Carlton Club. In 1974 this ladies club was joined by another, the Cowdray Club: both sets of lady members were offered associate status. Yet other institutions operate as 'clubs within a club' such as the arrangement with the Canning Club in 1972 for businessmen with links to Argentina and Latin America. The Canning Club has its own room at the In and Out where it holds its events and dinners.

Mergers with defunct naval clubs encouraged Prince Philip to consider accepting the role of president of the In and Out. It is a royal connection that has endured. Naval clubs under the 'In and Out' umbrella include the Goat Club which was brought into the fold in 1974. Named after the Goat public house, a favourite haunt of Admiralty staff during the First World War, the Goat was origi-nally a club for naval officers. The In and Out grew considerably from offering a home to members of the United Service Club, the 'Senior', when it was disbanded in 1975. In 1997 the In and Out offered a home to Den Norske Klub (DNK) which had been founded in 1887 to build strong links with Norway after the coun-try achieved its independence. DNK continues to operate as a 'club within a club'.

When the lease of the Naval and Military Club's rambling club-house on Piccadilly expired in February 1999, the club seized the opportunity to move. Fortuitously, the leasehold of a suitable St James's property had just become available. Once the home of MP and socialite Nancy Astor, the spacious house at the east corner of St James's Square provided the perfect setting for the In and Out's expanding membership. The new In and Out Club has enjoyed renewed popularity. Its latest acquisition was the women-only New Cavendish which joined the In and Out stable in 2014 after its members accepted that continuity was better than being disbanded.

Its former clubhouse on Piccadilly was not so fortunate. It lay empty and awaiting development for over ten years. At long last, it looks as if a developer is now planning to put this grand but increasingly derelict listed building to a new and imaginative use.

The grand palaces lining Pall Mall faced a particular problem. Despite their appearance of permanence, a number of long-established clubs began to encounter financial difficulties as expensive maintenance projects were delayed or deferred. Ninety-nine-year leases granted by Crown Estates were due for renewal during the early twentieth century and have been under review ever since.

In 1991 and with the lease on its building due to run out in thirty years, the Travellers Club entered into a negotiation with the landlord Crown Estates to renew its lease. This required a full valuation survey which arrived at the figure of £600,000 to extend the lease by a further sixty years. Members rallied to support their club with interest-free loans, while the club tried to raise the balance through a bank loan. It was not enough, although the club did manage to gather together £350,000, sufficient to buy a thirty-year lease extension and retain the same peppercorn ground rent. The club's future is assured until October 2053. At the Reform it was a similar story in the early 1970s when the club subscription was significantly raised to enable the club to fund a lease extension and essential building maintenance, making it for a short time one of the highest in Clubland. Today the Reform has a thriving tally of 2,700 members as well as a steady stream of income generation from renting out parts of the building as a film location. Most of the recent James Bond movies, including *Quantum of Solace*, use the Reform's library as 'M's' private office while the saloon was used for the sword fighting scenes in *Die Another Day*. Many TV dramas like *Smiley's People*, *Sherlock Holmes* and *Vanity Fair* have used the Reform's interiors as a backdrop. It is apparent that the entrepreneurial spirit evident in the seventeenth century and the financial acumen and energy of the Victorians are still available. To date over 100 films have used the Reform for some of their scenes.

A Family Tradition

Sons followed fathers into their clubs. One distinguished former member of the St James's Club describes joining the club in the early 1970s. A heady mix of hell-raising rakes, media types and highbrow diplomats made the St James's Club one of the most exciting in Clubland, but also a bit challenging for a newcomer. He recalls:

> I well remember walking into the club bar on my own, on the first occasion after being elected. As I passed Ludovic Kennedy playing backgammon with Lord Lucan all I could see was a solid wall of backs around the bar, an intimidating prospect for a 22-year-old, when in a sudden gap in this phalanx Johnnie McCrae, the barman, spotted me and beckoned me forward. 'Welcome, Sir. Let me introduce you to all the members here,' he said. And this he proceeded to do with the kindest tact imaginable. And then the sucker punch. 'You now know everyone, so it's your round, Sir!'*

---

* A former member of the St James's Club who has requested anonymity

By the early 1980s, Clubland was becoming the place to see and be seen. This renaissance was in part a bi-product of the Thatcher 'revolution' when a radical Tory government cut income tax, privatised nationalised industries, deregulated the City of London and unleashed a new entrepreneurial spirit. Old school attitudes counted for little. As John Martin Robinson comments in his book, *The Travellers Club: A Bicentennial History:*

> There were suddenly rich young men – commercial lawyers, merchant bankers, consultants, hedge fund managers, businessmen who for the first time since the 1950s wanted to live in large Georgian houses and join old-established gentlemen's clubs and could afford to do so.**

So how much would you have to pay to become a member of a traditional London club? Membership fees vary greatly according to the degree of exclusivity, the facilities on offer and the size of the club; generally, the bigger the membership, the lower the fee. Once your application has been approved there is an initial entrance fee which can range from £400 to £4,000 and above. Annual subscription rates range from £800 upwards. Exclusive clubs like Brooks's and White's are not necessarily the most expensive. Subscriptions are under £2,000 while Pratt's charges members £350. Most annual subscriptions hover around a median of £1,500 charged at standard rates. And there are reductions for special categories such as retired people or 'country members'.

Hefty subscription fees, lengthy waiting lists and a rigorous vetting procedure add to the popularity and cache of the elegant and exclusive eighteenth-century clubs of St James's Street, White's, Brooks's, and Boodle's. Well-managed and owning the freehold of their historic clubhouses, these institutions embody an aura of permanence. Old political rivalries are long forgotten. The clubmen of

---

** John Martin Robinson, *The Travellers Club: A Bicentennial History*, Libanus Press, London, 2018

St James's share a common bond of comradeship. In James Wyatt's immaculately restored coffee room, sixty members of White's sit down for lunch, swiftly choosing from an à la carte menu. Members make for their customary tables as the service runs like clockwork. Behind the scenes the chef and his brigade of cooks are well prepared. Above stairs, at tables laid with silver cutlery and cruets the service is cordial and flawless. Members are a mix of investment bankers, entrepreneurs, aristocrats and political grandees. Among the original founders, the Cecil and the Churchill families are still well represented.

To become a member of White's, widely regarded as the foremost gentlemen's club in London and arguably the world, thirty-five signatures are required from existing members willing to endorse an applicant's candidacy. Assuming this total is reached, there is a six-year waiting list. This rigorous selection process reinforces shared values and helps maintain trust between members.

Despite its colourful history, present-day Brooks's is apolitical and restrained. Bridge and chess have replaced backgammon and the club is friendly and inclusive. A unique feature of Brooks's is its strong family ties and the continuity that comes with it. Descendants of the sixth, seventh and eighth generation of families like Cavendish, Clive, Fox, Grey, Spencer, and Whitbread are members of Brooks's.

Part of the uniqueness depends on how a club is regarded by its members. Club ethos is a two-way street: it attracts members and as the years pass, they partake of it. At Brooks's, the spirit of Charles James Fox lives on, continuing to provide a focus for convivial events such as the twice-yearly Fox Club dinner. It is informative to consider why this club has survived for 250 years while so many others have closed. Member Charles Sebag-Montefiore comments:

Brooks's thrives because of its active group of like-minded members who regularly come to the Club, know each other and enjoy each other's company in a convivial setting for conversation, eating and drinking. The future depends on attracting younger members who enjoy the Club's traditions and history, and yet who can use the Club in their daily lives. It is a case of *plus ça change: plus c'est la même chose.*

Keeping Faith with the Past

'There is no coffee served in the coffee room and you are not allowed to smoke in the smoking room,' I was informed in deadpan manner during a visit to a well-known Pall Mall club. The names of rooms are part of a tradition: the 'coffee room', for example, is where luncheon and dinner are served. It is a nod to Clubland's origins in the eighteenth-century coffee-houses of St James's. And with the Victorian ritual of after-dinner cigar smoking consigned to history, and with entire clubs designated smoke-free zones, 'smoking rooms' have become private sitting rooms. It is infra dig to exchange business cards and should your mobile phone ring during a meal you must immediately switch it off. The identity of a club is built around its values and traditions. Clubs take great care to celebrate their history and the quirkiness that makes them unique.

A club is a repository of memories, a kind of collective consciousness that is seen in few other institutions. The walls of the Army and Navy Club in Pall Mall, for example, are hung with paintings of long forgotten battles and glass cases full of historic campaign medals and war trophies. Even the club's nickname is a badge of honour. Invariably referred to as the 'Rag', clubman and author Anthony Lejeune relates that in the club's early days, 'a certain Captain Billy Duff came in late one night and called for his supper. The bill of fare was so meagre that he described it angrily as a "rag and famish affair."'[*] The name stuck although the food has

---

[*] Anthony Lejeune, *The Gentlemen's Clubs of London*, Stacey International, London, 2012, p. 17

improved. Clubs take pride in presenting artefacts associated with members. This curatorial aspect is evident at Brooks's in whose entrance lobby hangs a recently acquired painting of Charles James Fox by Thomas Lawrence. In the members' room, people can view the club's original ballot box, an eighteenth-century gaming table and a death mask of Napoleon, the club's members being at one time strong supporters of the French emperor.

The origins of many clubs still resonate with today's members. Pratt's Club was established in 1841 as an informal dining club in the kitchen basement of 14 Park Place, a house owned by William Pratt, the Duke of Beaufort's steward. Informality and aristocratic connections are what makes this club unique. These qualities are highly prized. Pratt's was, and is still, a place where gentlemen can gather informally for dinner and a chat among friends. The clubhouse was bought by the Duke of Devonshire in 1937 in order to preserve a valuable heritage that might otherwise be lost. Pratt's is still owned by the Cavendish family and because of its small size and limited capacity is one of the most exclusive clubs in London. Its 600 members include no fewer than six knights of the garter. Relaxed informality is still the order of the day, despite its exclusivity, and the club room with its original dresser and its cast–iron range still looks as though it could function as a kitchen. Next door in the basement a dining table can seat fourteen people. Pratt's member John Martin Robinson values the intimate atmosphere as well as being able to drop in for a drink or an evening meal. 'The food is plain but if you order Morecambe Bay shrimps and a lamb chop you can't go far wrong. We have a tradition at Pratt's that the waiter is always called George. It saves confusion.' Robinson is also a member of the Beefsteak, a boisterous and convivial lunch club where waiters are addressed as Charles.

The character of many clubs has survived unaltered. The Travellers, for example, was always an aristocratic club. It had the largest number of dukes as members during the nineteenth century. It is also known as 'the silent club' because members respect one another's privacy – a valuable trait when the person sitting next to you could be the head of MI6 or an air vice marshal. It is thought that this reluctance to initiate conversation was the inspiration behind Conan Doyle's fictitious Diogenes Club frequented by Sherlock Holmes's brother Mycroft. The Travellers Club continues to have aristocratic overtones and, despite being referred to, tongue in cheek as 'a canteen for the Foreign Office', the club does not have so wide a membership as the Athenaeum, the Reform or the Oxford and Cambridge. In the 1980s, the Travellers made a conscious decision to get back to its roots in exploration and foreign travel. Long-term members like the author Patrick Leigh Fermor, his fellow veteran of SOE's Cretan campaign, Major Xan Fielding, and celebrated traveller Wilfred Thesiger were now joined by an influx of explorers and travel writers. Honorary membership was granted to, among others, Chris Bonington, Ranulph Fiennes, Colonel John Blashford-Snell and Eric Newby.

Other clubs have changed and adapted to suit the changing times. Politicians and Treasury mandarins are now in a minority at the Reform Club. The club has expanded to 2,700 members. Reflecting the diversity of interests, the Reform has societies aimed at economists, writers, journalists, historians, architects, and military intelligence officers, among others. The club has plenty of folklore. The spy Guy Burgess spent his last night on British soil at the Reform on 24 May 1951 before fleeing to Russia with his co-conspirator Donald Maclean.

One of the most fascinating and least known institutions is the Society of Dilettanti. Founded in 1732, the Society has never owned a building of its own. On the closure of the St James's Club, its former home, the Society accepted the invitation to transfer its pictures and to hold its dinners at Brooks's in St James's Street. Today, the Society flourishes with sixty members, a combination of landed aristocrats who own classical art works and academics, directors of museums and art galleries. The Society meets five times a year for convivial dinners at Brooks's and occasionally at the houses of its members. Its charitable trust gives grants towards the acquisition of archives and works of art and the conservation of historic buildings where there is a connection with the Society of Dilettanti.

The Society's tradition of commemorating its members in art is kept alive by portraiture commissions and paintings to celebrate special occasions. The role of Painter to the Society of Dilettanti is no mere honorary post. Its present incumbent David Hockney shows the Society continues to play an influential role in the British art establishment.

The Travellers Club preserves its own unique heritage. Architecturally, this has led to a detailed and academic restoration of the club's original decorative scheme laid down by its architect Charles Barry. This process took considerable detective work as layers of paint were scraped away and the original layer analysed to reproduce exactly the colours. An essential part of the Travellers Club heritage, its library contains an unrivalled collection of seventeenth, eighteenth and early nineteenth-century books on travel donated by the club's founding members. The collection forms the core of an important historic archive which is being constantly added to.

In line with its original mission, the Travellers Club cultivates close ties with affiliated clubs around the world. It has links with old established clubs in fifteen countries including Australia, Canada, India and South Africa, the United States, Austria, France, Spain, Portugal and, in the Far East, China, Korea, Taiwan, and Thailand. Members of the Travellers enjoy reciprocal hospitality in no fewer than seven major US cities and an equivalent number across Canada. Impressive though this is, it is eclipsed by the Carlton Club which boasts an overseas network of around 136 affiliated clubs in thirty-six countries worldwide.

Reading club histories and interviewing club secretaries indicates that almost all members' clubs have, at one time or another, fallen victim to fraud, financial mismanagement, and the theft of rare wines, silver, fine damask table napery and so on. This phenomenon is almost as old as the clubs themselves. In 1857, for example, it was discovered that the secretary of the Reform Club, a Mr W. King Norway who had died while in office, had siphoned nearly £900 of the club's money into his personal account. The money was never recovered. Thirty years later another club secretary, a certain G. Digges Latouche, was arrested at Liverpool docks about to board an Atlantic steamer bound for America with a portmanteau stuffed with cash. A hue and cry had been raised when it was found that his accounts were short by £500. Digges Latouche was sentenced to six months' hard labour, a verdict which sounds very lenient given the severity of the crime.

In the main the clubs themselves have been to blame. Their ethos of trust provides a perfect camouflage for determined criminality. Where clubs lack a robust and active management committee, much trust is devolved upon the secretary. Reliance on a single individual in this way creates intolerable temptation. This can only be combatted by a committee's proper oversight of finance and a fit for purpose reporting system. Before the war, the club secretary was usually an ex-services senior officer, but in recent years professional management has been recruited from the hotel and hospitality industries bringing a more commercial modus operandi to bear. Many of the managers hold recognised international qualifications in club management awarded by the Club Management Association of Europe. And if greater scrutiny is needed then British clubs could follow an example from the USA.

In America, an organisation, ClubCorp, runs a family of members' clubs for their committees as an outsourced service.

Clubs have fewer staff. At the Travellers, the modern upstairs kitchen is much smaller and more streamlined with a mixture of gas hobs and ovens with some electric ovens to keep food warm. The historic segregation of club staff into male and female roles once reflected the hierarchy of servants in a stately home. Women were generally confined to 'below stairs' roles. Nowadays, club meals are as likely to be served by a waitress as a waiter, and the wearing of livery in the form of a tailcoat or the wearing of in-club colours is kept for special occasions only. Service resembles any top-class hotel or restaurant. Members are expected to abide by a few simple rules. A lounge suit with shirt and tie is the accepted standard for men, with a black tie and dinner jacket for special occasions. Women's clothing is just as prescriptive. No trouser suits or any form of leisure wear is permitted, and stiletto heels or extreme fashion statements are forbidden. Servants are to be treated with respect.

Mohammed Anzaoui

Mohammed Anzaoui (51) has been club steward at the Reform Club for the past twenty-seven years, eight of them as club steward. He describes his role:

> I used to work at the Royal Overseas League and I once worked for a Meridian Hotel but the Reform Club is something unique. It is like a home from home in the way we treasure our members. Staff are like a big happy family. When I first came to the club in 1991 I worked in the chambers department, the thirty guest bedrooms which are run by the club's Chamberlain. I handled bookings and took advance reservations. In those days we had no en-suite bathrooms to our guest bedrooms. Now, many of the rooms have been upgraded to a modern standard. As Steward my job is to meet and greet and I work from 12.00 noon until 8.00 p.m. That covers lunch and dinner when the club is at its busiest. It's a big responsibility. We're expected to offer a personal service. I know every member by name and which club society they belong to and I will offer small services such as organising someone to sew on a missing button or supplying a replacement shoelace. You need to be observant and ensure small problems are ironed out. You can never say, this is not my job! I also act as a guide and will give a short history of the club if members'

guests want a guided tour. In the past, I have supervised banquets or occasions when the club is hired by a member for an event like a family wedding. If there are a large number of guests to cater for, we will often use agency staff to wait at table. For formal occasions and at Christmas I wear livery, a black cut–away coat with brass buttons. We compare ourselves to a five-star Michelin. We have 110 staff and there are seven women who serve in the Coffee Room and about forty women staff including chamber maids. I report to the Head of Buildings who reports directly to the Secretary.

Pressure for Change

The traditional clubs founded in the eighteenth century were never representative of society. They served the interests of an upper–middle class and aristocratic elite. And they performed that role very well. The new political clubs that came on the scene around the time of the Great Reform Act were, for a brief time, political powerhouses where being elected as an MP was suffi-cient to guarantee membership of a club with strong affiliations to your party. Here policy was hammered out behind closed doors while party strategists planned and often part-financed local election campaigns.

Since the 1960s, society has become more diverse and more meritocratic. Large numbers of women graduates have entered the workplace and risen to the top of their professions. Progressive equality legislation is ensuring women and ethnic minorities are fairly represented on company boardrooms and in the Civil Service, while in traditionally male careers like the military, women are now fully integrated.

It is instructive to consider how far today's clubs reflect changes in society. The old rules by which a member was nominated and then elected by ballot rarely apply as all but the most selective and traditional now adopt an inclusive recruitment policy. Even so, references are needed. At the Oriental Club, for example, references are required from your employer and two members of the club who can vouch for your social standing. Applicants must provide evidence of a link to the 'Orient' – whether family, business or diplomatic connection, or nationality. India, China, Japan, Malaysia or the United Arab Emirates are well represented among the club's diverse membership.

The old political clubs are no longer recognisable in the institutions that bear their name. Party organisation and funding has been removed from the clubs while any behind-the-scenes discussions with lobbyists have to be strictly minuted and accounted for. By the 1920s there were several women-only clubs like the Ladies' Empire Club founded in 1902 and the Ladies' Imperial Club which followed in 1906. Founded during the Great War, the New Cavendish, the Alexandra, and the Cowdray filled a need among women who volunteered for active service. Pressure to admit women gradually percolated into the mainstream. As these clubs became absorbed or amalgamated by gentlemen's clubs, a range of mixed-sex institutions was created. Above all clubs needed paying members and some were pleased to take them regardless of their sex.

Many clubs are adapting to a more fluid society. Some, like the Lansdowne Club in Berkeley Square, were well ahead of the trend. Established as the Bruton Club in 1935, the Lansdowne has always been a club for families where the gentlemen were encouraged to enrol wives and where children could be admitted from the age of 6. Family-friendly facilities include a swimming pool and ballroom. The club is popular with country members visiting London and looking for a calm oasis. It was an exception.

The pressure on clubs to admit women started to gather momentum during the 1960s. One by one, the gentlemen's clubs have given way with compromises such as inaugurating a ladies' night or establishing a 'ladies' annexe'. A small majority admit women on an equal basis to men and are encouraging more of them to apply for membership.

Women's membership was a thorny issue and club members often resist change until it becomes inevitable. The 'In and Out' Naval and Military Club was one of the first members' clubs to accept women as associate members in 1938. Women had their own drawing room on the second floor. But there were definite issues as women were only allowed in via a side entrance in Half Moon Street and could only join the men for dinner in the coffee room if they were at a table 'below the salt'. Pressure to extend full membership to ladies increased exponentially as the club began amalgamating with women's clubs. It finally offered women full membership in 1999.

The National Liberal Club was an early champion of women's members when it voted to accept women in 1976. Soon afterwards, the Reform Club welcomed lady members in 1981. The Army and Navy and Oxford and Cambridge followed in 1995 and 1996 and Pall Mall's foremost club, the Athenaeum, has admitted women from 2002. The Carlton Club voted to admit women as full members in 2008. The club's first full female member was Anne Widdecombe MP. Prime Minister Margaret Thatcher had been admitted as an honorary member since her election as Tory leader in 1975. In 2010 Mrs Thatcher was elected as the club's president. The Equality Act of 2010, however, has put the spotlight on Clubland's attempts to court women. But where the Act could have broken down barriers it has proved weak. It contains a 'protected characteristics' clause under which traditionally male-only clubs or male-only rooms within clubs can continue to exclude on the basis of gender.

However these small successes are spun, traditional clubs face a mountain to climb when it comes to attracting women, and reaching full equality remains an aspiration rather than a reality. Seth Alexander Thevoz, author of *Club Government*, and librarian at the National Liberal Club observes:

> I have long argued that clubs should be more representative of society in an age when so many women are at the top table. I imagine

life will become a lot harder for men-only clubs, as they become less viable.

The In and Out Naval and Military Club is among the most progressive of the clubs with 25 per cent women members.

The Reform Club has 19 per cent women members out of a total of 2,700 and is making big efforts to attract more. Subscriptions and membership manager Sheron Easter comments: 'Our women's section is growing largely because we encourage couples to join. It's a friendly and welcoming club with a lot of social events.'

But there is one institution which, if not a club in the strict sense of the word, occupies a Clubland palace and looks to the casual observer very like its neighbours. The United Service Club building in 116 Pall Mall has been home to the Institute of Directors since 1978. The historic club founded by Wellington was wound up but its immaculately preserved building has taken on a new life as the setting for business meetings, seminars and lunches for the bosses of Britain's burgeoning small and medium enterprise (SME) sector. Full-length oil portraits of royalty and military heroes stare down from the sumptuous flock-wall-papered walls. An amazingly versatile building, Nash's historic clubhouse now includes wine bars, lecture theatres, break-out rooms and spaces for hot-desking. The Institute of Directors, an organisation founded in 1903, now has over 30,000 members. Listing as Grade 1 has meant none of the full-length portraits of generals or royalty can be changed. But the club fits in to this cosy tradition. It has full Wi-Fi access and members set down their laptops in quiet corners on antique tables.

In 2014 the Archbishop of Canterbury resigned from the Travellers Club because its rules excluded women. Nobody noticed. And two years later Prime Minister David Cameron resigned from White's for similar reasons. If he was hoping that his act would reposition him as a 'man of the people' he must have been disappointed as it barely caused a stir. But in Clubland his manner of resignation was regarded as churlish and insulting.

The most elite and privileged clubs see no reason to change. The Garrick, White's, Brooks's, Boodle's, the East India, the Travellers and many others remain male only. In any case, the decision on whether to admit women as full members has to be approved by a two-thirds majority of members. Belonging to a male-only club is therefore a personal choice. It is part of the diverse range of institutions that make up London's Clubland. It is an important link to the past and an emblematic statement. At one traditional club the mood has swung against equality. Changing the composition of a club is no easy matter. The long waiting list for membership and the process of being proposed and seconded favours the status quo. In any case, the identity of these clubs rests with their being male spaces. One clubman told me: 'from a position where half the club was in favour of admitting women back in the 1980s, 60 per cent are now against. Younger members want to preserve the tradition of a gentlemen's club'. Any change to club rules has to be approved by a two-thirds majority.

Clubs are making efforts to attract younger members. Clubland's youth wing, 'Inter-club', is a mixed-sex, free-to-join social media platform for men and women members of traditional members' clubs aged 20–35. Members are enrolled by their host club on joining and thereafter as members of 'Inter-club' the group has free access to nineteen participating clubs. Each club has an appointed Inter-club ambassador, who helps organise a range of activities for young members such as bar crawls of London clubs, golf days, and discos.

Krishan Chudasama, the Oriental Club

Krishan (26) has been a club member for three years. He explains why clubs continue to be relevant for the new generation:

A former business colleague, who I knew from the time I used to work at Canary Wharf, knew about my interest in field sports and invited me for a day's competitive shooting at the gun maker Holland and Holland's grounds in north-west London. The day was organised by the Oriental Club. My team did well and I got talking to John Taylor, the secretary of the club's shooting society, who said I shot well. He invited me to the Oriental Club as his guest at the society's annual dinner. It was a black-tie evening and, as I didn't have a dinner jacket, I borrowed one. I felt at home as the Oriental isn't stuffy or intimidating like some London clubs. I was asked if I wanted to apply to join as a youth member. I fulfilled their entry criteria as I had a strong family connection to India through my Rajput ancestry. I needed two club members who could vouch for me and a social and professional reference. As I was under 25, the fee was reduced to £300. It will increase in stages until I reach the age of 35. I think I will remain a life member. I've been a member now for three years and it's been a brilliant experience. I can bring friends to the club for drinks or invite people to dine. I don't know anywhere else where you can eat so well for far less than you would pay in an equivalent restaurant. As well as fine dining, our chef Wesley Smalley makes some of the best curries in London. When you join as a young member you are eligible to join Inter-club, an online network of nineteen London clubs which host events for members aged 20–35. You simply tell Inter-club which club you belong to and await their approval. It's a great social scene. I work as a sales and marketing assistant for Savile Row tailors Richard Anderson and Company. Belonging to a club is useful in my work as it is a place where I can network or meet clients. There's always something going on at the club and always like-minded people to talk to when you want to relax and unwind after work. One of my most memorable days was when the Oriental Club hosted my civil marriage ceremony. Some of my bride's relatives came over from India to meet my family. After the ceremony, we had a reception at the club with free-flowing champagne and canapés. There were eighty guests. I think you could say I impressed my future father-in-law.

Palaces of Power

Clubs continue to exert influence, largely through their networks of members and by providing a meeting place where conversations can take place in relaxed surroundings. The first thing that strikes anyone entering a traditional club is the sheer scale of these buildings. Palace is no misnomer and any preconceptions you may have about the decor and the furnishings are entirely true. Huge gold-framed oil portraits of illustrious founders hang on the walls of the main reception rooms. Corridors are full of framed nineteenth-century cartoons by 'Spy' from the magazine *Vanity Fair*. The walls are a palimpsest of club history, making connections and a memorial to long-forgotten statesmen and generals – people once vital to the nation.

As you enter, one wonders whether the decor is designed to impress or intimidate the casual visitor. Or does it engender a sense of belonging and homeliness, or one of aspiration? The reception hall or saloon is lined with deep buttoned black leather chester-fields or club sofas. The impression given is that of a stately home. Penetrate the exterior and the club is warm and welcoming. There are coal fires and areas where one might perch on comfortable armchairs ideal for reading newspapers. The abiding impression is that clubs were intended to be aspirational, setting a standard both physically and emotionally.

Luxury Brands

With the influx of the international super-rich, real estate and luxury brands have undergone a revival. Brands like Burberry, Gieves and Hawkes and Hilditch and Key among others sell to a world market. Among the celebrated list of royal warrant-holders is vintner Berry Bross & Rudd, the royal grocer Fortnum and Mason, Floris, and Alfred Dunhill. St James's boasts more royal warrants than any other part of London. And you can still buy hats from Lock and Co.'s hatters in St James's Street or be measured for a personal last for bespoke shoes or a pair of cloth-topped Balmoral button boots at Lobb's in St James's Street or at Foster and Sons in Jermyn Street.

The Theatre Royal in Haymarket still has echoes of its Regency past. St James's has kept its traditional association with the arts. The arguments that raged among artists in the eighteenth century between classical and topographical paintings are being replayed in the Royal Academy's Turner Prize which has seen some outrageous conceptual art including videos or piles of bricks or dead sharks pickled in preservative. Institutions such as the Ritz and the Wolseley, named after the building's original occupant in the 1920s, the Wolseley car showroom, offer fine dining. The Burlington Arcade is still a location for luxury products.

Clubland Revived

From the immediate post-war era to years of boom and bust, the economics of running a traditional gentlemen's club have shifted. Many advertise for new members and relax previous stringent entry requirements. The huge rooms are costly to keep and are often let out for conferences and events. Some downsized and moved to less ostentatious premises. But formality exists in the shape of rules governing clothing appearance and even hairstyles. The Reform Club for example, keeps a selection of ties which will be loaned to any guest who has the temerity to pitch up with an open-necked shirt.

The rare combination of enterprise, imagination and application that has shaped St James's and the associated institutions designed to supply the needs and desires of the wealthy and aristocratic now attract a new international clientele. Global centres of power, influence and resources like London, Tokyo, New York, Paris and Berlin have a common thread of attracting and building enclaves of luxury and fashion. In London, and in St James's, this maelstrom began in 1700 with the burgeoning influence of creative and enterprising minds building institutions serving unimaginably wealthy aristocrats. This trend gathered pace with the winning of the Napoleonic Wars and the establishment of an empire that spanned the globe. For over 300 years, St James's has remained the location for London's most exclusive clubs. Throughout economic depression and even war, there has always been a demand for the services a members' club could provide: overnight accommodation, good food, refreshment and congenial company. These have remained a constant.

LIST OF CLUBS

The Army and Navy
    Club
36 Pall Mall SW1

The Arts Club
40 Dover Street, W1

The Athenaeum
107 Pall Mall, SW1

The Beefsteak Club
9 Irving Street, WC2

Boodle's
28 St James's Street, SW1

Brooks's
St James's Street, SW1

Buck's
18 Clifford Street, W1

The Caledonian Club
9 Halkin Street, SW1

The Carlton Club
69 St James's Street, SW1

Cavalry and Guards Club
127 Piccadilly, W1

The East India Club
16 St James's Square,
    SW1

The Farmers Club
3 Whitehall Court, SW1

The Garrick Club
15 Garrick Street, WC2

The Institute of
    Directors
Pall Mall, SW1

The Jockey Club
Pall Mall, SW1

The Lansdowne Club
9 Fitzmaurice Place,
    Berkeley Square, W1

The National Liberal
    Club
1 Whitehall Place, SW1

The Naval and Military
    Club (The In and
    Out)
4 St James's Square, SW1

The Oriental Club
Stratford Place, W1

Oxford and Cambridge
    Club
71–77 Pall Mall, SW1

Pratt's Club
14 Park Place, SW1

The RAF Club
128 Piccadilly, W1

The Reform Club
104 Pall Mall, SW1

The Royal Automobile
    Club
Pall Mall, SW1

The Royal Over-Seas
    League
Park Place, St James's
    Street, SW1

The Savage Club
1 Whitehall Place, SW1

The Saville Club
69 Brook Street, W1

The Travellers Club
106 Pall Mall, SW1

The Turf Club
5 Carlton House Terrace,
    SW1

White's
37 St James's Street, SW1

LIST OF SOURCES

Ackroyd, Peter, *Queer City: Gay London from the Romans to the Present Day* (Chatto & Windus, 2018)

Ambrose, Stephen, *The Supreme Commander: The War Years of General Dwight D. Eisenhower* (Cassell & Co., 1971)

Ambrose, Tom, *Prinny and his Pals: George IV and His Remarkable Gift of Friendship* (Peter Owen Publishers, 2009)

Anon., 'A monk of St Francis', *The Gaming Table: Its Votaries and Victims in All Times and Countries Especially in England and in France* (Patterson Smith reprint series in criminology. and social problems. Publication no. 96)

Armytage, Percy, *By the Clock of St James's* (John Murray, 1927)

The Athaneum, www.athenaeumclub.co.uk/

Athenaeum Liverpool, *The Athenaeum Liverpool, 1797–1997.*

Atkinson, Diane, *Rise Up, Women!: The Remarkable Lives of the Suffragettes* (Bloomsbury, 2018)

Baily, F.E., *The Love Story of Lady Palmerston* (Hutchinson & Co., 1938)

Beresford Chancellor, E., *Memorials of St James' Street* (Grant Richards, 1922)

Black, Barbara, *A Room of His Own: A Literary-Cultural Study of Victorian Clubland* (Ohio University Press, 2012)

Bourke, Algernon, *The History of Whites* (Waterlow and Sons, 1892)

Burlingham, Russell and Billis, Roger, *Reformed Characters: The Reform Club in History and Literature* (The Reform Club, 2005)

Clark, Peter, *British Clubs and Societies 1580–1800: The Origins of an Associational World* (Oxford University Press, 2000)

Clark, Peter, *The English Alehouse: A Social History 1200–1830* (Longman, 1983)

Colin, Sid and Staveacre, Anthony, *Al Bowlly* (Elm Tree Books, 1979)

Committee of the United Service Club, *History of the United Service Club* (Gale and Polden, 1937)

Croker, J. W., Letter from John Wilson Croker to Sir Humphry Davy sent from The Admiralty 12 March 1823. Source – The Athenaeum Club General Committee Minutes 1824–1826

Dixon, Anthony, *The Army and Navy Club 1837–2008* (The Army and Navy Club, 2009)

Egan, Pierce, *Boxiana or Sketches of Ancient and Modern Puglilism, from the Days of the Renowned Broughton and Slack to the Championship of Cribb, Volume 1* (Reprinted by Elibron Classics, 2006)

Egan, Pierce, *Life in London or the Day and Night Scenes of Jerry Hawthorn, Esq., And his Elegant Friend Corintian Tom in Their Rambles and Sprees Throughout the Metropolis* (Reprinted by Forgotten Books, 2015)

Ellis, Markman (ed), *Eighteenth Century Coffee-House Culture,* Volume 2 'The eighteenth-century satire'(Pickering and Chatto, 2006)

Escott, T.H.S., *Club Makers and Club Members* (T. Fisher Unwin, 1914)

Fielding, Daphne, *The Duchess of Jermyn Street* (Little Brown and Co., 1964)

Firebrace, Captain C.W., *The Brigand with Parrot The Army and Navy Club 1837–1933*, (John Murray, 1934)

Fitzroy, Sir Almeric, *History of the Travellers Club* (Allen & Unwin, 1927)

Forrest, Denys, *Foursome in St James's The Story of the East India, Devonshire, Sports and Public Schools Club* (The East Indian Devonshire Sports and Public School Club, 1982)

Forrest, Denys, *St James's Square*: People, Houses, Happenings (Quiller Press, 2001)

Fulford, Roger, *Boodle's 1762–1962: A Short History* (Eyre and Spottiswood, 1962)

Girtin, Tom, *The Abominable Clubman* (Hutchinson, 1964)

Goldsmith, Vivien. *The Daily Telegraph,* 24 November 2005

Griffiths, A.G.F., *Clubs and Clubmen* (Hutchinson & Co., 1907)

Gronow, Captain Rees, *The Reminiscences of Captain Gronow, Formerly of the Grenadier Guards and MP for Stafford, Smith* (Elder and Co., 1842)

Harris, Michael, *London Newspapers in the Age of Walpole: A Study of the Origins of the Modern English Press* (Fairleigh Dickenson University Presses, 1987)

Henrey, Robert, *A Village in Piccadilly* (J. M Dent, 1942)

Henrey, Robert, *The Siege of London* (J.M. Dent, 1946)

Jenkins, Roy, et al., *Armchair Athenians: Essays from Athenaeum Life* (The Athenaeum, 2001)

Kelly, Ian, *Beau Brummel: The Ultimate Dandy* (Hodder and Stoughton, 2005)

Kelly, Ian, *Mr Foote's Other Leg* (Picador, 2012)

Lake, J.W., *The Works of Lord Byron, Including the Suppressed Poems* (Henry Adams, 1829)

Lejeune, Anthony, *The Gentlemen's Clubs of London* (Stacey Publishing, 2012)

Lillywhite, Bryant, *London Coffee Houses* (Allen & Unwin, 1963)

Linnane, Fergus, *Madams: Bawds and Brothel-Keepers of London* (Sutton Publishing, 2005)

Lord, Evelyn, *The Hell-Fire Clubs: Sex, Satanism and Secret Societies* (Yale University Press, 2008)

Milne-Smith, Amy, *London Clubland: A Cultural History of Gender and Class in Late Victorian Britain* (Palgrave Macmillan, 2011)

Mosely, Leonard, *Backs to the Wall: London Under Fire 1939–45* (Book Club Associates, 1971)

Murphy, Robert, *Smash and Grab: Gangsters in the London Underground 1920–60* (Faber & Faber, 1993)

Nevill, Ralph, *London Clubs: Their History and Treasures* (Chatto & Windus, 1911)

Nichols, Beverley, *Twenty-Five: An Autobiography* (Pomona Books, 2006)

Pallett, Ray, *Goodnight Sweetheart: Life and Times of Al Bowlly* (Spellmount Ltd, 1986)

Pallett, Ray; *They Called Him Al: The Musical Life of Al Bowlly* (BearManor Media Ltd, 2010)

Pankhurst, E. Sylvia, *The Suffragette Movement: An Intimate Account of Persons and Ideals*, (Reprinted in Kraus and Co., 1971)

Pember Reeves, Maud, *Round About a Pound a Week* (Fabian Society, 1913)

Powell, Anthony, *To Keep the Ball Rolling: The Memoirs of Anthony Powell, Vol III*, (Heinemann, 1976)

Rubenhold, Hallie, *Harris's List of Covent Garden Ladies: Sex in the City in Georgian Britain* (Tempus, 2005)

Sadleir, Michael, *Blessington-D'Orsay: A Masquerade* (Constable, 1947)

Sala, George Augustus, *Twice Round the Clock or the Hours of the Day and Night in London* (John and Robert Maxwell, 1878)

Sebag-Montefiore, Charles and Mordaunt Crook, Joe (eds) *Brooks's 1764–2014 : The Story of a Whig Club* (Paul Holberton Publishing, 2013)

Steinmetz, Andrew, *The Gaming Table: Its Votaries and Victims* (Tinslet Brothers, 1870)

Thevoz, Seth Alexander, *Club Government: How the Early Victorian World was Ruled from London Clubs* (I.B. Tauris, 2018)

Timbs, John, *Clubs and Club Life in London* (John Camden Hotten, 1872)

Timbs, John, *Curiosities of London: Exhibiting the Most Rare and Remarkable Objects of Interest in the Metropolis* (David Bogue, London, 1855)

Uglow, Jenny, *Hogarth: A Life and a World* (Faber & Faber, 1997)

Waddy, H.T., *The Devonshire Club and Crockford's* (Eveleigh Nash, 1919)

Wainwright, David, *The British Tradition: Simpson's – A World of Style* (Quiller Press, 1996)

Ward, Humphrey, *History of the Athenaeum 1824–1925* (The Athenaeum, 1926)

White, Charles, *Almack's Revisited* (Saunders & Otley, 1828)

White, Jerry, *Mansions of Misery: A Biography of the Marshalsea Debtors' Prison* (Vintage Digital, 2016)

Wilson, Francis, *The Courtesan's Revenge: Harriette Wilson, The Woman Who Blackmailed the King* (Faber & Faber, 2003)

Wilson, Harriette, *The Memoirs of Harriette Wilson* (John Joseph Stockdale, 1825)

Windsor, Edward (formerly Edward VIII), *A Family Album* (Cassell, 1960)

Woodbridge, George, *The Reform Club 1836–1978: A History from the Club's Records* (The Reform Club in Association with Clearwater Publishing Company Inc., 1978)

Woodham-Smith, Cecil, 'The Man Who Invented Modern Cooking', *Harper's Magazine*, Vol. 217, December 1958

Wright, Thomas, *The Life of Colonel Fred Burnaby* (Everett & Co., 1908)

Ziegler, Philip and Stewart, Desmond (eds), *Brooks's: A Social History* (Constable, 1991)

INDEX

The
History
Press   The destination for history
        www.thehistorypress.co.uk